Innovative Teaching and Learning Practices in Higher Education

Innovative Teaching and Learning Practices in Higher Education

Kayoko Enomoto, Richard Warner
and Claus Nygaard

THE LEARNING IN HIGHER EDUCATION SERIES

LIBRI
PUBLISHING

First published in 2018 by Libri Publishing

ISBN 978-1-911450-35-1

A CIP catalogue record for this book is available from The British Library

Cover design by Helen Taylor

Design by Carnegie Publishing

Printed by Lightning Source

Libri Publishing
Brunel House
Volunteer Way
Faringdon
Oxfordshire
SN7 7YR

Tel: +44 (0)845 873 3837

www.libripublishing.co.uk

Contents

Foreword

This timely book by Enomoto, Warner and Nygaard provides a practical and inspiring review of innovation in teaching and learning. Innovation can be interpreted in different ways and in education it is often thought to be limited to the use of technology in the classroom. The various chapters in this book explore the wider nature of innovation, including stories of how teachers and institutions have introduced innovations that might be classified as breakthrough, disruptive, radical, incremental or sustainable. The book is rich in these stories as it takes a broad view of what innovation in education looks like. In the chapters, authors paint a picturesque canvas with broad brushstrokes for the reader to ponder and revise their perception of what constitutes innovation in education.

Innovation in teaching and learning is not a product or an artefact; it is a culture and a way of thinking and working. The culture of innovation can be found in the interactions between students and their peers, between students and teachers and between institutions and industry and the wider community. We can see innovation in the physical and virtual learning environments, in student support services that promotes the success of the individual; we see innovation in the design and delivery of educational offerings that serve a wider cross section of society, and in educational partnerships that allow commercial educational vendors to work with higher educational institutions to broaden our perception of what is possible in higher education. The chapters in this book are the stories of teachers who want to make a difference to their students.

At its core, educational innovation is about improvements in student learning, the enhanced quality of course offerings or services and new ways to fostering engagement. Innovation can be related to increased productivity and efficiency, but if this is the only point of innovation we would all be the poorer for its implementation. Innovation in teaching and learning is also about inspiring students, teachers and the community to contest the current state of education and propose new ways of doing our core business, or even to change the very nature of that core business. Sometimes these changes are evolutionary, consistent with incremental innovation. Other times the change is revolutionary, and we are taken by surprise by the speed with which an idea has spread. Sometimes innovation is about breaking down barriers that have been constructed over decades and are considered the foundations and standards upon which our perception of quality is built. Innovation normally involves a spark of inspiration, the courage to challenge current practices and a good dose of design thinking.

Sometimes we think of innovators as the mavericks, the teachers who undertake secret experiments with their class and hope that administrators will leave them alone to get on with their changes. This book shows that innovators are not mavericks, they are the ordinary teachers who have had the courage to do extraordinary things. These teachers want to share their stories; they want to let us know what was effective and what was not effective. These are the stories of teachers who wanted to make a difference to their students, to enhance the experiences and outcomes of those in their classes.

This book shows that innovation is not a solitary journey. Teachers need to hear the stories of their peers; teachers need support and scaffolding to join the culture of innovation. Importantly, teachers need the support of their institution and need recognition when they have contested and changed the way we do our core business in teaching and learning. This institutional support includes policies and practices that promote innovation and do not stifle teachers who want to contest the status quo.

Our students will be graduating into a world of complexity and ambiguity. They need to be immersed in a caring learning environment that engages them in situations that challenge their current thinking and promotes innovation. What better way to foster this type of environment than to have their teachers and institutions living the culture of innovation? Students should be an active participant in this culture, contributing to both incremental and breakthrough innovations in their own courses and institutions.

The use of technology in education is only innovative if it fundamentally changes the nature of the learning and assessment activities undertaken by students. Digitising an analogue experience may provide time or space efficiencies, but by itself it does not lead to a culture of innovation. We end up doing the same thing faster or for a lower cost. There is nothing inherently wrong with this, but we should not be misguided that this is innovation. Digitising traditional lectures and placing them online might allow for a more flexible timetable or for greater participation in a program, but if the content is the same, if the learning activities and the assessment tasks are the same, we have not really engaged with innovation. Replacing traditional lecture content with scenario-based group activities or role plays, or allowing students to design their own assessments to show they have mastered the required learning outcomes, are disruptive innovations.

So why is this book important? It is designed for all teachers; it contains the stories of those who have adopted the culture of innovation and have dared to challenge the traditional edifice of how teachers should teach and how students should learn. The chapters encourage us to reflect on our own practices and challenge us to have the courage to contest what is, and start doing what should be.

Professor Geoffrey Crisp
Pro-Vice Chancellor (Education)
The University of New South Wales

Preface

This book is the product of the symposium model invented by the Institute for Learning in Higher Education (LiHE), a not-for-profit academic association which, as intimated by its name, focuses entirely on learning at the post-secondary level. LiHE's scope is limited to colleges, universities, and other institutions of higher education. LiHE functions as a network, bringing together international academic researchers and practitioners within the sphere of higher education who share a common goal to advance the shift from a transmission-based philosophy to a student-centred, learning-based approach. This implementation of a learner-centred higher education philosophy has the overall goals in mind of improving learning outcomes for students, furthering their self-development and enhancing their employability in a rapidly changing world.

The principal activity of the association is a symposium. About 15 years ago, Professor Claus Nygaard, then at Copenhagen Business School, noted that academics attend conferences at which they present their research in a 10–20-minute session, receive a few comments, then very often 'head to the bar for a drink'. LiHE was instituted in order to contest this predictable academic conference format, with its large number of delegates, and (often) many parallel streams, some of which are poorly attended and/or geographically isolated and all of which normally leave very little time for discussion. He proposed an alternative, therefore, which *au contraire* returns to that ancient Greek format – the symposium – at which co-creation is key.

LiHE, through its symposium model, brings together small groups of academics, with teaching and learning expertise, from a variety of disciplines, in such a way that can promote joint research and collaboration in publishing. About 14 months prior to an LiHE symposium, which is output motivated, a call for chapter proposals – based upon a focused theme – is announced on the association's website and on various electronic mailing lists. Potential authors submit chapter proposals, which are then double-blind peer reviewed. If a proposal is accepted, its author is given 2 months to complete it. The whole chapter is again double-blind peer reviewed, and if it is accepted, the author is invited to attend the symposium. There, all authors revise their own chapters, work together to revise each other's chapters, and collaborate to assemble the book manuscript, which, approximately two months later, is submitted to the publisher, Libri Publishing, Oxfordshire, UK.

This particular book, the third in a trilogy addressing the timely issue of innovative teaching and learning, is a collaborative product of the 2018 Copenhagen Symposium on Innovative Teaching and Learning Practices in Higher Education, organised by the Institute for Learning in Higher Education. The symposium took place in Copenhagen, Denmark from May 14–16, 2018. The symposium itself was the culmination of the long writing and review process detailed above.

Before meeting in Copenhagen, invited authors were divided into three collegial work groups according to their chapters' common focus. Then, they were sent a collegial review plan, and asked to give supportive, constructive collegial reviews of the other chapters in their work group. This was undertaken for the purpose of helping others finalise their chapters for publication. Then, the common focus of the three collegial work groups became the title of the three sections of the book:

+ Section 1: Technology-Based Innovations

+ Section 2: Simulation-Based Innovations

+ Section 3: Practice-Based Innovations

During the symposium, the authors met and worked not only on their own chapters, they also wrote – on the fly – an introductory chapter for each of the three sections of the book. For example, the collegial work group responsible for the chapters on technology-based innovations, wrote the introductory chapter for technology-based innovations, and so on. As a result, each author left Copenhagen, with two chapters in this book, their original chapter and their joint introductory chapter for their own section of the book. Finally, in addition to these tangible outcomes of the symposium, it is our hope that all the authors also left Copenhagen with a sense of collegial accomplishment to move forward into other collaborative writing endeavours.

Chapter 1

The Why, What and How of Innovative Teaching and Learning in Higher Education

Kayoko Enomoto, Richard Warner & Claus Nygaard

Why should teaching and learning in higher education be innovative?

In business news, in trade reports, and in market and company analysis today, we most often hear a callout for innovative practices in companies. This counts for both private and public companies – and indeed is just as relevant to higher education. While such focus on being innovative is not at all new, it has become progressively more relevant with rapid technological developments and the unprecedented impact of the Internet, combined with the application of big data analysis, machine leaning, artificial intelligence and virtual realities. In the context of contemporary higher education, such rapid external changes are concurrent with an increasingly diverse student demographic as a changing internal environment. In particular, more students from non-traditional backgrounds and (even more) full-fee paying international students, are currently participating in the higher education sector. Both these externally and internally changing environments call for innovative practices in teaching and learning in order to survive in this increasingly competitive higher education market place.

In 1991, Michael Best wrote the book, *The New Competition*, which was one of the first books to thoroughly present a new paradigm for understanding the logic behind competitive forces in successful industrial areas, and such forces would also have impacts upon the higher education sector. According to Best (1991), the epoch of industrialisation with pre-programmed large-scaled transactional mass-production of products with long life cycles (what he called *The Old Competition*) was being replaced by an epoch of information (what he called *The New Competition*) with flexible specialisation, networked economies, open access to resources, and the use of technological solutions to go even beyond solving known problems. These are some of the building blocks to what Christensen and Raynor (2003) refer to as *disruptive innovation*. Both companies and competition have changed, and societies have transformed into more disruptive and rapidly moving entities. Thus, higher education has found itself under increasingly higher pressure with its institutionalised practices of delivering the 'right' knowledge and ways of thinking to students at the right time.

In the days of *The Old Competition* (Best, 1991), that is when companies could invent a product or a service and bring it to a well-defined market, under relatively stable conditions, it appeared that it was not too difficult for universities to educate students for their future career. This was because the labelling put on the student degree certificate more or less fitted 'a right shelf' in the job market. Under these circumstances, universities could transmit the right knowledge and ways of thinking to students in the practice of teaching and learning, with perhaps little thought given to any problems prevalent in the transition between higher education and the job market. Universities could define the curriculum, primarily focusing on academic expertise, teach students what was considered to be valuable knowledge within the given disciplinary domains, give students a grade according to their performance in tests and exams, and then have them graduate with a respected degree suitable for getting a job within a certain field.

The New Competition model (Best, 1991) challenged universities to remain as the principal providers of the right knowledge and ways of thinking. This is because, in many ways, societies and industries' perceptions appeared to have altered, questioning the role or relevance of universities as providers of new technologies, new means of communication and new forms of delivery of knowledge. Such perceptions have progressed further, as much of the world has become a complex mix of interaction and new innovations, enabled by the (aforementioned) Internet and technological developments, gradually diminishing physical distance in a 'virtual' world. Therefore, universities must respond to these challenges by embracing new technologies in teaching and learning, in an innovative way that also enhances employability-related transferable skills (Fallows & Steven, 2013) that students would need in the workplaces of the future. Indeed, many university students we teach today, are likely in future, to be doing types of jobs that do not even currently exist. Thus, much content of named degrees has to be deemed (by both students and employers) a good fit for the actual work that graduates will be doing in the workplace.

Given that universities are not necessarily perceived as being well-equipped to help students navigate through changing workplace needs, how does a university prepare its students for a job market with such tangible and intangible traits and dynamics? What seems to be needed is not the addition of more disciplinary content, but rather more employ-ability enhancing skills development in curricula, whilst ensuring universities are embracing the rise of new technologies in teaching and learning. Nevertheless, university academics need to be some of the most valuable experts within their disciplinary field. Rather than acting as experts who have to transfer their specialist knowledge to students, such academics (as educators) need to provide, through innovative curricula and practices, scope for students to clearly see that the embedded content not only enhances their disciplinary content knowledge, but also their employability. Such scope should foster students' adaptability and crea-tivity through transformative learning experiences that are relevant and valuable beyond their university studies.

Core to enhancing the employability of today's students is equipping them with learning skills, that is, learning 'how to learn', that bring about and nurture their adaptability and creativity. Such learning skills mean that students not only have to identify and solve well-known problems, but be proactive in their own study practices, so that they learn to reach new understandings of problem situations. This is what Koppenjan and Klijn (2004) label as the ability to solve *wicked-problems*. That is, to learn how to move from solving simple technical problems with well-known modus operandi, in order to master the complexities of problems which are neither fully understood, nor possess a prescribed solution or any appropriate tool to solve them. *Wicked-problems* necessitate what Argyris & Schön (1978) called *triple-loop learning*, the so-called ability of *learning to learn*. This involves students looking behind their own pre-considerations and to move their own horizons in the process of learning (Gadamer, 1997).

In reality, the notion of learning to learn has been much discussed in the literature. What is fundamental is whether universities are willing to embrace this notion and enact it through their curricula – in such a way that actively encourages students to develop their own adaptability and creativity, so they become creative problem solvers who are well equipped to thrive in a broad range of work environments. After all, many university students of today, could well be working in jobs and fields of expertise in future with no contemporary equivalents. Therefore, if universities are to survive as key institutional players, they have to reflect upon their ways of teaching and learning. They need to compete on the quality of their innovative methods of teaching and learning practices; not solely rely on the expert, discipline-specific knowledge of university academics. Teaching students how to *learn to learn* in order to understand and solve *wicked-problems* (Argyris & Schön, 1978) calls for a learning-centred approach. This is the credo for this book in which we show multiple cases of innovative teaching and learning practices.

What does it mean to be innovative in teaching and learning in higher education?

Having argued for the need for being innovative in teaching and learning from a macro-based market economic view, it is necessary to take a closer look at the practices of teaching and learning, in order to define more clearly what it means to be innovative in teaching and learning in higher education. For example, is it innovative to use an interactive whiteboard instead of a blackboard? Is it innovative to integrate drama when teaching medicine? Is it innovative to use polling software during lectures? Is it innovative to use peer-grading? Hørsted *et al.* (2017:4) argue that the success of higher education lies in the *"quality of its innovative methods of delivery"* and that *"innovation = invention + value"*. This means that, to be innovative in teaching and learning, one has to come up with an invention, which adds value. It is not enough to do something new, if it does not add value. For example, it is not innovative to use a new technology to merely replace a learning activity that can be equally done by pen and paper or 'talk and chalk'. Where the value of a product innovation is judged by the customer, the value of higher education is judged by both students and future employers. Yet, what then may be considered as being of value? Hørsted *et al.* (2017:3) argue that *"value = Σconsequences"*, which means that if the sum of consequences is considered positive, the innovation has a positive value. If not, it has a negative value. In teaching and learning then, an innovation equals an invention (doing something in a new way) which adds value in the sense that the sum of its consequences is positive.

However, it is all too easy to be seduced by the apparent value of (for example) a possible technological innovation. For contemporary students, the use of technology could well appear to be a given, rather than innovative of itself. We need to dig a little deeper to find the teaching and learning value for the student, asking the sorts of questions outlined in the paragraph above. Moreover, the waters get murkier when we judge value in terms of institutional constraints, such as budget, time and curricular assessment constraints. Adding to the mix, if an 'innovation' satisfies as many such constraints as possible, then it needs to be systematised, rather than a one off, if university academics are to be rewarded for such an innovation. Even something as simple as a whiteboard can be utilised in an innovative way, to engage a large proportion of the students through peer-to-peer dialogues, to give triggers for facilitating their reflective learning, and putting up example student work for peer-evaluation, resulting in better learning outcomes for students. Thus, innovative teaching need not be massively expensive, as here the sum of consequences could be judged as: higher engagement, guided reflection, orchestrated learning activity and student peer-evaluation, in which the students have more active involvement over their learning outcomes. Such consequences could then possibly lead to: better understanding, higher grades, greater engagement, raised motivation to learn, improved retention and degree completion rates, increased transferable knowledge, adaptability and creativity, and enhanced employability.

If the sum of the consequences can lead to the (above) outcomes, then Hørsted et al.'s (2017:3) equation can be seen to hold true: "*innovation = invention + value*" which, in such a case, is clearly a positive value. Yet, even this positive value on the part of any innovation, has to be offset against the demands of the market-driven higher education sectors of today. Herein lies the rub, higher education learning in the 21st century more often than not, lies within this economic rationalist model. If we stand still pedagogically, we risk getting 'left behind', there is a need for teaching and learning innovations as a counter-balance. However, this very self-same rationalist model demands such innovations be cost effective (or at the very least cost neutral) and be transferable to other disciplinary contexts, both of which put an even bigger burden on university academics and academic developers who strive to be innovative within the constraints of such a model.

We, as university academics involved in teaching and learning in the higher education sector face an uncertain future, as we endeavour to be innovative in a rapidly changing higher education landscape. That is to say, when we innovate, we need to show the value of such innovations across a number of categories, not the least of which is employability-related transferable skills (Fallows & Steven, 2013). The student as consumer model, set within the market-driven realities of the higher education sector, requires big things of us. By showing that we can successfully innovate (and against such benchmarks), we are showing a flexibility and ability over and above the so-called ivory tower days.

How does innovative teaching and learning in higher education look?

In this book, authors report of their own experiences with designing and conducting innovative teaching and learning practices in higher education. The chapters showcase innovative practices that evidence the notion: "innovation = invention + value" (Hørsted et al., 2017:3). Each chapter clearly shows the sum of consequences resulting in a positive value, demonstrating a wide range of consequences as evidence. We have divided the book into three sections, and each section holds examples of what is considered to be innovative teaching and learning. The three sections are:

- Section 1: Technology-Based Innovations;

- Section 2: Simulation-Based Innovations;

- Section 3: Practice-Based Innovations.

The chapters in these three sections showcase a wide variety of illustrative examples, transferable to other disciplinary contexts, of *what* innovative teaching and learning looks like and *how* it takes place.

Section 1, *Technology-Based Innovations*, holds five chapters. In Chapter 2, *An Introduction to Technology-Based Innovations in Higher Education*, Aikyo, DePew, Holt, Rigden and van Rensburg introduce and discuss the utilisation of technology as a tool for promoting innovations in their practice of teaching and learning, and as an enabler for active learning in higher education.

In Chapter 3, *Collaborating Pairs in Online Graduate Education*, DePew and Holt address innovations in teaching and learning by exploring the perspective of 'group work' in higher education, through the particular window of two students in pairs, collaborating to work together in the online environment. This chapter shows how carefully structured activities can bring about the benefits of collaborative pair work.

In Chapter 4, *Using a Learning Management System to Improve Students' English Writing Skills*, Van Han and van Rensburg present how a college developed learning platform was incorporated into degree programs, in order to provide English as a second language students with the opportunities to improve their English writing skills in Vietnam. In doing so, this chapter examines how the role of the language teacher has shifted from instructor to facilitator, and the role of the students from passive learners to active knowledge acquirers with the use of new technologies in language teaching in higher education.

In Chapter 5, *Using Screencasting to Provide Effective Feedback on Academic Writing Assignments*, Rigden disseminates how screencasting technologies can be used to give audio and visual feedback to English as a second language students, as an alternative to using written corrective feedback on academic writing assignments. This chapter shows the effectiveness of the use of screencasting in helping the students with different learning styles and enabling them to be more confident in their English writing ability.

In Chapter 6, *Teaching World Englishes through the Use of Skype as a Learning Tool*, Aikyo explores the use of Skype to teach the notion of 'World Englishes', whilst developing Japanese university students' English competence, through individual conversation lessons given by English teachers in the Philippines. The chapter demonstrates how the students became more confident in both using English and communicating in a different variety of English that reflects the linguistic and cultural characteristics of a particular country.

Section 2, *Simulation-Based Innovations*, holds four chapters. In Chapter 7, *Enhancing Student Engagement and Employability through the Use of Simulations*, Andersen, Elbarrad, Enomoto and Warner, introduce and argue for the use of simulation-based teaching and learning practice, as one effective way of enhancing student engagement while developing employability skills, such as teamwork and communication skills. They explore reasons for the use of simulations in contemporary higher education, in order to develop such employability skills in tandem with (and not at the expense of) developing academic, discipline-based knowledge and skills.

In Chapter 8, *Improving Students' Meta-Reflective Abilities through the Use of Scaffolded Simulation Exercises*, Andersen presents one innovative way of responding to the challenge of giving more 'speech time' to the students of German in a Danish university, through the use of simulation-based practice. The chapter also shows how real-world, authentic exercises such as role plays, are carefully scaffolded to be given to small groups of students, in order to enhance their meta reflection, one core element of their employability skills.

In Chapter 9, *Using a Simulation Game to Teach Students Principles of Cost Accounting*, Elbarrad and Saccucci address challenges of teaching the concepts of Cost Accounting, by using a hands-on, real-life example that allows student teams to build a house, applying cost concepts. The chapter shows how such simulation-based learning (by doing) discourages students from merely memorising the concepts without understanding, but instead, effectively enables students to meaningfully and deeply learn the concepts.

In Chapter 10, *Developing Undergraduate Students' Transferable Generic Skills through an Innovative Group Drama Project*, Enomoto and Warner present the innovative use of a group drama project, focusing on the development of teamwork and communication skills and intercultural competence in a Japanese language course in an Australian university. The chapter also demonstrates how the group project design makes it possible to engage both the engaged and the less engaged, reticent students by double-tasking both discipline and generic transferable skills development in the language curriculum.

Section 3, *Practice-Based Innovations*, holds five chapters. In Chapter 11, *An Introduction to Practice-Based Innovations in Higher Education*, Spratt, Armatas, Kalyn and Kepez argue for innovative practices to be firmly underpinned by the relevant literature to inform its design and implementation, and also to be guided by the notion of students as equal partners in the pedagogical process.

In Chapter 12, *Discourse Communities of Learning in Graduate School: An Authentic Transformative Experience*, Kalyn, Lemisko, Squires, and Balzer discuss their innovative approach to teaching and learning at the graduate school level, through the investigation of the journey of graduate students, who are already in the K-12 school system, in order to learn about the impact that graduate school had on their personal and professional lives. The chapter shows how the consistent and deliberate activation of student-centred learning that the students experienced at graduate school, in turn motivated and empowered them to become innovators themselves during their own learning journey.

In Chapter 13, *Steelcase Active Learning Centre as a Community Design Centre*, Kepez addresses innovations in teaching and learning by highlighting the role that both physical environment and pedagogy play on student learning experiences. The chapter shows how the Steelcase Active Learning Center in a Turkish University was innovatively designed, to allow for a participatory model that enables the environment to be used as a Community Design Centre.

In Chapter 14, *Steelcase Active Learning Centre as a Testbed for Engineering Design Projects*, Arsan and Kepez present the use of a new technology that helps track locations of users and furniture in an active learning center in a Turkish University. The chapter also shows how the use of this technology effectively supports teachers to assign an engineering design project to student teams, whilst also positively influencing teachers not to limit their interactions with students, within the confines of scheduled class and office hours.

In Chapter 15, *Evidence, Analysis, Action: Using Learning Analytics to Direct Curriculum Review and Improve Student Learning Outcomes*, Armatas and Spratt argue for the use of learning analytics data by teachers to conduct curriculum reviews for the purpose of improving their teaching and learning practices. The chapter shows how the application of learning analytics is informed by a theory-based model to conduct evidence-based, data-driven programme reviews across several disciplines for curriculum enhancement at a university in Hong Kong.

About the Authors

Kayoko Enomoto is a Senior Lecturer, Head of Asian Studies and Director, Student Experience in the Faculty of Arts at the University of Adelaide, Australia. She can be contacted at this e-mail: kayoko.enomoto@adelaide.edu.au

Richard Warner is a Lecturer in the School of Education in the Faculty of Arts at the University of Adelaide, Australia. He can be contacted at this e-mail: richard.warner@adelaide.edu.au

Dr. Professor Claus Nygaard is executive director of the Institute for Learning in Higher Education and executive director of cph:learning in Denmark. He can be contacted at this e-mail: info@lihe.info

Bibliography

Argyris, C., & Schön, D. A. (1978). *Organizational Learning: A Theory of Action Perspective*. Reading, MA: Addison-Wesley.

Best, M. (1991). *The New Competition*. Cambridge, MA: Harvard University Press.

Christensen, C. M., & Raynor, M. (2003). *The Innovator's Solution: Creating and Sustaining Successful Growth*. Boston, MA: Harvard Business Press.

Fallows, S., & Steven, C. (2013). *Integrating Key Skills in Higher Education: Employability, Transferable skills and Learning for Life*. London: Routledge.

Gadamer, H. G. (1997). *Truth and Method*. New York: Continuum.

Hørsted, A., Bartholomew, P., Branch, J., & Nygaard, C. (2017). A Possible Conceptualisation of Innovative Teaching and Learning in Higher Education. In Hørsted, A., Bartholomew, P., Branch, J., & Nygaard, C. (Eds.) (2017), *New Innovations in Teaching and Learning in Higher Education*. Oxfordshire, UK: Libri Publishing Ltd., pp. 1–22.

Koppenjan, J. F. M., & Klijn, E. H. (2004). *Managing Uncertainties in Networks. A Network Approach to Problem Solving and Decision Making*, London: Routledge.

Section I: Technology-Based Innovations

Chapter 2

An Introduction to Technology-Based Innovations in Higher Education

Mikiko Aikyo, Diane D. DePew, Karyn Holt,
Kristina Rigden & Henriette van Rensburg

Introduction

As our global society becomes more and more connected with technology, it also becomes expected that we actively integrate into our scholarship of teaching and learning, technology as a tool for promoting innovations. One of the obvious questions to ask, when dealing with technology in higher education is *"why technology?"*. While it may seem to be a silly question, our answers to that question may have far reaching impact on the way in which we think and design curricula. It is so, because technology should not be used for technology's sake. It should be used if – and only if – it enhances students' learning experiences and improves students' learning outcomes. In this first section of the book, we include four chapters, which demonstrate innovative teaching and learning practices, taking full advantage of technology to enhance students' learning experiences and improve students' learning outcomes.

According to *P21 Partnership for 21ˢᵗ Century Learning* (2015), citizens of the 21ˢᵗ century must be able to demonstrate critical thinking skills, related to information, media, and technology. Indeed, these skills are essential for students to be successful in the rapidly changing environment of work and society. The development of these essential skills can be made possible through technology-based innovative practices, by way of enabling students to actively acquire new knowledge and practise applying that knowledge through technology. In so doing, it is imperative that students become active participants – active learners in the construction of their knowledge (Nissim *et al.*, 2016).

Active learning

Active learning is defined *"as anything that involves students in doing things and thinking about things they are doing"* (Bonwell & Eison, 1991:2). Therefore, active learning necessarily demands student-centredness in our practice of teaching and learning. The notion of the student-centred approach can be novel or even a little intimidating to those who are more comfortable with the traditional teacher-centred approach, based on a "lecture-practice-test" method requiring the teacher to play the active role in the process of learning (Brooks, 2009). In contrast, a student-centred approach allows students to *"influence the content, activities, materials, and pace of learning"* (Michael, 2006:160). Therefore, shifting the educational paradigm from teacher-centred to student-centred, requires us to focus more on learning rather than teaching. Such a shift in focus necessitates retooling of educational content, learner activities and the instructor role, in order to create opportunities for more active student engagement in a student-centred learning environment.

In the student-centred approach, students are active participants in both learning and teaching, as they engage in a range of participatory learning activities, as well as actively engage with content and instructors. Moreover, a student-centred approach can also encourage students to continually monitor and assess their own learning and to consciously plan their next steps by identifying what needs to be modified in the learning process (Michael & Modell, 2003). For example, this can be achieved through an iterative process of providing formative feedback to the student. To enable a student-centred approach, technology has much to offer in creating an active learning environment.

Using technology

Using technology is not new to students in higher education. They are increasingly engaged in technology to provide communication, information, and entertainment (Drew & DePew, 2015). Technology can be used for teaching and learning in a variety of settings and for multiple purposes. The four chapters in this section of the book show different uses of technology. One university uses technology to enhance student peer learning, another uses it to improve students' English writing skills, a third uses it to provide visual and auditory feedback to students, and a fourth uses it to facilitate conversation in a foreign language. As these four chapters show, technology provides flexibility in accessing experts as well as peers, which can be very helpful in learning new skills. What is also shown in these four chapters is that advances in the use of technology have shifted the role of the teacher/educator from instructor to facilitator, and the role of the students from passive learners to active learners. The application of technologies also brings about a modification of existing pedagogies or may call for a completely new pedagogy with the learner-centred approach.

In the context of higher education, the integration of technology into our teaching and learning practice, could bring about improved students' employability at the same times improving student engagement and learning outcomes. Such integrated technologies need not be complex, and can include relatively simple, familiar technologies, such as screencasting (Chapter 5) and Skype (Chapter 6). However, such technology-based practices need to be carefully designed and scaffolded to develop students' employability skills, for example, teamwork, communication, critical thinking, problem-solving skills, and so on. Such design of technology-based practices, however, have to be achieved not at the expense of acquiring deep discipline knowledge; this design requirement is where innovations are called for.

Introduction to the chapters in this section of the book

For the purposes of this section of the book, innovation is defined as the use of a practice or idea in a new way or introduction of a new idea, which adds value to teaching and learning. Technology is a tool used in today's global society to bridge gaps in knowledge and to connect collaborators worldwide. The technology is not the primary focus, it is a tool, which resides quietly in the background of teaching and learning. The chapters which follow will share different and inspiring innovations in higher education that involve different technologies for teaching and learning.

In chapter 3, DePew and Holt share how faculty use technology to aid collaboration among online students. The tools within their learning management system provide the means for students to share documents, email, and communicate synchronously even when students may not be geographically near. In this way they use technology to enhance remote students' learning experience and through working as a collaborating pair with a scaffolded project throughout the semester students also improve their learning outcomes.

In chapter 4, Nguyen and van Rensburg show how they have incorporated technology into an English Foreign Language course to improve student's English writing skills. They have designed their own Learning Platform to engage students online, and work with a structured curriculum to encourage and motivate students to work systematically with writing assignments throughout the semester. Through this structured approach where students work progressively with essay reading and writing, they enhance students' learning experience. They also indicate that students' have improved their learning outcomes through this application of technology.

In chapter 5, Rigden presents the use of screencasting to give visual and audible feedback to students. She describes how the use of this Web 2.0 technology has enabled faculty to make writing relevant to students by providing engaging feedback throughout the programme. This way of methodologically combining student work with active feedback has enhanced students' learning experience. And as Rigden puts it, it has also improved students' learning outcomes, as the feedback enables them to reflect on their own work and over time progress to learn academic writing skills.

In chapter 6, Aikyo describes how the communication technology Skype has been used within three courses to help non-native English speaking students to enhance their English skills. Faculty has used the pedagogical concept of "World Englishes" (Kirkpatrick, 2007), where students learn through active engagement in communicative exercises. Using technology in this way, has improved students' learning experience as they have been able to take control of their learning. As Aikyo shows, it has also improved students' learning outcomes.

About the Authors

Mikiko Aikyo is Director of the Institute of Language Education and Professor of the Department of Global Citizenship Studies at Seisen University, Tokyo, Japan. She can be contacted at this e-mail: m-aikyo@ seisen-u.ac.jp

Diane D. DePew, PhD. is an Assistant Clinical Professor within the College of Nursing and Health Professions at Drexel University, Philadelphia, PA, USA. She can be contacted at this e-mail: d.depew@drexel.edu

Karyn Holt, PhD, is a Clinical Professor within the College of Nursing and Health Professions at Drexel University, Philadelphia, PA, USA. She can be contacted at this e-mail: keh36@drexel.edu

Kristina Rigden, EdD, is a TESOL Instructor at the University of California, Riverside Extension Center and the Director of Outreach Programs and Women in Engineering for the College of Engineering at California State Polytechnic University, Pomona, USA. She can be contacted at this e-mail: krigden@ucx.ucr.edu

Henriette van Rensburg, PhD, is an Associate Professor (Special Education) in the Faculty of Business, Education, Law and Arts, at the Toowoomba campus of the University of Southern Queensland, Australia. She can be contacted at this e-mail: vanrensb@usq.edu.au

Bibliography

Bonwell, C. C., & Eison, J. A. (1991). *Active learning: Creating excitement in the classroom.* ASHE-ERIC Higher Education Report No. 1, Washington, D.C.: The George Washington University, School of Education and Human Development.

Brooks, C. D. (2009). *Effects of process-oriented and product-oriented worked examples and prior knowledge on learner problem solving and attitude: A study in the domain of microeconomics* (Doctoral dissertation). Florida State University, Tallahassee, FL. http://purl.flvc.org/fsu/fd/FSU_migr_etd-2979

Drew, S., & DePew, D. D. (2015). Introducing the practice of technology-enhanced learning. In Branch, J., Bartholomew, P., & Nygaard, C. (Eds.), *Technology-enhanced learning in higher education*. Oxfordshire, UK: Libri Publishing Ltd, pp. 97–111.

Kirkpatrick, A. (2007). *World Englishes: Implications for international communication and English language teaching*. Cambridge, UK: Cambridge University Press.

Michael, J. (2006). Where's the evidence that active learning works? *Advances in Physiology Education*, 30(4), 159–167. https://doi.org/10.1152/advan.00053.2006

Michael, J. A., & Modell H. I. (2003). *Active learning in secondary and college science classrooms: A working model of helping the learning to learn*. Mahwah, NJ: Erlbaum.

Nissim, Y., Weissblueth, E., Scott-Webber, L., & Amar, S. (2016). The effect of a stimulating learning environment on pre-service teachers' motivation and 21st century skills. *Journal of Education and Learning*, 5(3), 29–39. https://doi.org/10.5539/jel.v5n3p29

P21 Partnership for 21st Century Learning. (2015). *P21 framework definitions*. Retrieved from http://www.p21.org/storage/documents/P21_Framework_Definitions.pdf

Chapter 3

Collaborating Pairs in Online Graduate Education

Diane D. DePew & Karyn Holt

Introduction

With our chapter, we contribute to this book *Innovative Teaching And Learning Practices In Higher Education* by examining how the pedagogical method of collaborating pairs has effectively encouraged students to translate their learned knowledge into skills that enhance their future employability, through collaborative learning experiences. The specific focus of this pedagogic method is on developing the 'ability to work with others' to prepare students for collaborative work, one of the key skills for improving employability in many professions, but particularly imperative in Nursing. This chapter will show how the pedagogical method of collaborating pairs can prepare students for real-life social and employment situations. Collaborating pairs consist of two students and is a form of group work based on peer-to-peer learning (what we call peer learning in this chapter). Collaborating pairs were set up in two of our graduate online nursing courses over one term, for the purpose of enabling peer learning for written assignments. We designed the use of collaborating pairs in such a way that promotes two-way discussions and deep exchange of ideas, whilst requiring students to identify each other's strengths and weaknesses and push each other to improve.

The pedagogic method of collaborating pairs builds on the theory of active learning which contains the following two precepts: 1) students learn best through active learning, and 2) learning takes place when students solve problems beyond their current developmental level with the support of their peers (Vygotsky, 1978; Mazer, 2016). Bonwell and Eison (1991:2) in their seminal work, *Active Learning: Creating Excitement in the Classroom*, defined active learning "as anything that 'involves students in doing things and thinking about things they are doing'." Active learning focuses on strategies where students are doing something such as reading, discussing, or writing and requires higher-order thinking in and of itself. In addition, crucial to such active learning is the timely provision of appropriate scaffolds (Enomoto & Warner, 2014). Therefore, we carefully designed our innovative practice with timely, relevant scaffolds to support collaborative pairs to work on a project throughout the course. This scaffolded project included three assignments within its collaborative learning focus. The social construct of collaborative learning (Bruffee, 1999) is based on these four principles:

+ the primary focus of instruction is the student;

+ interaction is paramount;

+ group work is important to learning;

+ approaches are structured

Mobilising peer group influence around learning, assumes *"learning occurs among people, not between people and things"* (Bruffee, 1999:84). Freeman *et al.* (2014), in their meta-analysis of 225 research studies, assert that students enrolled in a course with traditional lecturing have a failure rate 1.5 times higher than those students who are enrolled in courses with some active learning, such as collaborative group work. We see the pedagogic method of collaborating pairs as a strategy leading to active learning.

According to Social Learning Theory (Bandura, 1977), cognitive, behavioural and environmental influences and their continuous reciprocal interactions offer an explanation of human behaviour. Learning is a cognitive process which occurs in social situations; new behaviours are learned by observing and imitating others, or through direct instruction, often without practice or direct reinforcement. While being similar to Social Development Theory (Vygotsky, 1978) and Situated Learning Theory regarding the interplay between social situations and learning (Lave & Wenger, 1991), Bandura's (1977) Theory of Social Learning does differ somewhat. It does so by connecting behavioural and cognitive learning theories, in encompassing attention, memory, and motivation. Differing influences affect: 1) the amount of attention expended on learning; 2) the cognitive power used in retaining that which is learned and then converted into recall-able and reproducible information, and finally 3) the motivation to imitate that which has been modelled.

Reading this chapter, you will gain the following three insights:

1. collaborating pairs can produce the transfer of new knowledge from one student to another;

2. static pairing provides for the effective transfer of knowledge between a student with the added benefit of a sustained relationship with one other student throughout the course;

3. dynamic pairing can produce the transfer of new knowledge from one student to another by pooling the diverse strengths of the changing collaborating pairs.

Our chapter has four main sections. In Section 1, we describe our motivation for using the pedagogical method of collaborating pairs in our online graduate course. In Section 2, we describe what we see as the innovative aspects of using the pedagogical method of collaborating pairs. Here, we differentiate between dynamic pairing and static pairing. In Section 3, we discuss the student and teacher perspectives on the outcomes of using both static and dynamic pairing. It also summarises our conclusions. Taking a future focus, Section 4 sets out our hopes and expectations to apply collaborating pairs in other courses and with other teachers in different teaching and learning contexts.

Section 1: Our motivation to use collective pairs

The Masters of Science in Nursing (MSN) curriculum at the Drexel University College of Nursing and Health Professions is provided fully online. The online learning environment provides challenges to student engagement and collaboration. Students enter the program at differing times within their own plan of study. Courses in the curriculum may or may not have prerequisites or co-requisites. There are core courses that all MSN-students have to complete. The content of the core courses is based on the American Association of Colleges of Nursing MSN Essentials, i.e., expected learning outcomes for nurses from a graduate program. The core courses include:

+ Issues in Contemporary Health Care Environments;

+ Advanced Ethical Decision Making in Health Care;

+ Quality and Safety in Healthcare;

+ Research Methods and Biostatistics;

+ Evaluation and Translation of Health Research;

+ Advanced Pharmacology;

+ Advanced Pathophysiology;

+ Advanced Health Assessment and Diagnostic Reasoning.

Students individualise their curriculum based on their selected area or concentration of study such as Nurse Practitioner, Nurse Educator, Nursing Leadership, and Nurse Anaesthesia. Additional specialty courses and track specific courses may be required. Each specialty area's curriculum is based on the professional standards. For example, the Nurse Educator track is based on competencies from the National League of Nursing Teachers role and the American Nurses Credentialing Center's test plan for an educator in the Professional Development Role. The specialty courses for the Nurse Educator track are:

+ Foundations of Nursing Education;

+ Curriculum Design for Higher Level Cognition;

+ The Role and Responsibility of the Nursing Professor;

+ Assessment, Measurement, and Evaluation;

+ Teaching Methods in Nursing Education.

We found that our students were struggling to translate their learned knowledge into skillsets crucial to their employability. Such skillsets included the development of behavioural objectives, alignment of assessment measures with these objectives, and development of test items. We discussed several ways to solve this problem and came up with the idea of using group work, while students worked with a scaffolded project. However, we did have second thoughts, because in our experience, most graduate and undergraduate students do not like group work. When working in groups, there can be too many perspectives and getting to a consensus is a challenge. Because our course is taught online and thus uses asynchronous activities, the mode of class delivery, different time zones, and lack of schedule flexibility presented barriers to group work.

Indeed, some researchers (Hodges, 2017; Lencioni, 2002) point out the drawbacks of using group work. According to Hodges (2017), group work encompasses challenges of human social interactions including personality conflicts, inconsistent expectations, fear of criticism, and differences in buy-in or resistance to change. Often an assignment is tackled with a divide and conquer method, and the resulting product is not cohesive. Students often end up doing only part of the work of learning. Lencioni (2002) identifies the absence of trust, fear of conflict, lack of commitment, avoidance of accountability, and inattention to results as the five dysfunctions of teams.

To mitigate these challenges, but still utilise some of the advantages of peer learning, we chose the pedagogical method of collaborating pairs. We believe that, given an applicable context, collaborating pairs can outshine the results of working in larger collaborative teams. In paired collaborations, trust is built with one person at a time. When pairings change, new trust building must take place with a new partner. This can bring about extended trust across the wider team or class, whilst the trust between older pairs remain unchanged. Trust is more easily built between only two people than by including others. Working in a pair results in a healthy fear of wanting to help the other person succeed in the project and realising that if one team member does not do his work, the other team member will also fail – the results are not just individual but affect the team. Trust is built when constructive passionate debate must occur with a partner rather than artificial harmony or passive dispassionate inactivity in a larger group. With a paired collaboration, small commitments to a plan of action are made as the project progresses. The dyad promotes true buy-in of the project as a whole, as each step of the project is a negotiation and the result of two people's work. Having briefly sketched out the background for our use of the pedagogical method of collaborative pairs, we will now describe student and teacher practice in more detail.

Section 2: Collaborating pairs as an innovative practice

We present collaborating pairs as an innovative practice in teaching and learning, because this pedagogic method allows for students to translate their learned knowledge into skills that enhance their future employability through collaborative learning experiences. We set up collaborating pairs to enable peer learning for written assignments through a collaborative peer review process. Pairing two students helps us develop a learning community more rapidly than when using large groups. We believe the efforts of the individual student are more focused, and less negotiation is needed because there is only one other group member to negotiate with. The 'community' effort is an active one. We have used collaborating pairs in two ways: 1) static pairing and 2) dynamic pairing.

Firstly, with static pairing, the student pair is formed at the beginning of the course and work together on the assignments of a scaffolded project throughout the course. This static pairing provides increased familiarity between the two students working continuously together. It also provides enhanced accountability in the group, and quicker development of peer trust due to the intimate group size. The static collaborative pairing is used in the MSN Nurse Educator track course: "Assessment, Measurement, and Evaluation". The Nurse Educator track concludes with an applied practicum in the work setting of the student's choice: academia or nursing professional development. In a static pairing, the teacher has the learning management system randomly assign students at the beginning of the term into pairs. This randomisation mimics the work environment, where collaboration is often based on role and not on the person's personality or strengths. In the online course environment, students view the name of the other student with whom they have been partnered. The students access the integrated communication tools (discussion board, email, synchronous meeting) to connect with the other student. The experience has shown that students also use communication outside the course, such as telephone, video conferencing, and text messaging to collaborate in group work. The syllabus outlines the three assignments of the scaffolded project on which the pair will be working. Students are instructed to work collaboratively on each assignment. The teacher checks in with each pair to guide the collaborative peer review process. Even if the work is divided, students are to provide feedback to their peer on that person's work and collaboratively develop one paper for each assignment. Each student provides a self evaluation and a peer evaluation. The score of the self and peer evaluation is then weighted to five percent of each student's final course grade.

Secondly, in dynamic pairing, peers are strategically identified as the project progresses, and the composition of the pairs change after each step of the scaffolded project. While keeping the benefits of two people to a group, dynamic pairing boosts interaction and engagement among the entire class and adds different perspectives at different points in the project. The dynamic collaborative pairing is used in a post-Baccalaureate Certificate in Neuroscience, Learning & Online Instruction. This interdisciplinary certificate program is designed for two audiences: professionals who plan to instruct courses in online or blended environments, and graduate students who wish to expand their course of study to designing online and hybrid courses. The intentional dynamic pairing allows the teacher to exploit the diversity of this heterogeneous group. The pair changes with each component of the scaffolded project.

The certificate program is 12 quarter credit hours. The core courses include:

- ✦ Neuroscience of Learning and Online Instruction;

- ✦ Online Neuropedagogy, Regulations & Online Instruction;

- ✦ Capstone: Applying Neurobiology to Online Instruction.

In a dynamic pairing, the teacher purposely pairs students of differing knowledge, skills, and abilities in order to target the learning of specific skills. In using the diversity of the students' knowledge, skills, and abilities within the pair assignment, varying perspectives are brought to the scaffolded project with each assignment. The teacher considers discipline, culture, shifts worked, student age, life experiences, educational goals, and actual project topic to assign the pairings. About halfway through the course, students are informed who they will be paired with for the first assignment of the scaffolded project. This timing provides the first half of the course for the teacher to decide the best pairings for the students. Students provide evidence of their synchronous collaboration by posting a link to their archived meeting for the teacher to review. Software for this recording is the students' choice. They have used Skype, Screencast-O-Matic, Blackboard Collaborate, and Zoom thus far. By changing the student pairing over three assignments of the project, differing student perspectives provide a more varied outlook. Students submit an individual assignment for each aspect of the scaffolded project. Changes suggested by the different collaborative pairs as the project progressed are incorporated. This method boosts interaction and engagement among the entire class because, by the end of the course, students have had the opportunity to meet intimately with at least three of their classmates and have been offered feedback on their work from three perspectives. If all three indicate the same problem or magnificence, that perspective becomes stronger.

We see collaborating pairs as being a significant contribution to innovative teaching and learning practice. Its use removes the barriers inherent in group work while maintaining the positive impact on the learning process and outcomes. When two people are paired to complete a project, more time is spent in a one to one collaboration, which increases the accountability amongst the collaborators. Additionally, when only two are collaborating, less time is needed to communicate within the group. From scheduling meetings to debating points to negotiations, final work is much faster. Time for individual reflection and action can also be focused, since the perspective is only from one. Regardless of whether it be a static or dynamic pairing, collaboration supports student learning. For example, with only two people on a team, dysfunction, readily occurring in larger collaboration groups, rarely occurs. Accountability is squarely on two people, and each knows what has been done, what needs to be done, and by whom it was done. Two working as a paired collaboration makes negative behaviours completely transparent.

Preparation of the innovative practice

A means of randomly assigning students to a pair is required for static pairing. For us, the learning management system does this. Of course, one can also use a manual process to assign random pairs. Self and peer feedback is provided by a teacher-developed evaluation form distributed to all students at the onset of the term. The form uses a 4-point Likert scale to measure:

- contributed a fair share of work;

- work was accurate and complete;

- completed work on time;

- contributed positively;

- shared ideas and valued other's ideas.

This form is completed at the end of the scaffolded project. Initially, the form was in an electronic format that the student completed and emailed back to the teacher. The teacher then did hand calculations to determine the score for each student. Currently, the evaluation of self and peer is done via an online survey. Students have a link in the course to the evaluation that they then complete. The data is downloaded to a spreadsheet to complete the calculations. This has saved teacher time and decreased computational error.

To use dynamic collaborative pairing, there needs to be a requirement for students to introduce themselves early in the term, including details such as life experiences, student major, work specialty, and educational goals. The first assignment of the course would then be to share project topics. The teacher would use both information sources (class introduction and project topics) to pair students for their first project assignment. Dynamic pairing can be based on topic similarity or dissimilarity, discipline similarity and ultimately, pairing a stronger and a weaker student to develop each of them. This process is completed two more times for a total of three times during the project. Recommended (no cost to student) software to use to record their synchronous meetings were listed with links to obtain the software programs. Within the Learning Management System, a repository was set up so that the evidence of collaboration could be submitted and reviewed by the teacher.

As this practice and the capstone course have evolved, a constructivist approach has been applied. The students now self-select into the dynamic pairing. The scaffolded project is in the capstone course, the last in the program. Students have moved through the courses as a cohort and have become familiar with each other's strengths, weaknesses and areas of expertise. The collaboration occurs twice instead of three times throughout the term.

Section 3: Students' and teachers' perception of outcomes

In this section, we take a look at the outcomes seen from both students' and teachers' perspectives. The student perceptions of the outcomes of the collaborating pairs have been mostly positive.

"Working with a partner where we could challenge each other and exchange ideas was definitely a benefit during these assignments. . . Collaborating ideas enabled me to be able to work better as a partner but also feel free to offer suggestions freely and develop the different aspects of our assignments." (Student voice).

Some students voiced apprehension: *"I believe that working in pairs is scary at first, but it is a constructive way to learn to work together with someone on multiple levels."* (Student voice).

Others addressed the pros and cons of collaborative pairs: *"Personally, I found working with a partner a mixed blessing. It is a test of patience and professionality [sic] to work on a project with a person who differs in temperament, background, and availability. I did appreciate having someone to discuss ideas with or even be confused with at times. Having a varied perspective also helped me to shape my own ideas."* (Student voice).

Before implementing the collaborating pairs in the Nurse Educator track, the average individual scores on the three assignments were 87.2. With the collaborating pairs, the average is 89.4. Separate from the grade, peer learning and teaching has been shown to improve learning (Stone et al., 2013; Vickerman, 2009). Using collaborating pairs resulted in the achievement of higher grades than in previous terms when there was no use of collaborating pairs for peer review in those same assignments.

For us, the teachers, the first-time static collaborating pairs was introduced the practice was functional. Students worked together, and scores showed improved skills. The following term the practice of collaborating pairs did not go as well. In two of the fifteen groups, one of the students was either not responsive or non-contributive. It is harder to 'hide' in a group of two, and we did not expect this type of behaviour from graduate students. In each case, the functional student reached out to the teacher and was guided on communication tactics. The teacher then required of the whole class to visually post pair communication (via discussion board) as a means of oversight to pair function. Subsequently, it was deemed necessary to provide a structure for the collaborating pairs to follow on ground rules and accountability. A review of student feedback and scores was conducted, which gave us further insights. One result which we had not really anticipated, is that we have found that since collaborative pairs were introduced into the course, there have been fewer contacts with the professor for assistance. It seems as if a measure of 'peer tutoring' has been occurring and that this outcome appears indicative of students scaffolding and taking ownership of each other's active learning as well as their own.

When using dynamic pairing collaborations, the reflective papers have improved with each pairing. The teacher burden has been reduced in the process of revising because the student pairings do not have a history working together, it is a 'new' pairing each assignment. This requires that each pair study the assignment and provide a new perspective that is most likely not previously shared. If it was shared, that advice was even stronger, and usually accepted by the authoring student. The final projects have had higher grades by 2.0 points than those without the pairings and has helped reduce teacher workload as the teacher has spent less time providing help for enrolled students.

Section 4: Moving forward

With what we have learned, from our experiences with collaborating pairs in our scaffolded project, in the course Assessment, Measurement, and Evaluation, we would like to expand the use of collaborating pairs to other courses in the MSN curriculum. The practice is being added to the course on curriculum development within the Education Track and in one of the core courses of the MSN Curriculum. Embedding collaborative pairs throughout key courses in the curriculum, would provide a means of boosting student confidence in their employability skills, and provide an experience similar to what the work environment will be upon graduation. However, one thing that we have learned, through enacting our scaffolded projects, is that requiring the collaborating pairs to submit ground rules for communication and expectations should be offered, to ensure accountability of all. Indeed, such an option will be offered in the upcoming term in our curriculum. Our university is known for its capability and capacity to equip students with the ability to work with others through collaborative learning experiences and we feel that our curriculum is but a small (but valuable) part of the bigger picture – preparing students for collaborative work, key in our discipline and in the workplace of their future.

Conclusion

In this chapter, we have described and explored the pedagogic method of collaborating pairs. We have examined two types of pairing, static pairing and dynamic pairing. In static pairing, the teacher randomly assigns pairs to mimic the work environment. The pair works together on a scaffolded project throughout the term. In dynamic pairing, the teacher changes the collaborating pairs throughout the term providing differing partners, perspectives, and strengths throughout the term. Collaborating pairs effectively promotes and inspires two-way discussion and an exchange of ideas in which students measure their strengths and weaknesses pushing each other to improvement. The transfer of knowledge between the students not only leads to mastery but builds learning skills and abilities, (perhaps including peer tutoring) that the student can then apply in the future.

About the Authors

Diane D. DePew, PhD. is an Assistant Clinical Professor within the College of Nursing and Health Professions, Drexel University, Philadelphia, PA, USA. She can be contacted at this e-mail: d.depew@drexel.edu

Karyn Holt, PhD, is a Clinical Professor within the College of Nursing and Health Professions at Drexel University, Philadelphia, PA, USA. She can be contacted at this e-mail: keh36@drexel.edu

Bibliography

Bandura, A. (1977). *Social learning theory*. New York, NY: General Learning Press.

Bonwell, C. C., & Eison, J. A. (1991). *Active learning: Creating excitement in the classroom*. ASH#ERIC Higher Education Report No. 1, Washington, D.C.: The George Washington University, School of Education and Human Development.

Bruffee, K. A. (1999). *Collaborative learning: Higher education, interdependence, and the authority of knowledge* (2nd ed.). Baltimore, MD: The Johns Hopkins University Press.

Enomoto, K., & Warner, R. (2014). Promoting student reflection through considerate design of a virtual learning space. In Scott-Webber, L., Branch, J., Bartholomew, P., & Nygaard C. (Eds.), *Learning space design in higher education* (pp. 127–150). Oxfordshire: Libri Publishing Ltd.

Freeman, S., Eddy, S. L., McDonough, M., Smith, M. K., Okoroafor, N., Jordt, H., & Wenderoth, M. P. (2014). Active learning increases student performance in science, engineering, and mathematics. Proceedings of the National Academy of Sciences USA 111, pp. 8410–8415.

Hodges, L. C. (2017). Ten research-based steps for effective group work. IDEA Paper #65. Manhattan, KS:IDEA

Lave, J., & Wenger, E. (1991). *Situated learning: Legitimate peripheral participation*. Cambridge, U.K.: Cambridge University Press.

Lencioni, P. (2002). *Five dysfunctions of a team: A leadership fable*. San Francisco, CA: Jossey-Bass.

Mazer, E. (2016). *Peer instruction blog*. http://www.peerinstructionblog.net

Stone, R., Cooper, S., & Cant, R. (2013). The value of peer learning in undergraduate nursing education: A systemic review. *International Scholarly Research Notices Nursing* (Article ID 930901) http://dx.doi.org/10.1155/2013/930901

Vickerman, P. (2009). Student perspectives on formative peer assessment: An attempt to deepen learning? *Assessment & Evaluation in Higher Education*, 24(2), 221–230. doi: 10.1080/02602930801955986

Vygotsky, L. S. (1978). *Mind in society: The development for higher psychological processes*. Cambridge, MA: Harvard University Press.

Chapter 4

Using a Learning Management System to Improve Students' English Writing Skills

Nguyen Van Han & Henriette van Rensburg

Introduction

With our chapter, we contribute to the book *Innovative Teahing And Learning Practices In Higher Education* by describing how we utilised a Learning Management System (LMS) to improve the English writing skills of English as a Foreign Language (EFL) students at the College of Finance and Customs in Vietnam. We show how we have designed an English Writing Course as an integrated part of a LMS, and how the use of the LMS as an online platform for the English Writing Course, has helped us engage students as autonomous learners. An autonomous learner can be defined as possessing the aptitude for formulating cognisant decisions relevant to their own learning (Najeeb, 2012). We detail our use of the LMS and illustrate how it provides students with good opportunities to improve their English writing skills, whilst, as they function as autonomous learners, encouraging them to experiment with and adopt a new writing practice approach.

Using information and communications technology to engage students and improve learning outcomes is not new. Our experience shows us that advances in the use of technology have helped shift the role of the language teacher from instructor to facilitator, and the role of the students from largely passive learners to more active learners. Thus, the application of technology brings about a re-adjustment of existing pedagogies and calls for a new learner-centred pedagogy. We argue that designing the LMS in such a way that encourages students to embrace a new English writing practice approach, ensures active participation from students in the learning process and improves their English writing skills. That is what we are going to demonstrate in our chapter. Reading the chapter, you will gain the following:

1. inspiration to design a LMS which supports the improvement of EFL students' English writing skills;

2. insight into the application of a LMS-based writing skills practice that encourages EFL students to become autonomous language learners;

3. motivation to use technology to teach English writing skills in EFL contexts.

Our chapter is arranged in four sections. In Section 1, we provide the background to our innovative practice by positioning our use of the LMS-based English Writing Course within contemporary literature. In Section 2, we present the LMS-based English Writing Course in more detail by providing an in-depth account of our initiative. The outcome of our innovation is narrated in Section 3, which leads into Section 4, outlining how we believe the innovative practice can be advanced further.

Section 1: The background to our innovative practice

One of the main aims of foreign language education is to educate students to fully utilise their language proficiency, as a positive contributor to their personal and social development. In the context of EFL teaching and learning, language learners need to develop their linguistic communicative competencies (Canale, 2014), in tandem with improving their evaluation skills to assess their own learning performance as well as performance of peers in the process of learning. Such enhanced evaluation skills can then lead to learner autonomy. Autonomous language learners are less reliant on the teacher and teacher-directed instruction, and can engage more in their independent learning than non-autonomous learners (Benson, 2011). Therefore, in foreign language education, equipping students with such evaluation skills is equally important as developing their linguistic communicative competencies. When teaching foreign languages, university language educators have to employ techniques, means and forms that can help students develop such skills and competencies to become autonomous learners. This called for our innovative design of an LMS-based English Writing Course, requiring changes to both teachers' and students' roles, as well as their responsibilities in the teaching and learning process of English writing skills.

With respect to writing skills in particular, technology may be utilised to encourage language students to think of writing in English in new and positive ways, as compared to writing in non-technology environments (Pennington, 1996). Similarly, Phinney (1996:140) points to the importance of technology in writing and recognises the following postmodernist paradigm shift: "*As part of the changing culture of composition instruction, there is a new emphasis on de-centering authority, coupled with a recognition of the importance of collaborative learning, and a realisation of the need for new models of writing and rhetoric.*"

It is worth mentioning that there are many publications describing the use of LMS for developing the writing skills of EFL students. Some of the research investigates the impact of different aspects of LMS on language writing skills. For example, Beauvois (1998) concluded that students could increase their interaction, leading to the improvement of their written works. Bikowski and Kessler (2002) also revealed that students had positive attitudes towards LMS interactivity and they also had positive in relation to LMS feedback capacity. Particularly crucial to the context of an LMS and learner autonomy, Yan and Xiaoqing (2009) indicated that students were able to develop their learning responsibility and learner autonomy when engaging in LMS.

Having recognised a number of the learning based benefits that LMS offers, we noted that the integration of this tool into teaching English writing had the potential to bring some tangible benefits to our students in language education in Vietnam. As we decided to use an LMS as the backbone of our English Writing Course for EFL students, it became natural for us to design the LMS in such a way that it catered for some of the possible positive effects as mentioned in the research above. In the next section of our chapter, we describe the LMS-based English Writing Course and the practices it governs in more detail.

Section 2: The design and use of the LMS

LMS is considered to be one of the useful solutions for both students and educators in e-learning environments (Al-Busaidi & Al-Shihi, 2012). LMS is a web-based technology that helps plan, distribute, and evaluate a specific learning process. The LMS that underpins our English Writing Course is Web 2.0 which means that it uses user generated Websites that emphasise both content and usability for its users. This system contains software applications and features, which provide students with learning materials and content that are easily accessible and managed.

However, any use of LMS needs to be well structured by a pedagogical process that underpins the students' learning. In our case, this pedagogical process consists of four stages:

1. *Organisational stage:* introduction of the course aim; familiarisation with the LMS operation; familiarisation of students with criteria for evaluating their performance;

2. *Preparatory-technical stage:* registration of students on LMS site; posting trial messages; compiling the list of topics for writing by the teacher and students;

3. *Procedural stage:* brainstorming and searching for relevant information on specific topic, analysis and synthesis of the information obtained; reaching a certain educational goal (posting questions and answers); monitoring students' performance; presentation of students' written works in the groups at LMS site;

4. *Evaluating stage:* reflection; self-evaluation; evaluation of students' performance by the teacher.

Thus, following these four stages, we provided students with opportunities to improve their English writing skills, whilst encouraging them to adopt new writing practice approaches, as autonomous learners.

When we designed the LMS-based English Writing Course, we used the framework developed by Aifudin (2016:139). She defines eight important characteristics of the LMS needed to enhance the quality of students' learning performance.

"*1. reliable and accessible support;*

2. involving collaboration components;

3. continuous, constructive and timely feedback;

4. contextual teaching and learning;

5. timely feedback and support;

6. using reliable technology and assisting the mastery of sufficient technological skills and knowledge;

7. involving experimental learning activities;
8. product-oriented course activities."

Our LMS-based English Writing Course is a collaborative and user-friendly platform that was designed by teachers at the College of Finance and Customs in Vietnam and approved for integration into the curriculum by the college's senior management. Students enrol in this course for a duration of thirteen weeks. One week before the course begins, students receive instructions on how to log in to LMS and register by inserting their full name, and also upload a photo of themselves.

The LMS-based English Writing Course adapts interactivity dimensions (Table 1) developed by Chou (2003) in order to increase the learning interaction among students.

Interactivity dimensions	Brief description
Choice	Ability to access information of varying types (i.e., multimedia)
Non-sequential access of choice	Ability to choose a route through information
Responsiveness to learner	System responds to users' requests quickly
System responds to users' requests quickly	System collects data about users and their use patterns Users can access data about their use
Personal-choice helper	Information helps learner to make better choice of the content
Adaptability	System adapts learning experience to individual users
Playfulness	Information arouses curiosity and encourages learners to play and explore
Facilitation of interpersonal communication	Users (educators and students) can communicate with each other online
Ease of adding information	Users (educators and students) can add information to the system

Table 1: Interactivity dimensions (adapted from Chou, 2003).

The first (navigation) page of the LMS-based English Writing Course contains different activities in which students can participate and interact with the content, educators and classmates, as shown in Figure 1.

Figure 1: LMS-based English Writing Course navigation page.

The *Topics* section provides students with the list of twelve topics, which cover a variety of subjects from daily life to business settings. In addition to viewing the list and the tasks requirements, students have the option of viewing the sample of essays related to the certain topic. During the first week of the course, students need to know all twelve topics and they are required to write an essay on a weekly topic.

The *Brainstorming* section provides students with the opportunity for in-depth work with essays based on ideas. Students are able to brainstorm ideas that is important section before start writing a complete essay. As such, they are supposed to spend a great deal of time on brainstorming. Here, students can look at their peers' brainstorming, in their capacity as an autonomous evaluator, in order to develop their ideas effectively and the quality of their own content may be enhanced as a result. Teachers can correct any idea-related errors and give feedback when necessary.

The *Essay* section permits students to post their completed writing in a Word format. Students also have the opportunity to download and read their peers' writing to learn about the weaknesses and strengths of each essay, where students can develop their evaluation skills through critical thinking, as a further indicator of autonomous learning. The teacher acts as a facilitator in assigning one student's essay to another student, who is responsible for marking it and giving constructive feedback.

The *Discussion* section enables the students to submit their evaluation and comments on the essay. It is expected of the students that they identify and analyse certain error types, for example, grammatical errors and lexical errors. Then, finally, the teacher downloads and marks the essays using the code scheme adapted from Hegelheimer and Fisher (2003). In addition, each week the teacher randomly selects one student's essay and uses the 'Track Changes' feature along with oral comments, recorded with Camtasia, a program that allows users to create professional videos and screencasts. This file is then uploaded for students to watch, aiming to assist them in recognising and learning from these errors.

The *Dictionary* section allows students to take the initiative, as autonomous learners, to look up vocabulary in order to use it accurately and appropriately in their writing. Students also have access to an online dictionary, leading to their overall development in choosing and using the academic words effectively. Students are encouraged to use a wide range of topic-related vocabulary.

The *Help* section enables students to post questions or inquiries about the writing tasks. Both the educators and their peers can provide appropriate answers and solutions throughout this section.

Our LMS-based English writing skills practice fully utilises all of the aforementioned sections. In the writing of the weekly topics, the LMS actively facilitates EFL students to develop both their linguistic communicative competencies and evaluation skills – by way of evaluating own learning performance and performance of peers, thereby promoting autonomous language learning.

Section 3: The outcome

The deviation from traditional teaching and learning practice, through collaboration with a writing LMS application, added variety for students and encouraged students to adopt new writing practice approaches. Students were more actively involved in the learning of a foreign language, in this case English, and more responsible for their learning tasks. The students were developing capacities to develop as autonomous learners. The project was also an opportunity for students to recognise how their writing skills could be enhanced as a consequence of related activities. When students evaluated the written work, we found that they showed increased cognitive activities, creativity and independence. They also improved their English writing skills, as well as improved time management, communication, peer learning and reflection.

More specifically, our design and use of the LMS-based English Writing Course has proven effective and valuable to the students and the practice has contributed to students' overall improved English writing skills in a number of ways, such as:

- developing greater confidence in giving opinions and evaluative feedback;

- greater exposure to learning activities;

- raising grammatical awareness;

- being accountable for learning performance;

- encouraging learner autonomy;

- gaining benefits from more psychological and comfortable learning environment; and

- demonstrating ability for critical thinking.

In relation to the research mentioned earlier, we found that our LMS-based Writing Course succeeded in increasing student interaction, another indicator of increasing learner autonomy, leading to the improvement evidenced in their written works, which concords with the findings of Beauvois (1998). We also found that the LMS-based Writing Course had positive affect on students' attitudes towards interactivity and feedback, findings which support those made by Bikowski and Kessler (2002). Finally, and echoing the findings Yan and Xiaoqing (2009), we found that students were able to develop their learning responsibility and learner autonomy when engaging in the LMS-based Writing Course.

Section 4: Moving Forward

The LMS creates a convincing simulation of reality and can trigger both writing quality and motivation, which is capable of expanding the boundaries of traditional education. Based on our experiences with the LMS-based English Writing Course, we predict that the students' experiences of this course should yield greater levels of satisfaction than previous iterations. This in turn could be evidenced in the depth of understanding displayed by students in the assessments evaluated during the course.

The college has succeeded in designing and integrating a LMS course into the curriculum to assist students to effectively improve their English writing skills. The benefits of this integration are evidenced through students' positive learning outcomes. In our view, this LMS-based English Writing Course is a prototype of smart and dynamic online learning, which will enhance the future of language learning in Vietnam. In order to enhance students' experiences in an innovative way, and encouraging of learner autonomy, the following conditions should be considered in the future:

- greater attention to the didactic properties of a LMS (e.g. brevity, publicity, linearity);

- combining social, cultural and psychological components;

- boosting students' motivation for self-learning and autonomy; and

- relating interactivity dimensions to students' needs and instructor goals.

With the success of the LMS integration into English writing skill teaching, the College of Finance and Customs will introduce this model to students in the third year and fourth year from 2019 onwards. In addition, this model is being considered for implementation in other universities in Vietnam and, where conditions are appropriate, has a transferability potential to be used in other second language learning scenarios in other countries, both regionally and beyond.

Conclusion

This chapter has covered an introduction to LMS, as an innovative teaching and learning tool for EFL-students to improve their English writing skills and develop as autonomous learners. We discussed how to design the content of LMS, and how LMS can be used to facilitate writing skills in class. Our innovative practice also demonstrated that LMS successfully provided the students with useful and authentic activities, which motivated students in their language learning, and enabled them to actively engage in the learning process as autonomous learners. This LMS has showed itself to be valuable in a Vietnamese tertiary education setting with EFL students. We also believe that students' English writing skills have improved significantly due to this innovative application of learning technology.

About the Authors

Nguyen Van Han is currently undertaking his PhD in Education at University of Southern Queensland. He can be contacted at this e-mail: nguyenvanhantesol@gmail.com

Henriette van Rensburg, PhD, is an Associate Professor (Special Education) in the Faculty of Business, Education, Law and Arts, at the Toowoomba campus of the University of Southern Queensland, Australia. She can be contacted at this e-mail: vanrensb@usq.edu.au

Bibliography

Aifundin, M. S. (2016). *Training language teachers online: a study of computer-assisted language learning (CALL) teacher training in Indonesia*. PhD thesis, University of Southern Queensland.

Al-Busaidi, K., & Al-Shihi, H. (2012). Key factors to instructors' satisfaction of learning management systems in blended learning. *Journal of Computing in Higher Education*, 24, 18–39.

Beauvois, M. H. (1998). Conversations in slow motion: computer-mediated communication in the foreign language classroom. *The Canadian Modern Language Review*, 54(2), 198–217.

Benson, P. (2011). Teaching and Researching: Autonomy in Language Learning. Harlow: Longman.

Bikowski, D., & Kessler, G. (2002). Making the Most of Discussion Boards in the ESL Classroom. *TESOL Journal*, 11(43), 27–30.

Canale, M., (2014). From communicative competence to communicative language pedagogy. In *Language and communication*, pp. 14–40. London: Routledge.

Chou, C. (2003). Interactivity and interactive functions in web-based learning systems: A technical framework for designers. *British Journal of Educational Technology*, 34(3), 265–279.

Hegelheimer, V., & Fisher, D. (2003). Grammar, writing, and technology: A sample technology supported approaches to teaching grammar and improving writing for ESL learners. *CALICO Journal*, 23(2), 257–259.

Najeeb, S. S. (2012). Learner autonomy in language learning. *Procedia-Social and Behavioral Sciences*, 70, 1238–1242.

Pennington, M. C. (1996). *The computer and the non-native writer: A natural partnership*. Cresskill, NJ: Hampton Press.

Phinney, M. (1996). Exploring the virtual world: Computers in the second language writing classroom. In M. Pennington (Ed.), *The Power of CALL*. Houston, TX: Athelstan, pp. 137–152.

Yan, G., & Xiaoqing, Q. (2009). Chinese College English Learners' Attitudes and Behaviors in Computer-Assisted Autonomous Language Learning. *The Journal of ASIA TEFL*, 6(2), 207–231.

Chapter 5

Using Screencasting to Provide Effective Feedback on Academic Writing Assignments

Kristina Rigden

Introduction

With my chapter, I contribute to the book *Innovative Teaching And Learning Practices In Higher Education* by showing how I use screencasting to provide effective feedback on academic writing assignments at the University of California in the United States. Screencasting is a video recording of the computer screen captured over a period of time, usually with audio narration. Such use of technology has become a vital and expected part of higher education over the past decades, as technology has evolved rapidly and students have become more reliant on technology. With my use of a Web 2.0 technology like screencasting, I enable my students to become immersed in 21st century learning skills. I have chosen to use screencasting technology for feedback, because it has been shown that many students struggle with written feedback because it is time-consuming to read all of the teacher's comments, the teacher's handwriting is sometimes illegible (Yoke *et al.*, 2013), or the feedback comments are not written in a way that students can easily understand. As one way to address these shortcomings, I introduced screencasting technology as a mean for teachers to give high-quality feedback on students' writing assignments – as an alternative to written corrective feedback. If used successfully, Henderson and Phillips (2015) state that feedback through screencasting can be student-centered, personal, authentic, constructive, supportive, stronger and clearer than written corrective feedback. Moreover, feedback through screencasting can be made available in both face-to-face and distance learning settings, because it can be accessed and watched at the convenience of students (Chu & Leung, 2003; Ali, 2016). According to Middleton (2016), this learning flexibility is important for contemporary students, as it provides an extension to the existing physical or virtual learning environment. Therefore, all these aspects of screencasting technology help encourage students to actively engage with the process of feedback.

Reading this chapter, you will gain the following three insights:

1. how to use screencasting technology to create clear and engaging feedback that effectively encourages students to watch, understand and use;

2. advantages and disadvantages of screencasting technology;

3. reflection on practical applications of screencasting technology.

The chapter has four main sections. In Section 1, I describe my background as an English as a Second Language Instructor at the University of California, Riverside Extension Center in the United States, putting forward the need for the incorporation of technology into the classroom. In Section 2, I discuss in more detail the innovative practice of using screencasting technology. In Section 3, I examine student's perspectives as receivers of such feedback and add my teacher reflections on screencasting as a means to provide feedback. In Section 4, I look ahead and discuss how the use of screencasting may be moved forward. All of these sections are presented from my perspective as a teacher.

Section 1: How I became aware of screencasting technology

As an English as a Second Language (ESL) Instructor in an Intensive English Program at a University, I was researching to find effective ways to teach pronunciation to the international students in my oral (pronunciation) skills course. One of my fellow instructors commented that she records her voice as a form of audio feedback to the students, so that they can hear the correct pronunciation. I implemented this technique and the students, indeed, valued such audio feedback. Replicating the findings of a study by Wang and Young (2015), the use of this technique effectively enabled students to notice their pronunciation errors. As the students continued to improve their pronunciation through the use of audio feedback, they also became more confident in taking oral (including pronunciation) tests with the knowledge that their pronunciation was improving. With this method being so effective for student learning of English pronunciation, I then applied this method in my other courses that involved writing. Concurring with Aoki's study (2014), I also found that audio recording feedback was useful to my ESL students in such writing skills courses. At the same time, however, I strongly felt the need to find an innovative way to visually represent what I was saying to the students, when giving feedback on their writing.

This led me to research the flipped learning strategy, that requires students to complete pre-class activities before coming to class. In the flipped learning context, pre-class activities typically involve transmission of content information in the forms of short videos or pre-readings, to be completed before class, in order to allow class time to be largely spent on project-building and interactive student activities. Such pre-class short videos are often produced with screencasting technology. This is how I started to incorporate the use of screencasting into my feedback practice. The following section outlines the innovative use of screencasting technology that makes feedback clear, understandable and usable.

Section 2: The practices of screencasting

Screencasting is a video recording of the computer screen, often accompanied by audio narration. Screencasting can be done simply through audio narrating a PowerPoint presentation or through other screecasting programs. Past research findings suggest that using screencasting to give academic writing feedback, instead of written corrective feedback, has changed the way students learn and master academic writing, as it enables the teacher to provide more feedback in greater detail (Dagen *et al.*, 2006). Similarly, Ali (2016) observes that such screencasting feedback practice is clear, personal, specific, supportive, constructive and engaging. Henderson and Phillips (2015) state that feedback through screencasting can be student-centered, personal, authentic, constructive, supportive, stronger and clearer than written corrective feedback. These findings strongly suggest that, if screencasting is effectively incorporated into academic writing feedback, it can generate a positive impact on student's writing. Furthermore, several studies have shown that students learn better with other forms of feedback than they do with written corrective feedback. Such other forms include in-person writers' conferences, video feedback and screencasting. For example, in Henderson and Phillips' (2015) study on video feedback, they found that 98% of post-secondary students positively rated videos as the primary form of feedback. Likewise, Ali's (2016) study reported that university freshmen in an academic writing course, evaluated video feedback as helpful, because it assisted them to reshape their ideas, to organise their essays and to vary their sentence structures. Similar results were also found in Edwards *et al.* (2012) study on screencasting as a form of feedback on an essay. Their results showed that personal feedback was helpful and students felt that it was easier to accept, and that the visual cues and explanations helped clarify the points of the professor. All these findings strongly support the use of screencasting technology as a form of feedback that can bring about positive outcomes on the part of the students.

Preparation of screencasting

For anyone new to the technology of screencasting, it is important to test out the variety of screencasting options that are available, such as Jing, Screencast-o-matic, Cam Studio, Camtasia Studio and Screencastify to determine, which is going to be the best fit for one's needs. With many of the different screencasting programs available, it is necessary to create an account to use the program. In addition, some of the programs will require a download of the software and signing an agreement stating they have a right to view one's screen, audio and webcam when using the program. With screencasting, I would first recommend starting by experimenting with the free programs that are available. (Currently, I use Screencast-o-matic because it has a free and paid version. It gives the option to record audio and computer screen only, or audio, computer screen and a video using the webcam on the user's computer). After downloading this software, preparation of screencasting can begin.

Preparation of screencasting will require giving students a writing assignment, teacher time to write comments on the student's paper and record a screencasting, time for the students to reflect on their corrective feedback for their writing assignment, and student time to rewrite the first draft. The following teacher actions will need to take place in order to prepare for screencasting:

- A writing assignment notice;

- A marking rubric accompanied by guidelines showing how the teacher is going to give feedback, drawing upon Straub's (2000) seven principles for effective feedback (outlined below);

- Time to write comments or notes on the student's writing assignment in preparation of recording the screencasting;

- Schedule a time to record a screencasting for every student in the class that submitted the writing assignment;

- Record the screencasting;

- Time to disseminate teacher's screencasting recording to the students;

- Student time to reflect and revise the first draft of their writing assignment.

After the teacher has given students a writing assignment and students submit them digitally, the process can begin for screencasting. The teacher should write feedback and have those comments ready before starting screencasting. It is important to remember to identify patterns of strengths and weaknesses in the writing assignment (Dagen *et al.*, 2006), in addition to utilising Straub's (2000) seven principles for effective feedback to student writing:

1. turning comments into a conversation;

2. not taking control over the student's text;

3. giving priority to content, context, organisation and purpose;

4. limiting scope and number of comments presented;

5. focusing the comments on the maturity and stage of the writing;

6. directing the comments to the individual student; and

7. using praise often.

Once the screencasting program is ready to go on the computer and the document is uploaded to the computer screen, the screencasting can start. This involves clicking the record button on the screen and there will be a 3-2-1 countdown on the screen. It is helpful to speak to the student through the recording as if speaking to them during an informal conference or office hours (Dagen *et al.*, 2006). When speaking, voice volume, pitch and intonation should be varied to keep the students interested and engaged in the feedback process. Also, it is important to move the computer mouse around the screen and highlight the text of what one is discussing. In some screencasting programs, the mouse moving around the screen is able to highlight the text and change colours to bring the listener's focus to the screen. During the recording, also note if the webcam feature is to be used or not. If it is to be used, the webcam should be at eye level and the lighting is in front of the computer so there is not a shadow on the user's face. Once the recording has finished, press the stop button. Listen to the first few minutes of the recording and note the following elements:

+ Was the volume loud enough?

+ Were all of the words enunciated? (Remember the students need to understand the speech patterns of the feedback provider).

+ Did pitch and intonation vary so as to keep the students interested and engaged in audio feedback?

+ When the mouse moved across the screen, was it disrupting or did it help point to what was being described?

+ Is the webcam image distracting, clear and not blurry? (When I was teaching pronunciation, the students found it very helpful to watch me speak as they could watch my mouth placement when I was speaking phonemic sounds that they struggled with. When teaching writing, the students found the video in the corner distracting from the content that was being spoken).

+ If brave, the screencasting can be shared with a colleague to get additional feedback.

It is important to note that depending on which screencasting program used, editing may not be possible. For example, Screencast-o-matic can only record for a maximum of 15 minutes in the free version and editing is not possible. In the paid for version Screencast-o-matic, one can make longer recordings that can be made and edited, and have audio feedback captioned for students.

There are a few ways to disseminate a screencasting recording to the students: email the link of the recording to the student (confidential), send the recording via a cloud-computing service like Dropbox or Google Drive (confidential), or post the recording in the digital classroom, like Google classroom, Moodle, or Wikispaces (public). Since I have experience with Screencast-o-matic, this screencasting program enables the user to send a link with the recording (under 15 minutes) directly to the recipient. The recipient can click on the link and the screencasting video will pop up. The student does not have to download any software or have an account with Screencast-o-matic to view the recording. This link can even be watched on a mobile device which enables flexibility with the user.

Section 3: Students' and teachers' perspectives on the use of screencasting technology

In order to evaluate the use of screencasting technology for giving effective feedback, two qualitative survey interviews were administered with two groups: one consisted of students and the other consisted of pre-service ESL teachers. The first interview survey was conducted with 11 students enrolled in an intermediate academic writing course. The students were given two one-page writing assignments in order to assess their academic writing ability in ESL. To give effective teacher feedback on the writing assignment by way of screencasting, I drew upon Straub's (2000) seven principles for effective teacher response to student writing as I mentioned earlier in the chapter. Closely following these principles, feedback was created by way of screencasting and sent to each student. The same process was repeated for the second writing assignment. This survey was administered, after the second screencasting was given to the students.

The second interview survey was given to nine current and former pre-service ESL teachers enrolled in a TESOL (Teaching English to Speakers of Other Languages) technology class. The questions in this survey were designed to evaluate their (teachers') ability to use the screencasting program in their feedback practice, how they felt when they were given feedback through this screencasting technology, and their own experience as teachers using screencasting to give feedback to their students.

The outcome

Overall results obtained from the two interview surveys clearly indicated that the use of screencasting in my feedback practice has been positively received by both students and TESOL pre-service teachers in the classroom.

In the first interview survey, all of the students expressed their experience of receiving this form of feedback positively. In particular, all of the four students from Saudi Arabia commented that the verbal explanation on their writing really helped them understand the constant grammar mistakes they were making in their writing. Similarly, one student from Japan commented that she liked hearing my voice as it sounded like I was talking to her directly. These comments concur with the aforementioned previous research findings. In addition, one of the students from Saudi Arabia commented that she sent the screencasting link to her parents to also watch. She told me that she did this because she was proud of her positive feedback on this specific writing assignment and she wanted her parents to see her progress writing in English. While this is the only situation that I have been informed about of a student sharing a link of a screencasting, it is important to note that this element of technology can be shared with anybody once the student has a link of one's voice/webcam image giving him/her feedback on an assignment. In addition to the interview comments, unsolicited emails containing positive, excited responses were also received from several students immediately after the feedback links were sent to them: *"thank you for this feedback, it really helped me understand"*. Such emails from the students revealed that my feedback through screencasting improved their writing and that they felt more confident completing the next writing assignment.

The results from the second interview survey was also positive. When the pre-service teachers used screencasting to practice with the technology, they noted that the technology was easy to master. The dilemma for the pre-service teachers was writing down notes and making comments about what to say as many of them forgot what they were going to say once the recorder was on. The pre-service teachers noted the importance of good quality feedback to give the students as this was a learning tool for the students in the classroom. One pre-service teacher remarked that the screencasting program can create a *"...non-threatening [classroom] atmosphere that is highly conducive to learning"*. The pre-service teachers also remarked that this process was very time consuming with a larger class and sometimes this may not be possible to do weekly, but possibly monthly with the students. When the pre-service teachers used the screencasting in the classroom with their students, the students could not believe that this technology existed and thought it was *"so cool"* to hear their teacher's voice speaking directly to them.

Teacher perspective – my own reflections

The outcome for myself as an educator has been remarkable as I observe the growth of my students and TESOL pre-service teachers. I have learned that although using screencasting to give writing feedback can be time consuming with a larger class, the results are highly effective; especially with ESL students or those students who struggle with academic writing in a university setting. I have learned that it takes time to give students feedback on academic writing when using technology. There is an investment in reading the students writing assignment, making quality notes and specific comments on the writing assignment, recording feedback with screencasting, and then sending the digital link to the student. This time commitment needs to be shared with one's class because the students cannot expect this with every writing assignment. In my academic writing class, I only used screencasting three times during the quarter with three different writing assignments.

Regarding the recording, college students' attention spans appear to average around ten minutes long (Barefoot, 2000; Worley, 2011). Therefore, I would keep the recording under ten minutes. I never made a recording over five minutes because it is tedious for a student to listen to me speak that continuously and it makes it easier for me to have a time limit on each recording. Furthermore, a student's grade should never be disclosed on the recording, because the student can share the link with friends or family, as evidenced by the example I shared of a Saudi student sharing the link with her parents, who then shared it with all members of the extended family. Using screencasting to give feedback on academic writing is time consuming for the teacher, but the results have proven effective and it is important to incorporate technology in the classroom.

Section 4: Moving forward

My experience moving forward with screencasting is to continue to use it with my students and TESOL pre-service teachers. The students in my class have seen the powerful impact a screencasting can have on their academic writing and how their confidence improves in the English language. With my pre-service teachers, they have been very responsive to this technology. They understand the time commitment and are ready to make that commitment to see their students' progress and growth in academic writing. They are excited in the technological innovations that can be applied in the classroom. These pre-service teachers are the future teachers and university professors; they are enthusiastic and ready to step into the classroom and teach the next generation.

Beyond ESL students, this practice can be used with other non-language disciplines, such as the social sciences and humanities to give effective feedback in academic writing. This practice can be applied to these diverse contexts in order to facilitate student learning. The applicability of this innovative technology can result in positive outcomes and academic growth in university students.

Conclusion

It is important to incorporate technology into the classroom and make writing relevant in the 21st century (Ali, 2016). Screencasting can make this happen and become a learning and teaching tool for teachers. This technology is meant as an alternative option to traditional written corrective feedback. There is a lot of versatility with this method of multi-sensory feedback delivery that can help students who are still comprehending writing in English or learning how to write academically. Yet it also has the potential to be utilised beyond the parameters of a language learning context in the teaching of other disciplines. This innovative technological idea can have a profound effect on students in higher education.

About the Author

Kristina Rigden, EdD, is a TESOL Instructor at the University of California, Riverside Extension Center and the Director of Outreach Programs and Women in Engineering for the College of Engineering at California State Polytechnic University, Pomona, USA. She can be contacted at this e-mail: krigden@ucx.ucr.edu

Bibliography

Ali, A. D. (2016). Effectiveness of using screencast feedback on EFL students' writing and perception. *English Language Teaching*, 9(8). doi: 10.5539/elt.v9n8p106

Aoki, S. (2014). Potential of voice recording tools in language instruction. *Teachers College, Columbia University*, 14(2). doi: 10.7916/D80P1BPD

Barefoot, B. O. (2000). The first-year experience: Are we making it any better? *About Campus*. Retrieved from http://www.unb.ca/saintjohn/teachlearn/_resources/bb.pdf

Chu, K. C., & Leung, D. (2003). Flexible learning via web-based virtual teaching and virtual laboratory systems. *Journal of Technology Studies*, 29(2), 82–87.

Dagen, A. S., Mader, C., Rinehart, S., & Ice, P. (2006). Can you hear me now? Providing feedback using audio commenting technology. In Foote, M. M., Szabo, S., Falk-Ross, F., & Sampson, M. B. (Eds.), *Navigating the literacy waters: Research, praxis, and advocacy. The twenty-ninth yearbook: A peer reviewed publication of the college reading association*, Provo, UT: College Reading Association pp. 166–180.

Edwards, K., Dujardin, A. F., & Williams, N. (2012). Screencast feedback for essays on a distance learning MA in professional communication: An action research project. *Journal of Academic Writing*, 2(1), 95–126.

Henderson, M., & Phillips, M. (2015). Video-based feedback on student assessment: Scarily personal. *Australasian Journal of Educational Technology*, 31(1). doi: 10.14742/ajet.1878

Middleton, A. (2016). Reconsidering the role of recorded audio as a rich, flexible, and engaging learning space. *Research in Learning Technology*, 24.

Straub, R. (2000). The student, the text, and the classroom context: A cast study of teacher response. *Assessing Writing*, 7, 23–55.

Wang, Y. H., & Young, S. S. C. (2015). Effectiveness of feedback for enhancing English pronunciation in an ASR-based CALL system. *Journal of Computer Assisted Learning*, 31, 493–504. doi: 10.1111/jcal.12079

Worley, K. (2011). Educating college students of the net generation. *Adult Learning*. Retrieved from http://journals.sagepub.com/doi/pdf/10.1177/104515951102200305

Yoke, S. K., Rajendran, C. B., Sain, N., Kamaludin, P. N. H., Nawi, S. M., & Yusof, S. N. (2013). The use of online corrective feedback in academic writing in L1 Malay learners. *Canadian Center of Science and Education, 6*(12), 175–180. doi: 10.5539/elt.v6n12p175

Chapter 6

Teaching World Englishes through the Use of Skype as a Learning Tool

Mikiko Aikyo

Introduction

With my chapter, I contribute to this book *Innovative Teaching And Learning Practices In Higher Education* by describing how we use Skype as a learning tool by combining it with introduction of the concept of World Englishes for English language learning at the Department of Global Citizenship Studies at Seisen University in Tokyo, Japan. Originally, we taught the First-year English course as a face-to-face class only. The English skills learned by students during that course were to be used in the subsequent Fieldwork course, where our students go abroad to do fieldwork in an international setting. As we teach English at Seisen University, we use the concept called World Englishes, which is defined by Kirkpatrick (2007:3) as *"…those indigenous, nativised varieties that have developed around the world and that reflect the cultural and pragmatic norms of their speakers."*

Traditionally, British English and American English have been taught in Japan, exposing students to what we could call "native speakers' English". However, it is a relatively new approach to have students exposed to World Englishes, what we could call "non-native speakers' English". We decided, to further advance the English communication skills of our students, to develop a new Skype conversation class as part of the First-year English course. Using Skype as an online learning tool, we have our students communicate in English with teachers in the Philippines, through which they are introduced to nativised varieties (Kirkpatrick, 2007) of English, rather than the English spoken by native British or Americans in pre-published audio-visual learning materials. This is in contrast to most countries, including Japan, where English is taught as a foreign language. Here students are often expected to acquire accurate grammar and pronunciation similar to those of native speakers in the UK or the United States (Kamiya, 2008; Kirkpatrick, 2007).

I believe that using the concept of World Englishes improves the communication skills of language students, just as I believe the same is the case when adding Skype as an online learning tool. I consider our combination of the concept of World Englishes and the online tool, Skype to be innovative because of the following two reasons:

1. by providing our students with one-to-one conversation lessons with highly qualified teachers of English in the Philippines (though their mother tongue is not English) through Skype, they learn to speak English autonomously, feeling more free and confident to communicate in English, even when their English is not perfect;

2. by promoting the concept of World Englishes through the Skype lessons, the students become increasingly aware that their English does not necessarily have to be a perfect copy of British English or American English.

Reading this chapter, you will gain the following three insights:

1. become familiarised with the concept of World Englishes and how it affects language learning;

2. learn how we use Skype as an online learning tool; and

3. learn how we structured the curriculum to improve our students' English communication skills by combining the concept of World Englishes with Skype as an online learning tool.

The chapter has four main sections. In Section 1, I introduce the concept of World Englishes to motivate our development of the course World Englishes, in addition to the two courses, First-year English and Field-work. In Section 2, I describe the innovative aspects of using Skype as an online learning tool. I also show the curriculum and the requirements we put on our students when they follow our English courses. In Section 3, I present the outcomes of combining Skype as an online learning tool with the concept of World Englishes. This is based on pre- and post-qualitative studies. In this section, I also present the reflections of the teachers who taught these courses. In Section 4, I explain future applications of the findings of this project.

Section I: Understanding the concept of World Englishes

The concept of World Englishes was first introduced by Smith (1983) who pointed out that as a language becomes international, it cannot be bound by its original culture – or any culture for that sake. He explained World Englishes through the case of a Japanese involved in a business scenario with a Malaysian, and argued that none of them needed to understand British culture to be able to communicate in English. Nor is their understanding of English language bound by English culture itself. Other linguists approached the concept of World Englishes from a global communicative perspective and promoted its use internationally (Kachru et al., 2006; Kirkpatrick, 2007). In the context of this chapter, I define World Englishes as a variety of English reflecting the diverse natures of the countries where it is used. It serves as a communication medium in international situations.

There is a concern that speakers of different varieties of English will eventually become incomprehensible to one another. Crystal (1988) maintains the idea that the new varieties of English will evolve, however, he still believes in the importance of Standard English, because it fosters outward-looking communication between a local community and the rest of the world. He argues that it is necessary for people to acquire both Standard English and those new Englishes. This is because the existence of Standard English (to promote mutual intelligibility) is different from the reason for the existence of new Englishes (to promote local identity). Thus, Crystal (1988) advocates *a World English*, while Smith (1992) and Kirkpatrick (2007) argue for *World Englishes* with greater socio-cultural emphasis. Moreover, Smith (1992:75) contends that it is a natural phenomenon that nativised varieties exist and that there is no need for concern, arguing that "*Our speech or writing in English needs to be intelligible only to those with whom we wish to communicate in English.*" Also, Yazan (2015) emphasises that intelligibility is achieved through accommodation while people retain their own accents, and that language learners can be trained towards mutual understanding with a focus on the responsibility of both the speaker and the hearer.

Teaching English in Japan, the concept of World Englishes becomes interesting. It is so because Japanese are said to be weak at communicating in English. Research done by linguists such as Sakai (2008) shows that the longer a person is exposed to a language, the faster and the better the language is mastered. Torikai (2006) argues that the total time for the Japanese students to be exposed to English is extremely short. She mentions that a 10-year-old native speakers of English would be exposed to English for approximately 10 hours a day, which will total 36,500 hours in ten years. On the other hand, Japanese students spend only about 1,000 hours learning English at school for ten years (Torikai, 2006). In addition, unfortunately, there are limited situations in which Japanese students are exposed to and speak English out of school in their daily life, mostly due to Japan's geographical position. Even though Japanese students study English at school for a long period of time and have a good knowledge of the language, they only have few opportunities to practice English communication. Many Japanese students are reserved and do not feel free to speak out (Wakamoto et al., 2017). Needless to say, they are not outspoken, especially in English.

In relation to the particular context of this chapter, and the concept of intelligibility, it is important that our students become aware of who uses English, where it is used in the world and understand how and why the concept of World Englishes appeared. They should choose the kind of English they prefer and should not feel ashamed of not sounding just like native speakers of English. They should realise that every non-native speaker should be confident of speaking English unique to him or her.

We assumed, therefore, that our students need three important things to improve their English communication skills: 1) support; 2) enough time; and 3) relevant occasions for practicing their speaking. We were certain that introducing the concept of World Englishes played a significant role as a motivating factor for our students to learn English, yet we wanted to explore ways in which this motivation could be further developed through expanding study time exposure to 'real' English. This is why we developed the World Englishes course and implemented Skype as an online technology in the First-year English course.

The idea for this innovation was developed to help our students to have an ample amount of time and opportunities to practice speaking English, before they go out for Fieldwork in various countries. We offer a Fieldwork course in such countries as India, Indonesia, the Philippines, Taiwan, Korea, Malawi, New Zealand, Canada, England, and the

United States, to name but a few. These Fieldwork courses require the students to research on their theme of interest on site. They must interact with the local people and interview them in English. The teachers who accompany the students to these sites of Fieldwork, do so in the hope that their students would become more confident to speak with the local people freely and frankly for the sake of a good research outcome. So, our World Englishes course started in 2016, with the aim of encouraging our students to become confident in speaking English and accustomed to listening to non-native speakers' English. In the next section, I will look at our use of World Englishes as a pedagogical practice.

Section 2: Our use of Skype as a learning tool

With the aim of increasing the number of hours our students communicate in English, we integrated Skype as an online tool and developed a number of conversation lessons in which the students are individually engaged in an unattended class. However, we were mindful of Nakata (2006), who argues that it is difficult for students to make significant language development through autonomous language learning. Therefore, we undertook a pilot study on the effects of Skype conversation lessons with 74 students as subjects in the academic year, 2017–2018. A total of 13 students (3 third-year students and 10 second-year students) were going to Malawi in the Fieldwork course during the summer break. The rest of the 61 students were all third-year-students who did not participate in the Fieldwork course. The former (Malawi) group was surveyed through the first and second semesters, whereas the latter group was surveyed during the first semester. Both groups took Skype conversation lessons given by teachers from an English language school in the Philippines autonomously – during their free time out of regular class hours, in the computer room on campus or at home. They had to take at least three 25-minute sessions a week. The latter group was told that their participation would be counted in the grade of their seminar class in which they are enrolled, while that of the Malawi group was partially counted in their grade in the Fieldwork course. Achievement was assessed in such a way that the learners gained a score of 100% when they engaged in three 25-minute sessions a week. Assessment was made according to the number of sessions they took. The following are the findings of this pilot study.

1. very few third-year students in the latter group took the Skype conversation lessons, in spite of the fact that their achievement was counted partially in the grade of a seminar. The average score was only 21%;

2. those who undertook the lessons enthusiastically were the students in the former group who were participating in the Fieldwork course in Malawi. The average score of the third-year students was 71% and that of the second-year students was 59%.

Based on these findings of the pilot study, we learned two important considerations, in order to obtain optimum results, regarding the students' autonomous learning development in the Skype lessons.

1. the immediate need for the communication skills in English motivates the students;

2. for autonomous learning to occur, there is a requirement for an elaborate system including: a) venue: computer room, b) detailed lesson plan, and c) reminder and encouragement.

Therefore, as a result of the pilot study, we decided to develop a new Skype conversation class. This was to be in addition to the face-to-face (rather than online) First-year English course. This necessitated the organisation of a collaboration with the World Englishes course, in order to bring about optimal results in the Fieldwork course by means of using Skype as virtual fieldwork. Below is a brief description of the three courses.

The First-year English course

In the First-year English course, the students meet once a week in class, where they learn four skills (reading, writing, speaking and listening) using a textbook. In addition to this face-to-face class, they go to a computer room to have the individual Skype lessons with the online teachers in the Philippines. They must actually have one-to-one conversation with the teacher online and after each session, they have to reserve the next session. They are required to take at least two exams online: They must give virtual presentations which will be evaluated as part of the grade of First-year English. In one presentation, the students introduce themselves, explaining such topics as their major at university, hobbies, personality, their family and hometown. In the other presentation, they introduce their university and the Department of Global Citizenship Studies. They explain the objectives of the university, curriculum of the department, and student life. These presentations can serve as preparation for the actual presentation they will make when they participate in Fieldwork.

The Fieldwork course

The students of the Department of Global Citizenship Studies are required to take at least 4 credits in Fieldwork in order to graduate. This Fieldwork is research-based and is far from being a sight-seeing tour, or an intensive language program in which students are required to do research on their theme of interest. They study in detail the area they are visiting, during fifteen weeks in the first semester, before they actually visit the fieldwork site. Then they see the real situation with their own eyes and try to find how they could commit themselves to the problem areas. For example, in the Philippines, some students research into as to why there are numerous street children in the city and their methods of survival. Some other students survey the causes and effects of the low literacy rate of women in India. Other students learn about the Native Americans' life in the past and present. They are encouraged to get first-hand information which can be obtained only by interacting with the local people in English.

The World Englishes course

In the World Englishes course, students learn that out of the world population which is approximately seven billion, 1.75 billion are English users (25%) and 5.25 billion are non-users of English (75%). Out of 1.75 billion English users, only 390 million are native speakers (22%), and 1.36 billion are non-native speakers (78%) (Harvard Business Review, 2012). The Japanese students are encouraged to communicate in English after learning the fact that there are many more non-native speakers of English than native speakers and therefore there are even more chances for the non-native speakers to communicate with each other.

After being introduced to the general concept of World Englishes, the students become encouraged to overcome any possible negative attitudes toward English, and become free from psychological, cultural and socio-logical barriers which could stand in the way of their advancement of communication skills in English. As it is explained in more detail in Section 3, before taking the World Englishes course, the students were more nervous and were not confident in speaking English, but after taking the course, they became more relaxed and motivated to study English. Then they would have chances to listen to and speak to non-native speakers of English through Skype. The teachers have strong networks in various parts of the world and their friends and colleagues could collaborate with them.

A brief overview of the curriculum

Both First-year English and World Englishes are half-year courses which consist of 15 class sessions. Each session lasts for 90 minutes. World Englishes is the so-called omnibus course in which four teachers take turns teaching. They all had experiences studying, researching or working in the part of the world where English is not a native language. The four teachers are marked as A, B, C, and D. Each teacher's responsibilities (for example, in 2017) were as follows:

1. Lecture on the concept of World Englishes. (Coordinating teacher A)
2. Self-introduction by teacher B. How and where he learned English. (B)
3. The difference between American English and British English. (B)
4. English in the Philippines and Australia. (B)
5. Communicating with people in the Philippines through Skype. (B)
6. Self-introduction by teacher C. How he started to learn English. (C)
7. Communicating with people in Malawi through Skype. (C)
8. Communicating with a graduate of our department who works as a medical doctor in Sweden through Skype. (C)
9. Communicating with people in India through Skype. (C)
10. More about World Englishes. (A)
11. Self-introduction by teacher D. (D)
12. Listen to a variety of English through YouTube. (D)

13. Interview foreign students on campus. (D)
14. Campus tour with foreign students. (D)
15. Wrap-up. (A)

In addition, Table 1 (below) shows the content-based class plan for First-year English.

Week	Face-to-Face Class	Skype Class
1	Orientation	Orientation
2–3	Talking about Myself	Hobbies/Sports
4–5	Family	Family
6–7	Hometown and Neighbour	Hometown and Neighbour
		Exam: Presentation on Talking about Myself
8–9	Campus Life	Campus Life
10–11	My Kind of Career	Career
12–13	Travel and Correspondence	Travel and Correspondence
14	Interview Practice	Exam: Introduction of the Department
15	Interview Practice	
	Vocabulary Exam	

Table 1: Content-based class plan in First-year English.

In the Fieldwork course, the students meet once a week to study about the fieldwork site and decide the topic of their research in the first semester. They start preparing for their research by communicating with the local people introduced by the teachers. They visit the fieldwork site during the summer break. In the second semester, they have reflections upon the fieldwork, and write fieldwork reports both in Japanese and English. The Skype conversation teachers help them write the English version of the reports.

Organisation of the innovative practice

World Englishes and First-year English are carried out based on the class plan. YouTube videos also give the students chances to listen to a variety of World Englishes. Using their own networks, the teachers introduce their friends through Skype and the students talk to the local people, for example, those in the Philippines, India, Malawi, and Ethiopia. The students also interact with foreign students who are studying at our university, introducing themselves, interviewing each other and showing them around the university campus.

Preparation of the innovative practice

In this innovative practice, it was crucial for teachers to prepare well for the classes, in order to ensure that the teachers effectively facilitate the students to participate in the class actively, interacting not only with their classmates but also with the people who took part in the class such as overseas interviewees, and foreign students. The following are the materials and preparation needed:

- Thorough discussion among teachers in charge of World Englishes, First-year English, and Fieldwork courses for the smooth coordination and cooperation;
- Arrange budget for Skype lessons;
- Contract with the Skype English school;
- Assign a teaching assistant;
- Reserve a computer room;
- Make the clear schedule for the students;
- Plan a guidance for using Skype;
- Prepare lecture materials;
- Prepare power point;
- Select YouTube materials;
- Make appointments with overseas collaborators to talk through Skype;
- Decide Report topics.

In the face-to-face classes of Fieldwork prior to the actual visit, and in addition to the regular classes learning about the fieldwork site and the fieldwork method, the teachers connect the students with the people living in the fieldwork site through Skype. The students can talk to them in person on Skype before they see them on-site. This helps students to become prepared for the on-site research. In this way, we make the best use of Skype in three different courses to produce the multiplier effect of it.

Section 3: The outcome

Two questionnaires were administered with those students who took the World Englishes course in 2017: pre-World Englishes and post-World Englishes questionnaires. A total of 19 students participated in the pre-World Englishes questionnaire and 16 participated in the post-World Englishes questionnaire. Table 2 (below) shows the yes/no questions and the number of responses.

Questions	Yes (%)	No (%)	No answer (%)
Pre-World Englishes: Do you want to speak English like American or British people?	17 (89.5%)	2 (10.5%)	–
Post-World Englishes: Did you want to speak English like American or British people?	11 (68.7%)	5 (31.3%)	–
Pre-World Englishes: Is it true that you don't want to speak Japanese English?	11 (57.9%)	6 (31.6%)	2 (10.5%)
Post-World Englishes: Was it true that you didn't want to speak Japanese English?	8 (50%)	8 (50%)	–
Post-World Englishes: Did your attitude toward learning English change?	15 (93.8%)	1 (6.1%)	–

Table 2: Results of pre-World Englishes and post-World Englishes questionnaires.

In answering the question, "Do you want to speak English like native speakers such as American or British people?", 17 out of 19 students answered "Yes" (89.5%) and only 2 answered "No" (10.5%) before the students took the World Englishes course. After they took the course, 11 out of 16 said "Yes" (68.7%) and 5 said "No" (31.3%). To the question, "Is it true you do not want to speak Japanese English?", 11 out of 19 said "Yes" (57.9%), 6 said "No" (31.6%) and 2 did not answer before the course. After the course, 8 said "Yes" (50%) and 8 said "No" (50%). The interesting result to the question, "Did your attitude toward learning English change after taking World Englishes?" was that 15 out of 16 students said that it changed. The following are some comments that the students wrote in the post-course questionnaire.

+ *"I realized that pronunciation is not the most important element of English."*

+ *"I used to like to copy the native speakers' English, because those who speak native-like English are superior, but now I understand that there are many different kinds of English in the world and I have become confident of speaking my English."*

+ *"I didn't like English but now I love to learn English."*

+ *"I was very nervous when I speak English before, but now I am relaxed after I learned "World Englishes". I want to speak English!"*

+ *"I enjoyed talking with foreign students studying in our university, and I became motivated to learn English because it was fun to make friends with them."*

These comments appear to show that there was significant positive impact from World Englishes, on both students desire to learn and use English and an understanding of the value of the concept of World Englishes. As with the effect of the Skype conversation lessons on the students' English competence, the following results of the two exams conducted at the beginning and the end of the Fieldwork course show substantial improvement. The perfect score of the exams was 300 each which indicates the assessment of the following 6 areas: 1) ability to convey intentions, feelings, information, 2) pronunciation, 3) sentence structure, 4) grammar, 5) comprehension, and 6) fluency.

A total of 10 students got higher scores in the second exam than in the first exam by 1 to 40 points, while 3 students got lower scores by 3 to 5 points. They showed the most improvement in the first area, their ability to convey their intentions, feelings and information and the third area, and ability to make structured sentences.

Student perspective

After they learned about World Englishes and had a series of Skype conversation lessons, the students said that they realised the significance of World Englishes. They became more confident about speaking English and at the same time they became more cooperative when listening to and trying to understand English spoken by non-native speakers of English. One of them wrote in the questionnaire that she enjoyed talking with foreign students studying at our university, and she became motivated to learn English because it was fun to make friends with them. The pilot study on the Skype conversation lessons showed improvement in the students' English speaking ability. Those who had immediate need to communicate in English in fieldwork said that they had strong motivation to take the Skype conversation lessons. Linking World Englishes and Skype English lessons in First-year English, proved to work out very well.

Teacher perspective – my reflections

Through questionnaires carried out in the World Englishes course, we found that the students' attitude and behaviour toward English changed positively after learning about the concept of the World Englishes. The students became more relaxed, motivated and confident of speaking English, even though they know their English does not sound like that of the native speakers'. One student mentioned in the post-World Englishes course questionnaire that she used to like to copy the native speakers' English, because she thought their English is highly evaluated, but after learning about World Englishes she understood that there were many different kinds of English in the world and she became more confident in speaking her English. In this case at least, World Englishes seemed to serve as a motivating factor.

The teachers who took the students to overseas Fieldwork were also requested to answer the interview questions to determine if they noticed any difference in the students' communication skills and attitude and behaviour toward English when compared to that of the students from previous years. One student, before she went to Malawi, took the World Englishes course in 2016 and the Skype conversation lessons in 2017. The teacher who took the students to Malawi explained in the interview I conducted in September, 2017, that the student was rather reserved at the beginning of the fieldwork. However, she gradually started to take the initiative in asking questions to interviewees as a leader of the group. The teacher thinks that she owes her changes in her attitude and behaviour to the World Englishes course and the Skype conversation lessons she had with the non-native English speakers.

The other teacher, who took the students to India, in answering my interview questions, also said that she found the two students who took the World Englishes course and the Skype conversation lessons interacted positively with local people and asked them many questions. In particular, one of them facilitated the discussion and made a presentation on the findings of the discussion in English. The teacher also felt a positive impact on these students from the World Englishes course and the Skype conversation lessons.

Section 4: Moving forward

Based on the results of the pilot study, the questionnaires, and the interviews, we are now confident in utilising Skype conversation lessons, especially in conjunction with the World Englishes course. The Skype conversation lessons are currently offered only to our first-year-students. However, we could extend the offering to our second-, third-, and fourth-year students in the same manner. Furthermore, this innovative utilisation of Skype could be incorporated into the teaching and learning of other foreign languages, such as French, German, Italian, Greek, Chinese, and Korean that we teach at the university. Likewise, we have a course for Teaching Japanese to Speakers of Other Languages in Japanese Language and Literature Department. Therefore, it would be feasible for us to share our findings with the Japanese language teachers and those students who are aiming to obtain a teacher's certificate in Japanese language teaching.

Conclusion

In the Skype lessons, the students certainly have more time to be exposed to English. They are also given opportunities to speak in English at first hand. It is a valuable experience for the Japanese students who do not have many chances in their daily life to have one-to-one conversations with English speakers. Especially after acquiring the knowledge of World Englishes, speaking with the teachers in the Philippines online is even more effective as it puts the knowledge into practice. At the beginning, they could have a little difficulty in understanding the English spoken by the teachers which is different from what they have been accustomed to because they have mostly been exposed to American English or British English and encouraged to speak it in high school. However, the students will gradually become used to listening to it and at the same time, they feel more confident about speaking English which could be as unique as that of the teachers'. The results of the questionnaires show that there was definitely a positive impact of introducing the concept of World Englishes and Skype lessons on our students to improve their communication competence in English.

This project also gave us an insight about how to motivate our students. Quite a few survey results including that of Nakata (2006) indicate that it is difficult for students to achieve success in autonomous language learning. Especially, Asian students including Japanese students tend not to participate in unattended classes autonomously (Nakata, 2006). However, this project showed that the students may actively learn in the unattended classes autonomously if they have immediate need to learn English.

To enable students' active learning, teachers should encourage the students to participate in more Fieldwork and interact with foreign students studying on our campus. We could also create a joint class with foreign schools in the neighbourhood and invite guest speakers to make a speech in English followed by a question and answer session. It would be advisable to tailor such opportunities more frequently to make our students feel motivated by the immediate need to speak English. In addition, teachers should be able to afford much time and effort to make plans for well-systematised lessons and commit it to memory that their words of encouragement and reminders may have a big impact on the students' attitudes and behaviour to become autonomous learners of English.

About the Author

Mikiko Aikyo is Director of the Institute of Language Education and Professor of the Department of Global Citizenship Studies at Seisen University, Tokyo, Japan. She can be contacted at this e-mail: m-aikyo@ seisen-u.ac.jp

Bibliography

Crystal, D. (1988). *The English Language*. London: Penguin Books.

Kachru, B. B., Kachru, Y., & Nelson, C. L. (Eds.) (2006). *The Handbook of World Englishes*. Chichester: Blackwell Publishing.

Kamiya, M. (2008). Nihonjin ha dareno eigo wo manabubekika, *Sophia Junior College Faculty Journal, 28*.

Kirkpatrick, A. (2007). *World Englishes: Implications for International Communication and English Language Teaching*. Cambridge: Cambridge University Press.

Nakata, Y. (2006). *Motivation and Experience in Foreign Language Learning*. Bern: Peter Lang Pub Inc.

Sakai, S. (2008). Eigokyouiku ni okeru jiritsushita gakushushayousei to ICT. *Journal of Multimedia Aided Education Research 5(1)*.

Smith, L. E. (1983). *Readings in English as an International Language*. Oxford: Pergamon Press.

Smith, L. E. (1992). Spread of English and Issues of intelligibility. In Kachru, B. B. (Ed.) *The Other Tongue: English across Cultures*, Chicago: Illinois University Press.

Torikai, K. (2006). *Ayaushi! Shougakkoueigo*. Tokyo: Bungeishunju.

Wakamoto, N., Imai, Y., Ohtsuka, A., & Sugimori, N. (2017). *Kokusaigo toshiteno Eigo*. Tokyo, Shohakusha.

Yazan, B. (2015). Intelligibility, *ELT Journal, 69(2)*, 202–203. doi:10.1093/elt/ccu073

Section 2: Simulation-Based Innovations

Chapter 7

Enhancing Student Engagement and Employability through the Use of Simulations

Mette Skovgaard Andersen, Sherif Elbarrad,

Kayoko Enomoto & Richard Warner

Introduction

Contemporary higher education worldwide is characterised by continuous and rapid change, in terms of ways of not only promoting student active learning but also in achieving learning outcomes. Given this context, higher education institutions are obliged to respond to an increasing demand for closely aligning the learning outcomes of their degree programmes with the needs of the workplace. This demand-driven response can be observed in the different legal and semi-legal requirements that universities must meet when getting new programmes approved. Thus, more and more universities publically espouse these learning outcome requirements of their graduates, in the form of graduate attributes. Many of such attributes statements typically allude to transferable generic skills, including critical thinking, teamwork and communication skills, leadership readiness and intercultural competency.

Though the implementation of these learning outcomes differ across universities, there seems to be little doubt, that these so-called *"Employability issues are at the very core of contemporary Higher Education"* (Cranmer 2007:169). However, the raison d'etre for universities is also to provide students with deep discipline knowledge and relevant academic skills that can be harnessed in their future learning settings in an ever changing society. This puts universities in a dilemma: on one hand, universities are asked to meet rapidly changing workplace needs and to equip students with 'employability skills', and on the other, universities must also teach students deep discipline knowledge and relevant academic skills.

Indeed, as Cranmer (2007) points out, the development of employability skills in higher education can be seen as a complex area lacking definitive answers. Furthermore, Cherry and Khan (2012:86) also stress the importance of a shift from a *"linear instructionist paradigm to an immersive constructionist one"* in higher education. Such a paradigm shift allows students to be confronted by changing and challenging situations, and to learn to be flexible in their responses. This facilitates their ability to learn to cope with issues in question, thus generating a shift towards an *"immersive simulation environment"* (Cherry & Khan, 2012:87). Such an immersion and its thinking-on-your-feet focus are just as pertinent to the workplace, as they are to the academic classroom.

Therefore, in the chapters in this section, we build upon the arguments of Cherry and Khan (2012) to show examples of student-centred and process-focused ways to deal with the so-called employability skills versus academic skills/knowledge dilemma – by way of using simulation-based innovations in different discipline contexts. As Lane (1995) states, simulations are core to the transmission of learning into reality, in our case, the workplace beyond the higher education environment. Whilst simulation-based learning can also bring about unexpected, additional learning outcomes (see, for instance, Enomoto & Warner; Elbarrad & Saccucci, in this volume), the chapters will outline how we can use simulations in order to effectively deliver both academic (discipline) standards and employability skills.

Background

The idea of using simulations in teaching and learning might, at first, seem neither to be particularly innovative, nor a particular priority in addressing the aforementioned discipline knowledge versus employability dilemma. Indeed, and interestingly enough, Bonk and Kim's (2005) study surveyed future anticipated directionality in learning, and found that out of twelve didactic practices, simulations and role play was prioritised only in fifth place. Even when blended strategies of learning were considered, a majority of university academics stated that under 20% of their students were involved in any type of blended learning, including simulations. However, when Bonk and Kim (2005) extended their study to workplace trainers, they discovered that many had simulations listed second in priority. This markedly different ranking by employers, at that time, suggested that higher education was still hidebound by more tradi-tional 'talk and chalk' teaching and learning philosophies; not matching how employers expected universities to teach.

Some years later, these figures might be not as representative of the contemporary higher education sector, particularly with its increased focus on (often technology-driven) blended-learning. Nonetheless, these figures are perhaps still suggestive of a sector lagging behind in ways in which universities can engage students in appreciating the nexus between university and the workplace. For this reason, in this section, we show how simulation-based innovative teaching and learning practices can help students in promoting their perception of this nexus by allowing them to make decisions and take risks, to take responsibility and problem solve – yet all done within a safe cocoon, which is the supportive university learning environment.

Why use simulations?

The three chapters in this section are simulation-based, and they all in some way, simulate a reality in their innovative practice. The notions of simulations and role plays overlap with each other. However, they also differ in that students are themselves in simulations, whereas, in role plays, students take on a character. Role playing is *"an experiential learning technique with learners acting out roles in case scenarios to provide targeted practice and feedback to train skills"* (Ertmer et al., 2010:75). The notion of games also overlap with both simulations and role plays. In addition, games are normally experienced from a third-person point of view, detached from the consequences (Petroski, 2012). In contrast, simulations are normally experienced from a first- or second-person point of view, which creates more attachment to the consequences (Petroski, 2012). Figure 1 below illustrates how the three chapters are positioned as simulation-based innovations.

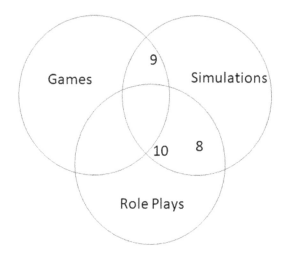

Figure 1: Overlaps between Games, Simulations and Role Plays (Adapted from Leigh et al., 2012:6).

First of all, the use of simulations, although requiring the suspension of disbelief, enables students to bridge between a concept and its real-world application by highlighting certain elements of that reality: *"students take on a decision making persona that might let them diverge from the confines of their normal self-imposed limitations or boundaries"*, and *"...transcend and think beyond the confines of the classroom setting"* (Carleton University, 2018:NP). Similarly, the use of simulations can enable us to naturally draw students' attention to the actual relevance of their (often factual) course materials, to the real-world application. In this way, simulations provide students with an approximation of real world experience in a safe, supportive learning environment.

Secondly, the use of simulations, when group-based projects are assigned, can effectively encourage students to identify and draw upon each other's relative strengths (and weaknesses) within their existing skill sets (Enomoto & Warner in this volume; Sutcliffe, 2002). In so doing, through simulations we are able to take students out of their comfort zones, challenging students to step into the unfamiliar. If successful, this can also bring about positive impact on class dynamics through new friendships and fun (Enomoto & Warner in this volume; Sutcliffe, 2002).

Thirdly, when participating in a simulation, students sit on the inside of the tasks/activities rather than being passive observers. They are able to make decisions for themselves, act on those decisions and take ownership and responsibility for the outcomes of those decisions. As Cherry and Khan (2012) point out, if a simulation has been well-constructed [with appropriate, timely scaffolds] and is interactive, it is not static and hence will not lead to a single probable outcome. Such a simulation will require transferable skills and resilience on the part of the students involved; such skills and resilience are indeed relevant and applicable to the 'real-world'.

Fourthly, the integration of simulations into our teaching and learning practice allows us to achieve not only intended learning outcomes, but also enhanced student engagement and learning experiences. Moreover, if designed appropriately, the use of simulations can also contribute positively to the development of a broad range of key transferable skills. Such key transferables include:

+ teamwork skills;

+ communication skills;

+ critical thinking skills;

+ problem solving skills; and

+ self-regulated learning skills.

In addition to these, students also need to develop their resilience and skills to cope with unpredictable outcomes – another area in which simulations can play a crucial part in preparing our students for their futures in an increasingly and rapidly changing work environment.

Each of the three chapters in this section shows innovative practice that can effectively help motivate students through simulations, to learn new knowledge and skills in a practical, engaging way. The chapters also demonstrate that some of the (aforementioned) employability-enhancing transferable skills can be also targeted and achieved through our practice of simulation-based innovations. However, these transferable skills are not obtained at the expense of deep discipline knowledge, nor academic standards.

Brief description of chapters

This section showcases ways in which we can address the gap between the traditional knowledge transmission model of learning and teaching (Enomoto *et al.*, in this volume) and the rapidly changing demands of stakeholders and industries.

In Chapter 8, Andersen focuses on innovative practices both on an organisational level and on a teaching level. The simulation-based innovations consist of different authentic or semi-authentic scaffolded learning activities, primarily role plays. Through the scaffolded design of learning activities, the author successfully creates a learning environment that effectively encourages students' participation and engagement.

In Chapter 9, Elbarrad and Saccucci use a simulation paper-based game to introduce the (often perceived as being 'dry') concepts of cost accounting, which includes budgeting, direct and indirect costs, and variance analysis. The game involves students actively role-playing in a situation simulating real life. This innovative way of using a non-traditional approach to teach students the cost accounting concepts, has resulted in enhanced students' course engagement, in addition to improved understanding of the concepts as measured by their performance scores.

In Chapter 10, Enomoto and Warner present an innovative design of a group drama project that can effectively develop both discipline and generic skills, using the context of a Japanese language course. Drawing upon students' existing skill sets, the design of the group project is carefully scaffolded to foster teamwork and communication skills, and intercultural competence. The group drama project makes it possible to engage both the engaged and the less engaged by double-tasking discipline and generic skills development, through means of the simulation.

It does us no harm to remember the words of Geurts and Duke (2012: x):"*Those in higher education do not play enough*". So, it is our hope that the chapters in this section will inspire you to consider utilising simulation-based practices in your own teaching and learning contexts.

About the Authors

Mette Skovgaard Andersen, Ph.D, Master of Foreign Languages, is the director of the newly established Danish National Center of Foreign

Languages (East) at Copenhagen University. She can be contacted at this e-mail: msandersen@hum.ku.dk

Sherif Elbarrad, Ph.D., CPA, CMA, is a Professor and Associate Dean – Students, at MacEwan University in Alberta, Canada. He can be contacted at this e-mail: elbarrads@macewan.ca

Kayoko Enomoto is a Senior Lecturer, Head of Asian Studies and Director, Student Experience in the Faculty of Arts at the University of Adelaide, Australia. She can be contacted at this e-mail: kayoko. enomoto@adelaide.edu.au

Richard Warner is a Lecturer in the School of Education in the Faculty of Arts at the University of Adelaide, Australia. He can be contacted at this e-mail: richard.warner@adelaide.edu.au

Bibliography

Bonk, C. J., &. Kim, K. J. (2005). Future directions of blended learning in higher education and workplace learning settings. In Bonk, C. J., & Graham, C. R. (Eds.), *Handbook of blended learning: Global Perspectives local designs*. San Francisco: Pfeiffer Publishing.

Carleton University (2018). Starting point-teaching entry-level geoscience. Retrieved from https://serc.carleton.edu/introgeo/interactive/roleplay.html

Cherry, S., & Khan, A. (2012). The changing mind: a transformative journey towards immersive learning. In Nygaard, C., Courtney, N., & Leigh, E. (Eds.), *Simulations, Games and Role Play in University Education*. Oxfordshire: Libri Publishing Ltd., pp. 85–102.

Cranmer, S. (2007). Enhancing graduate employability: best intentions and mixed outcomes. *Studies in Higher Education*, 31(2), 169–184.

Ertmer, P. A., Strobel, J., Cheng, C., Kim, H., Olesova, L., Chen, X., Sadaf, A., & Tomory, A. (2010). Expressions of critical thinking in role-playing simulations: Comparisons across roles. *Journal of Computing in Higher Education*, 22(2), 73–94.

Geurts, J., & Duke, R. D. (2012). Foreword. In Nygaard, C., Courtney, N., & Leigh, E. (Eds.), *Simulations, Games and Role Play in University Education*. Oxfordshire: Libri Publishing Ltd., pp. ix–xvii.

Lane, D. C. (1995). On a resurgence of management simulations and games. *The Journal of the Operational Research Society*, 46, 604–625.

Leigh, E., Courtney, N., & Nygaard, C. (2012). The coming of age of simulations, games and role play in higher education. In Nygaard, C., Courtney, N., & Leigh, E. (Eds.), *Simulations, Games and Role Play in University Education*. Oxfordshire: Libri Publishing Ltd., pp. 1–22.

Petroski, A. (2012). Games vs. simulations: when simulations may be a better approach. *TD Magazine*, 66(2), 27–29.

Sutcliffe, M. (2002) Simulations, games and role-play. In *The Handbook for Economics Lecturers*. Bristol: Economics LTSN, pp. 1–26.

Chapter 8

Improving Students' Meta-Reflective Abilities through the Use of Scaffolded Simulation Exercises

Mette Skovgaard Andersen

Introduction

With my chapter, I contribute to this book *Innovative Teaching And Learning Practices In Higher Education* by showing how we have used scaffolded simulation exercises as an innovative pedagogy to improve students' meta-reflective abilities in an oral proficiency course, *Interpersonal Discourse in German*. Following Baregheh *et al.*'s (2009) integrated definition of innovation, I view innovative teaching and learning as constituting a field of tension between new and old teaching methods and learning processes (Paulsen, 2012). From this viewpoint, I argue that on a macro (institutional) level, the development of the course, *Interpersonal Discourse in German*, could be seen as innovative, because the course incorporates learning approaches that are fundamentally different between two separate higher education institutions: The University of Copenhagen and Copenhagen Business School. On a micro level, I also argue that the organisation of the course and the combination of scaffolded simulation exercises, formative feedback and a focus on students' meta-reflection could also be regarded as an innovative practice. This is because such a practice, as this chapter will show, can lead to an increased level of student engagement, while increasing the amount of time spent on practising students' oral proficiency in German, at the same time.

Reading the chapter, you will get the following three insights:

1. (new) ways of strengthening students' oral proficiency/organising classes in oral proficiency;

2. (new) ways of improving students' meta-reflective abilities;

3. the difficulty of striking a balance between authenticity and test reliability and validity.

The chapter consists of four main sections. In Section 1, I briefly outline the background and the ideas behind the course and my reasons for considering the teaching to be innovative. In Section 2, I outline my teaching practice. Here I adopt Richards and Rodgers' (1982) ADP (approach, design and procedure) model in order to facilitate the reading of the chapter. According to Richards and Rodgers (1982) planning/presentation of teaching should account for: 1) the approach, referring to the teacher's understanding of language and language learning; 2) the design, referring to the curriculum, learning materials and activities; and 3) the procedure, referring to practice and actual teaching in the classroom. In Section 3, I focus on the outcome, seen from both student and teacher perspectives. The paragraph concerned with teacher perspective also concentrates on the assessment dilemma, which is connected with the teaching and the course's aim of authenticity. In Section 4, I discuss ways to move forward.

Section 1: The background

The course in question was developed in conjunction by representatives from Copenhagen Business School and The University of Copenhagen. Copenhagen Business School is an institution that, to a large extent, advocates case-based teaching and learning and teachers teach from a conviction that these cases should be as authentic as possible. This can also be observed in many of the examinations, which aim at simulating some kind of reality. A teaching and learning approach of this type can be termed 'contextual' (Berns & Erickson, 2001). By contrast, The University of Copenhagen is an institution which, to a greater extent, advocates a universal knowledge approach and consequently examinations typically mirror the idea that some knowledge is more central to the field, and therefore part of the curriculum, than other knowledge.

When Copenhagen Business School and The University of Copenhagen, in 2016, decided to offer a joint postgraduate degree in *Intercultural Market Studies* in the languages German, Spanish and French, it appeared that there was a clash of different teaching and learning approaches

(Andersen, 2016). Having been on the steering group and having taught various courses on this master's degree, I am able to draw on some experience with this new programme and below I shall describe a specific course, *Interpersonal Discourse in German*, in which the two approaches are combined, both in the actual classes and in the examinations. The result can be described as 'innovative' in Paulsen's (2012) sense of the word, as the course represents a tension field between new and old teaching methods and learning processes stemming from two different institutions. From my experience, courses of oral proficiency have been under prioritised, in comparison with courses with 'harder' competencies, like business knowledge courses at Copenhagen Business School and literature and history courses at The University of Copenhagen. The programme is a joint degree and consists of language courses and marketing courses. The course in question is mandatory and one out of four courses devoted to German.

Interpersonal Discourse is a course with the stated purpose of enhancing students' oral proficiency in professional contexts and their ability to interact and meta-reflect. This focus on meta-reflection can also be said to be an innovative contribution to communicative language learning (CLL), (see below, section 2), which has traditionally focused mainly on meta-pragmatics (Verschueren, 2000).

Section 2: The practice

Although the notion of Communicative Language Learning (CLL) has been defined in many different ways (Littlewood, 2011) my understanding of the approach is based on a communicative functional view of language. I believe that language skills can only successfully be developed and learned in social interaction (Long, 1998). Language develops in social contexts and it is necessary to allow students to make errors, so that they can develop an interlanguage, in the sense of Selinker (1972), through hypothesis testing (Ellis, 1997). From my perspective, it seems difficult to sustain the idea of a constant and prescriptive L2 norm with the purpose of the communicative language teaching being to gain near-native competence, as such a prescriptive position implies that there is merely a single way to interact. I constantly emphasise this difficulty during my teaching (see below).

The learning objectives in this course are rather broad and specify a number of competencies. According to the study regulations, by the end of the course students should be able to:

+ *"communicate effectively orally, in the sense that their speech should on the whole be correct and unambiguous;*

+ *moderate and negotiate in the foreign language;*

+ *navigate strategically in intercultural contexts and relations;*

+ *reflect on their own and their interlocutor's communication in the foreign language;*

+ *analyse cultural diversity;*

+ *handle potential cultural dichotomies on an interpersonal and organizational level;*

+ *work systematically, goal-oriented and strategically appropriate;*

+ *structure argumentation in the foreign language."* (Studieordningen for Interkulturelle Markedsstudier:NP).

It appears that these learning objectives can be related to the notion of 'intercultural communicative competence' as first coined by Byram (1997). Using his five *savoirs: 1) savoirs* (referring to knowledge of self and other and of interaction); 2) *savoir-comprendre,* referring to interpretation and relation skills; 3) *savoir s'engager,* referring to political education and critical cultural awareness; 4) *savoir-apprendre/faire,* referring to discovery and/or interaction skills and finally 5) *savoir-être,* referring primarily to attitudes, we can see that each learning objective can be said to be either merely one of the *savoirs* or a combination of the *savoirs.* The overall goal of the course *Interpersonal Discourse* is to develop students' oral intercultural communicative competence, yet the title was actually made before development of the course. Given the implementation it would actually be more appropriate to call the course *Interpersonal Communication.* The many learning objectives make planning complex, especially given the regulations give no indication as to how to prioritise or differentiate between the different areas of competence. With other words, it is up to the teachers' organisation and pedagogic principles to work towards the goals within only eight double classes and five lectures and to handle students with very different ability levels.

We, as teachers in the three languages, tried to solve this problem by actively working with the notions of declarative and procedural knowledge, albeit without accepting the traditional Piagetian cognitive-constructivist premise of declarative knowledge being a prerequisite for procedural knowledge. We believe that the two knowledge forms constantly interact and inform each other. However, as an organisational principle, the distinction has had two positive effects, both in terms of meeting both institutions' fundamental teaching approach as outlined above and ensuring consensus on how to interpret the many learning objectives.

Table 1 shows the structure of the course: five lectures primarily focusing on different (declarative) knowledge aspects of intercultural interpersonal communication and eight double classes (each double class 1½ hours) devoted to practice (procedural knowledge). The lectures centre on traditional pragmatics and consist of presentations of the notions of speech acts and speech act theory, turn taking, face theory, argumentation and intercultural interactions and negotiations. Each of the lectures is followed by one (or more) double classes, where students are expected to practise and reflect on their interactions. The specific activities are outlined in the next section and differ from language to language. Below, I describe the German classes together with my considerations. The course is assessed by means of a 30-minute exam with 30 minutes' preparation time.

Week	Activity
0	Producing a video to apply for course attendance
1	Lecture – speech acts
2	Practice – double classes
3	Lecture – turn taking
4	Practice – double classes
5	Lecture – face
6	Practice – double classes

Week	Activity
7	Lecture – argumentation and intercultural interactions
8+9	Practice – double classes
10	Lecture – intercultural negotiations
11+12+13	Practice – double classes

Table 1: Organisation of the course.

Procedure – organisation of the innovative practice

From my impression and experience, many language classes culminate in giving more speech time to the teacher than to the students. In my classes, approximately 15 students of German participated. The motto of the course is: *Sprechen lernt man nur durch sprechen* (i.e. the only way to learn to speak is to speak). In line with my approach, I constantly emphasise that it is not only unavoidable but even desirable to make errors and feel frustrated. I therefore discuss language acquisition processes and the importance of ensuring both input, output and interaction. I do this in order to make the students accept the central principles of my classes, which are task-based role plays and formative feedback. Role plays can be challenging both for students and teachers, for students because they have *"to take on the persona of someone other than themselves"* (Abeywick-rama & Brown, 2010:214; see also Enomoto & Warner in this volume), which can be a threat to their identity, and for teachers because they have to orchestrate the role play both in terms of content and time. However, the role play method can also, so to speak, set the students free and can create situations that are closer to real-world pragmatics and for that reason might be conceived of by the students as more motivating.

This is the reason that I have chosen role plays as a central principle, but I also use readings, various exercises, interaction tools and a great deal of recorded material from the internet as a basis for analysis. The readings in German are not discussed but only meant to give the students the necessary vocabulary. Another purpose of using internet materials is to ensure sufficient input. Generally, the role plays I developed can be conceived of as tasks (Willis, 1996) and were inspired by Ambjørn's (2001) three-level model: 1) focus on understanding and theory 2) focus on a production exercise with a specific task 3) focus on a production exercise with a more open task. Not every role play goes through all stages, but every role play is assessed in summative and formative peer and teacher feedback, often with the help of an assessment scheme closely related to the topic in question and some of the learning objectives of the course. I try to devise miscellaneous role plays isolating one specific pragmatic aspect, thereby ensuring a kind of progression. At the end of the course we practise professional negotiations based on specific cases and implement all the components.

Preparation of the innovative practice

As Table 2 shows, the German classes are all conducted in German and planned as follows. In addition to the materials shown below, I use short exercises, often also inspired by the world of theatre, and often executed individually by the students. The idea behind these additional exercises is to enhance students' self-efficacy in the sense of Bandura (1977). Examples would be reading aloud alone in different modes, whispering a story, simulating talking to persons behind doors.

Week	Activity
0	Producing a video to apply for course attendance
1	Lecture – speech acts
2	Readings in German about speech acts
	Exercises – speech acts
	✦ watch specific videos and try to find types of speech acts
	✦ role play – make a person leave the room with and without the use of directives
	Feedback
	✦ discussions about feelings and effects
3	Lecture – turn taking

Week	Activity
4	Readings in German about turn taking Exercises – turn taking • watch videos of interviews and try to find out how German-speaking persons interrupt, agree, etc. • role play – role play in groups of three with specific tasks, for instance 'try to interrupt, try to signal that you agree, try to signal that you are listening' etc. • interview each other in groups of three about a topic from the interviews Feedback • feedback on the basis of an observation scheme
5	Lecture – face
6	Readings in German about face Exercises – face • watch videos of talk shows and try to discover how German-speaking persons interrupt, agree, etc. • role play – arguing about positions (e.g. price) in specific situations with opposing interests and positions and different tasks like 'try to agree with everything, try to disagree with everything, try to use face-threatening acts/be rude' etc. in groups of three Feedback • feedback on the basis of an observation scheme
7	Lecture – argumentation and intercultural interactions
8	Readings in German about argumentation Exercises – argumentation and intercultural interactions • role play – discussing a case describing an intercultural interaction in groups of three with different types of argumentation (logos, pathos and ethos) Feedback • feedback on the basis of an observation scheme
9	Exercises – argumentation and intercultural interactions role play – with more focus on argumentation Like week 8
10	Lecture – intercultural negotiations

Week	Activity
11	Readings in German about intercultural negotiations
	Exercises – intercultural negotiations
	✦ role play – resembling exam situation
12	Practice – double classes
	Similar to week 11
13	Practice – double classes
	Similar to week 11
X	Final assessment – exam

Table 2: Organisation of hours.

Due to limitations of space, it is not possible to describe each role play and all teaching material in detail. Therefore, I have chosen to focus on three stages in the learning activities: 1) the beginning – before the classes start 2) the middle – an example of how a specific topic (turn taking) is structured in class and my use of evaluation schemes 3) the end – the final assessment.

Before attending the first class the students are asked to make a video in which they apply for participation in the course. In the case material, it is stated that there are not sufficient places for all applicants and that students therefore have to convince the person teaching this very advanced course that they should be offered a place. The purpose is to set the scene but it also gives:

- ✦ the teacher valuable information on the students' level of oral proficiency;

- ✦ the teacher and students the opportunity to discuss in theoretical terms both the content and the form of the applications in class;

- ✦ the opportunity for students to compare, discuss and grade, i.e. give the different applications (formative) peer feedback at home before coming to the first class (all students have access to all applications).

The participants are asked to find the three students who in their view are most suitable for the course and provide the reasons for their assessments in a plenary discussion. This task is not as such meant as a competition element (see also Elbarrad & Saccucci in this volume), but it broadens the discussion in class to include different assessment criteria such as content, arguments, mode of expression, language skills and in this way, students will indirectly become familiar with many of the learning objectives mentioned above.

The classes dealing with turn taking are organised as follows. First the students are asked to watch different videos containing German interviews at home and instructed to find ways of interrupting, agreeing, taking the floor, keeping the floor etc. In class they are asked to participate in a role play in groups of three, where one person has to take on the persona of a German-speaking person and talk about one of the topics in the interviews. Another person is given the task of trying to interrupt, signal that s/he agrees, is listening etc. The third person is asked to observe and give feedback on the basis of the observation scheme shown in Table 3. The use of observation schemes makes it easier for the students to focus on specific elements and can be said to scaffold their learning (Bruner, 1978). Each observation scheme is different depending on the topic. As Table 3 shows, the observation scheme for turn taking is divided into three parts: 1) observed behaviour with regard to interaction and interactional turn-taking elements, 2) observed behaviour with regard to language and 3) conclusions – advice and learning points.

Observed behaviour – interaction level	Comments
✦ Did you notice how the conversation started?	
✦ Did you notice if anyone tried to interrupt? And if so which turn-taking elements did they use (gambits)?	
✦ Did you notice if anyone tried to signal that they agreed? If so, which turn-taking elements did they use (gambits)?	
✦ Did you notice if anyone tried to take the floor? If so, which turn-taking elements did they use (gambits)	
✦ Did you notice if anyone tried to keep the floor? And if so which turn taking elements did they use (gambits)?	

Observed behaviour – interaction level	Comments
✦ Did you notice if anyone tried to pass the floor to somebody else? If so, which turn-taking elements did they use (gambits)?	
✦ Overall: Did the turn-taking work?	
Observed behaviour – language level	
✦ Was the pronunciation understandable and mostly correct?	
✦ Was the vocabulary adequate and differentiated?	
✦ Did the speaker speak fluently?	
✦ Was the speaker understandable and mostly correct?	
Conclusions – advice and learning points	
✦ If you had to give the speaker one piece of advice for future interactions – what would it be?	
✦ What did you learn from the observation?	

Table 3: Observation scheme – turn taking.

Finally, the students are asked to interview each other – again in groups of three – about their attitudes towards one of the other topics in the video interviews, this time without an observation scheme. The task here is to try to have a smooth conversation and notice anything that could be relevant for the understanding of turn taking. The session is concluded with a selection of my observations. The scaffolded role plays enable the students – so to speak – to experience 'real world' interactions and to reflect upon their own behaviour.

At the end of the course, there is an assessment, an exam. Also, in exam the students are asked to take part in a short role play, but they are also required to engage in meta-reflections about their own behaviour and answer questions on the curriculum. In this way both learning approaches of the participating universities were met. For the Copenhagen Business School teacher's it was of significant importance to the teaching corps that we actually tested the students' ability to enter into interactions that resembled a real-world professional context. We wanted the interactions to take place without prior preparation, in the sense that the students were not given any information on the precise interaction situation. In order to adhere to the way in which real-world negotiations actually take place, we chose to incorporate components from the students' marketing courses and asked them to hand in a short marketing report of a self-chosen firm's entry strategy of a self-chosen product.

This marketing report served two significant purposes. Firstly, it enabled the teacher to make a realistic case/role play that could serve as an exam question. Secondly, having written a marketing report, the students would have acquired some knowledge of the topic in real-world situations, where one would never negotiate a matter without having sufficient knowledge of the topic and having considered the pros and cons first. During the time allocated for preparation, students were asked to plan a negotiation where they had to play a representative from their 'own' firm in a particular situation. Approximately 8–10 minutes of the exam was devoted to this interaction.

The rest of the exam was a discussion of the negotiation, the students' meta-reflections, and the teacher's questions on their declarative knowledge. The latter was a special wish from the The University of Copenhagen teachers. In this way, the exam mirrored the aims of the course and the learning objectives, as well as the two institutions involved and their different approaches. However, as the assessment consists only of one grade, and as there are no regulations for the grading of the different micro and macro competencies of the learning objectives, the validity of the exam can be questioned (see below) even though a grading scheme was employed that was similar to the evaluation schemes used during course.

To prepare for the classes outlined above, teachers have to carefully select input material according to the topics in question, design relevant role plays and other exercises, make different observation schemes and constantly encourage students to combat their fear of public speaking (see, for instance, MacIntyre & Gardner, 1991). This is a challenging task, but in my experience organising the classes as illustrated above can be very fruitful and enhanced students' engagement considerably.

Section 3: The outcome

For the assessment of the outcome of this practice, all of the 15 students took part in the formal student evaluations. Overall, comments received from the students demonstrate that they enjoyed and engaged in the classes, and felt that they had learnt something, although they felt challenged. For example, the following two comments from the qualitative part of the evaluation (translation by the author from Danish) revealed:

+ *"Without any doubt, the teaching encourages active participation in classes. This means that you have to be well prepared to classes in order to gain from the teaching activities, this I find very positive."*

+ *"I have the impression that we are being challenged and learn something in the classes."*

This could suggest that the course organisation and learning activities have led to classes where the students were motivated to work – in a Vygotskian sense (Vygotski, 1978: 86), they worked within *"the zone of proximal development"*. On the other hand, the course evaluations did reveal some frustration that student felt with the amount and variety of exercises, whilst accepting the rationale and recognising a clear connection between theory and practice:

+ *"(...) it is difficult with the many exercises. To be fair, they are all rather well conceived, and I know that the only way to learn to speak is to speak, but sometimes it is really hard."*

+ *"It really works well that we do not have to read a lot prior to the classes, but primarily do exercises because this makes the course more varied. In addition, the exercises are very tangible and creative, which means that you are challenged in a different way than you used to be."*

+ *"I enjoy the close connection between joint lessons and practice classes."*

+ *"In the exercises, I'm a great fan of the teacher's attempts to do everything differently each time. It is really nice to be challenged in your learning style and in the group work – we are all in the same boat."*

Curiously, some students also expressed frustration with not just having to attend classes, but having to prepare for them:

+ *"With regard to role play, I have the impression that you cannot just turn up without being prepared and that you need mental resources to be able to participate in the role play."*

As a long-standing university educator, I have been struggling to accept that we 'only' do exercises in classes, even though we draw on theory in the evaluations and discussions. Also, the feeling of losing control and not being able to constantly monitor every group has been a challenge, as has finding new creative exercises for each topic. Some topics are more suitable for the generation of ideas. However, in my view the advantages clearly outweigh the disadvantages. Based on the level of activity, the students' questions and reflections and the students' engagement in discussions it was my distinct impression that I had more active and engaged students, more motivated students and more enthusiastic students, and even though it is difficult to provide documentation for this, my impression was that the students benefited from the approach and actually improved their oral proficiency and notably their meta-reflective abilities. All of the above evaluative comments strongly support this impression.

Section 4: Moving forward

The described innovative practice can be further developed and specified both within oral proficiency courses, but presumably also within other foreign language courses at university level. 'Cutting up' the learning objectives in authentic or semi-authentic exercises with different foci, scaffolding the activities in different ways and letting the students reflect upon their own behaviour might be a way to enhance students' motivation and engagement and make the students more competent. However, more research on this specific combination is needed.

Changes in teaching methods and teaching activities like the above described will often lead to reflections about assessment. The current assessment form might not be the most adequate as both validity and reliability can be questioned. In line with Li (2011), I understand reliability as factors not primarily related directly to the exam but to external factors, whereas validity concerns test-internal factors. By definition, oral examinations will to a certain degree be challenged with regard to reliability (Andersen & Tofteskov, 2016). By no doubt, this also is valid for the above described course assessment. Owing to the many learning objectives and the above-mentioned lack of differentiation, the so-called test-related reliability (Aberywickrama & Brown, 2010) can be questioned. The examiner and co-examiner have to find ways to assess and grade the different levels of competencies outlined in each learning objective according to stringent criteria. Nevertheless, the learning objectives are located on different levels and require different grading systems and it is most likely that the examiner and co-examiner have different interpretations of the levels and the grading system.

One way to move forward would therefore be to change the exam form and replace it with a portfolio exam. This would probably improve the learning outcomes and ensure that each of the learning objectives is tested more consistently. However, if teaching activities are to be assessed continuously and linked to different learning objectives, it will also require us to rethink some of the teaching activities.

Conclusion

This chapter has shown how the detailed planning and organisation of an oral proficiency course, in this case, *Interpersonal Discourse in German*, can effectively encourage students' course engagement. If successful, this innovative practice could also enhance their learning outcomes. The organisational principle of the course was based on the concepts of declarative and procedural knowledge. During the course, authentic scaffolded learning activities, formative feedback and students' meta-reflective abilities were given priority, thereby forming the core of the course. I believe that the organisational principle and the design of an oral proficiency course could be transferable to be utilised in other languages disciplines – particularly when there is a need to address similar issues at macro (institutional) level and/or at micro (course) level.

About the Author

Mette Skovgaard Andersen, Ph.D, Master of Foreign Languages, is the director of the newly established Danish National Center of Foreign Languages (East) at Copenhagen University. She can be contacted at this e-mail: msandersen@hum.ku.dk

Bibliography

Abeywickrama, P., & Brown, H. D. (2010). *Language assessment: Principles and classroom practices.* NY: Pearson Longman.

Ambjørn, L. (2001). Talt interaktion anskuet i et diskursivt, pragmatisk og strategisk perspektiv. *Webpublikation.* Retrieved March 25, 2018 from http://www.forskningsdatabasen.dk/en/catalog/2389212819

Andersen, H., & Tofteskov, J. (2016). *Eksamen og eksamensformer.* Frederiksberg: Samfundslitteratur.

Andersen, M. S. (2016). Et viden- og kulturmøde mellem Copenhagen Business School og Københavns Universitet: Integrerede kompetencer. *Sprogforum, 22*(62), 58–65.

Bandura, A. (1977). Self-efficacy: toward a unifying theory of behavioral change. *Psychological review, 84*(2), 191.

Baregheh, A., Rowley, J., & Sambrook, S. (2009). Towards a multidisciplinary definition of innovation. *Management Decision, 47*(8), 1323–1339.

Berns, R. G., & Erickson, P. M. (2001). Contextual Teaching and Learning: Preparing Students for the New Economy. *The Highlight Zone: Research@ Work No. 5.*

Bruner, J. S. (1978). The role of dialogue in language acquisition. In Sinclair, A., Jarvella, R., & Levelt, W. J. M. (Eds.), *The child's conception of language.* New York: Springer-Verlag.

Byram, M. (1997). *Teaching and assessing intercultural communicative competence.* Clevedon, UK: Multilingual Matters.

Ellis, R. (1997). Interlanguage. In Ellis, R. (Ed.), *Second Language Acquisition.* Oxford University Press.

Li, W. (Januar 2011). Validity Considerations in Designing Oral Test. *Journal of Language Teaching and Research, 2*(1), 267–269.

Littlewood, W. (2011). Communicative Language Teaching. In Hinkel, E. (Ed.), *Handbook of research in second language teaching and learning* (Vol. 2). Routledge.

Long, M. H. (1998). Focus on form Theory, research, and practice. In Long, M. H., & Robinson, P. (Eds.), *Focus on form in classroom second language acquisition*, 15, 15–41.

MacIntyre, P. D., & Gardner, R. C. (1991). Methods and results in the study of anxiety and language learning: A review of the literature. *Language learning*, 41(1), 85–117.

Paulsen, M. (2012). Innovationsbegrebets dialektik i en uddannelseskontekst– en strid mellem forskellige innovationsforståelser. In: Paulsen, M., & Klausen, S. H. (Eds.), *Innovation og Læring*, pp. 13–46.

Richards, J. C., & Rodgers, T. (1982). Method: Approach, design, and procedure. *Tesol Quarterly*, 16(2), 153–168.

Selinker, L. (1972). Interlanguage. *IRAL-International Review of Applied Linguistics in Language Teaching*, 10(1–4), 209–232.

Studieordningen for Interkulturelle Markedsstudier (n.d.). Retrieved April 26, 2018, from http://hum.ku.dk/uddannelser/aktuelle_studieordninger/ interkulturelle_markedsstudier/interkulturelle_markedsstudier_ka.pdf

Verschueren, J. (2000). Notes on the role of metapragmatic awareness in language use. *Pragmatics. Quarterly Publication of the International Pragmatics Association (IPrA)*, 10(4), 439–456.

Vygotsky, L. S. (1978). *Mind in society*. Cambridge, MA: Harvard University Press.

Willis, J. (1996). A flexible framework for task-based learning. Harlow: Longman.

Chapter 9

Using a Simulation Game to Teach Students Principles of Cost Accounting

Sherif Elbarrad & Frank Saccucci

Introduction

With our chapter, we contribute to this book *Innovative Teaching And Learning Practices In Higher Education* by showing how we have used a simulation game to teach students principles of cost accounting. Our teaching and learning practice outlined in this chapter, is innovative in the sense that it effectively helps students actively visualise the cost concepts in cost accounting. Understanding basic cost concepts and terminology can be challenging for many students, particularly in first-year introductory managerial accounting courses. This challenge largely stems from the fact that students seem not to share a common understanding of managerial information to which the instructor can refer. Thus, the idea of incorporating a game into our practice of teaching cost accounting, was developed to bring about students' experiential learning by doing. We adapted a multiplayer roleplaying game, as it creates a sense of excitement and engagement in class. Then, we carefully embedded several cost accounting concepts and topics within the game so it naturally attracted students' attention – as a simulation game, providing students (the participants) with a simulated environment in which they play. According to Cruickshank and Telfer (2010), simulation games are intended to provide students with insight into a process, or an event from the real world that is being simulated.

In this chapter, we illustrate the design and process stages of the stimulation game and describe how it was used to engage students, and led to effective achievement of the learning outcomes of the course. When reading this chapter, you will gain the following three insights:

1. an understanding of the design and process stages of using simulation games in order to teach undergraduate students principles of cost accounting, whilst appreciating that the use of game need not to be complex;

2. a recognition of the role of the simulation game plays in facilitating students' understanding of the cost concepts being taught;

3. knowledge about how you can incorporate a simulation game into your own teaching and learning practice to promote deep learning and understanding through simulated experiences.

The chapter consists of four main sections. In Section 1, we first discuss the use of simulation games in terms of its advantages and disadvantages. In Section 2, we illustrate how we designed and used the simulation game in an educational context, followed by the explanation of how to prepare and use the game from an instructor's perspective. In Section 3, we describe the outcome of the use of this simulation game, which is based on our study which was conducted to assess the effectiveness of using this simulation game for enhancing students' understanding and engagement. In Section 4, we show the possibility of using other products as the focus of the simulation game, as well as extending the use of this simulation game method in other classes in business disciplines.

Section 1: The use of simulation games in an educational context

Before we introduce the design and process stages of our simulation game, it is important to distinguish between what is a simulation and what is a game, and also explain why a simulation game is utilised in our teaching practice of cost accounting. Cruickshank (1977) as cited in Cruickshank and Telfer (2010:75) sees simulations as *"the products that result when one creates the appearance and effect of something else"*. Leigh (2003) takes this somewhat static definition further, in her belief that simulations *"...include all interactive representations of perceived reality past, present, future – used for learning purposes"*. For their part, games can be seen as challenges whereby players operate under rules to attain stated goal(s) or objective(s) (Cruickshank & Telfer, 2010). In our practice, we combine both into one innovative educational practice: we simulate a manufacturing work environment, where we ask each student group to work on a cost accounting task taking place in that particular environment. Then, the class celebrate the group that completes the task first, approximating a game contest situation but carried out in friendly, fun competition. According to Cruickshank and Telfer (2010), there are both advantages and drawbacks of using simulation games in educational settings. These advantages include: allowing the participants to get a real-world experience, having students solve difficult problems on their own instead of observing someone else preparing the solution, participants engage psychologically, making decisions and facing the consequences, and finally, games are played in a safe and enjoyable environment. On the other hand, Cruickshank and Telfer (2010) point out that there are some drawbacks with educational simulation games, which include: instructor's lack of familiarity with the game, games may at times be time-consuming, participants may occasionally need to possess more than merely the basic skills, and the games may be costly to develop and use.

When designing the use of the simulation game in our practice, all of these advantages and drawbacks were taken into consideration. For example, we made the design of the simulation game as simple as possible, taking around only 25 minutes of the class time, using inexpensive materials – pen and paper – which allowed all students to participate in the simulation game. The instructions for the simulation game were also made concise and clear for the students' comprehension, taking less than ten minutes to explain to the students. In addition, whilst fun and competition elements were also introduced, a conscious decision was also made not to stress the competition element of a game. Yet, the faculty member facilitating the simulation game observed a great deal of excitement during the simulation game – students did get excited to see who is going to finish the work faster and can make all cost calculations correctly.

We believe that following such methodology will minimise the drawbacks of using this paper-based simulation game. We asked a student from Engineering to draw a prototype house using cardboard and then to use the building experience of the house to identify the different cost concepts and topics. Students are to work in groups, and we started by identification of the role of each group member. The roles included one student to keep track of time, one student to manage the dispensing of tape and two students to cut and tape the house. The student keeping time would equate to a payroll function in industry, while the student dispensing the tape would equate to warehousing/supply chain management and lastly the two students cutting and taping the house would equate to an operation's function. All the students would then reflect on the accounting aspects of this simulation game, being forecasting, costing and variance analysis. Then we related the experience of planning and building the house to the cost principles.

Section 2: The practice

Using a class activity *"that can provide a common framework that the instructor can reference to teach new concepts and thus build students' knowledge"* is one way to overcome students' lack of engagement (King & McConnell, 2010:37). Evolution occurs everywhere, especially with learners. Learners today are different from learners of the past due to many reasons, including but not limited to: our advanced technology development, parents being more active in their learning progress and direction, the increasing number of sensory stimulations during their growing informative years. Consequently, it has become vital for instructors to ascertain the most effective methods for educating the current generation of accounting students; maximising the opportunity for cognitive retention (Hicks, 2007). Other researchers, such as Fouché and Visser (2009), believe that accounting education must change for the contemporary world and confront those number of educators' proving resistant to calls for change and do this through the development of a teaching methodology that can make a difference. This reluctance to change has also been observed by Boyd *et al.* (2000) and that it also devours their valuable time. Such arguments interested us in developing an activity that would get students engaged, minimize the class time "lost" on this activity. Based on student feedback, they (the students) were able to understand the main concepts of cost accounting differently and interestingly. The practice that we used involves designing an educational tool that fulfils these above-mentioned objectives. This is done by using a pre-designed design of a house printed on a light cardboard paper. We provide students with scissors, adhesive tape (the pieces of tape are requested by the students, and the design of the house represents direct material) and a printed worksheet that has some information and tables that they fill out during the game. The students use the house design to build the house and the worksheet to estimate and calculate estimated and actual material, direct labour, and overhead costs as well as calculating variances at the end of the game.

From an instructor perspective, this practice provides a tool that allows them to use the simulation game as an example, when referring to cost concepts in the class room with links to related book chapters. The instructor can be proficient in facilitating the simulation game within five minutes of preparation time. The simulation game requires less than one dollar/Euro of supplies per team of 5 students; the competitive component to determine which team finishes first adds a significant component of student engagement and fun.

The game is divided into three phases:

+ in the first phase, the students plan for the work and prepare material, labour, and overhead budgets;

+ in the second phase, they start working on building the product;

+ in the third phase, they record the actual data and analyse the variances.

Relating the simulation game to the curriculum

Any innovation in teaching and learning needs to be congruent to the demands and outcomes of the curriculum in which it is embedded. With that in mind, we ensured that this simulation was pertinent to the course. There were ten learning outcomes in this cost accounting course and the simulation game was designed to draw the student's attention to three of them. These three outcomes are listed below:

+ determine the cost of products in a manufacturing/job cost environment under the traditional costing method;

+ prepare and use budgets and analyse budget variances;

+ prepare a relevant cost and revenue analysis for management decisions including outsourcing and special-order pricing.

The simulation game is introduced in a core course within the Bachelor of Commerce. Students taking this course are majoring in different majors including but not limited to accounting, such as marketing, supply chain, international business. When planning the course outline, we plan for the game to be introduced after introducing the main cost concepts and before explaining variance analysis. The timing of introducing the game reinforces the main concepts of cost accounting, including direct material, labour, and overheads. The game also emphasises budgeting, by showing how to estimate the budgeted figures. Later on, while we are illustrating the variance analysis, we return to the figures emergent from the game and relate the topic to the game. At this point, the students understand how to calculate the variance and how to analyse them. Having this common reference point is very valuable, given that the average student would not normally cross paths with this subject area before enrolling in this class.

Organisation of the innovative practice

Before the class, the instructor would prepare for the game by preparing a single set of the game for each group. In our case, the class is composed of 40 students, so, we prepare eight sets. Each set is composed of scissors, adhesive tape, one design of a house and one worksheet. Before distributing the sets, the instructor forms groups of five students each. Students are then instructed to assign two group members to play the role of workers (who are to build the house model using the material provided) another group member is to be a timekeeper (where the student calculates each minute at a certain dollar payroll rate), another group member acts a warehouse controller, and another member records information on the worksheet. Each group is then asked to estimate the labour time that they expect it would take to build the house. They have to estimate the pieces of tapes that they will use (each tape is one inch long). If students ran out of tape, there were additional pieces of tape provided (each piece represented a certain non-refundable cost). The timekeeper starts calculating the time spent. The warehouse controller records the number of pieces of tapes used, and all information is recorded in the worksheet provided to the students (a copy is provided later in this chapter).

This worksheet is divided into four main sections. The required tasks are listed at the top of each section. The first section is used to record the budgeted figures at the beginning of the game. Students have to estimate the number of tape pieces that they are going to use and the labour time to build the house. This exercise prepares them for how to prepare a budget. The second section records the actual cost of purchasing materials. The price of the material is different from the budgeted price. The educator states a different purchase price for the tape to create a price variance. So, even if the students used the budgeted number of tapes, which is a rare case, they would have at least a price variance. If the pieces of tapes differed from the budgeted, they would have quantity variance as well.

The third section records the actual costs incurred for labour and overhead. Usually, the time that the students estimated is different from the actual time they spent in building the house. The fourth section is used to calculate the variance. In this section, the students compare their budgeted figures with the actual figures and calculate the variance for material, labour and overhead. After completing the game, the cost accounting concepts are emphasised by relating them to the game. For example, direct material and direct labour are linked to the material that the students used, and the time they spent in building the house respectively. We illustrate the difference between the budgeted and the actual. We then introduce the concept of variance analysis. It is easy for students at this point to analyse the total variance for each element and further analyse it into a change in price/rate and quantity/efficiency. The following pages show the two sheets that are distributed to students.

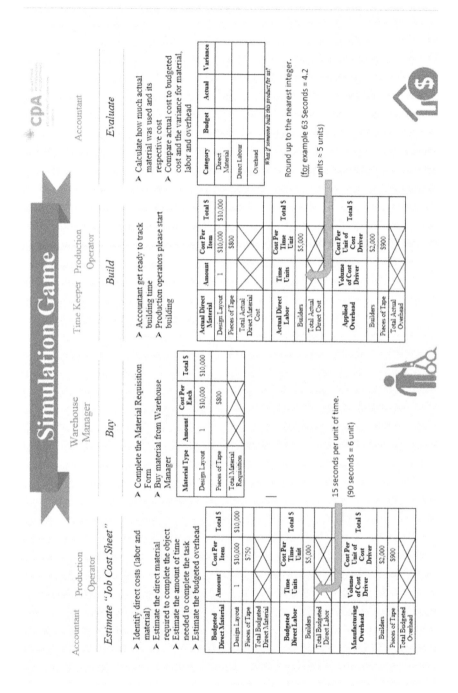

Figure 1: Worksheet handed out to students (Elbarrad & Saccucci, 2016).

The house layout

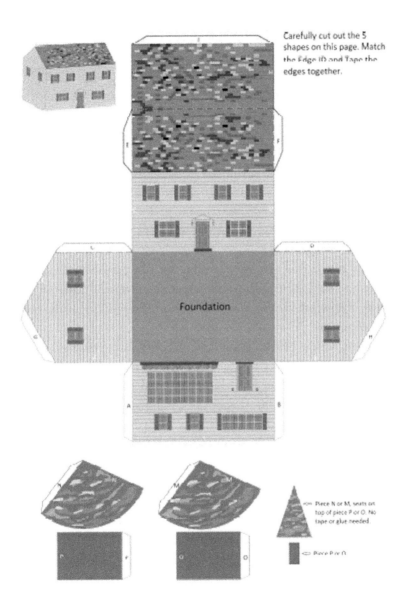

Carefully cut out the 5 shapes on this page. Match the Edge ID and Tape the edges together.

Foundation

Figure 2: House layout handed out to students (Elbarrad & Saccucci, 2016).

Section 3: The outcome

We previously conducted a study (Elbarrad & Saccucci, 2016) in order to measure the students' understanding of the cost accounting concepts, comparing before and after using this game exercise. In our previous study, we measured the quiz scores of forty students in two quizzes. One quiz was taken before playing the game, and the other was taken after the game. The pre-quiz and post-quiz both had ten multiple choice questions, while the multiple-choice questions were different for both quizzes. At the same time, it was ensured that the two quizzes were at the same difficulty level. Both quizzes were taken within a week of each other, therefore, very little in terms of new content material was introduced and discussed in class between the two quizzes. The student performance results of the quizzes were compared using a *t*-paired test. The *t*-test results revealed that there was a significant improvement ($p < 0.05$) in the students understanding of the concepts between the two test performance scores (Elbarrad & Saccucci, 2016). Thus, the statistical analysis evidenced the effectiveness of this practice in terms of their understanding of the cost accounting concepts.

The current study builds upon and extends our previous study (Elbarrad & Saccucci, 2016) – by way of incorporating students' reflective comments as qualitative data into the score-based quantitative analysis we previously conducted. Our reason for adding such qualitative data is that the use of this mixed (quantitative and qualitative) method, not only further supports the effectiveness of our innovative practice, but also offers more insights in terms of the students' learning experiences and their perspectives, than the *t*-test result alone can reveal to us.

Following the game exercise, a paper-based survey was administered with the students in class. The survey asked for an open-ended reflection on their learning experiences with the game exercise. The faculty member circulated the survey and then stepped out of the room while the students completed the survey. The surveys were anonymously completed, and all students participated.

Student's perspective

The obtained students' reflective comments overall reveal that they really saw the value in the use of this game exercise to achieve their learning outcomes. They thoroughly enjoyed having the hands-on experience and also relating what they have experienced with the cost accounting concepts that we introduced to them. As an additional, somewhat unexpected benefit, it was also noted that the students were able to meet new students in their class, because the groups were randomly selected by the faculty teaching the course.

The students enjoyed the game, and by the end of the game, the concepts were more solid in their minds. Quotes of students' reflections included, but are not limited to, the following:

+ *"Enjoyed the opportunity to meet other students."*

+ *"Glad it did not consume a significant amount of time."*

+ *"Like the layout of the game."*

+ *"It was easy to understand."*

+ *"I like how it visually and hands-on demonstrated the concepts."*

+ *"It was fun and increased my knowledge base."*

+ *"Different and brief method of learning the concepts."*

+ *"Gave a good sense of possible hurdles forecasters may have in the industry."*

+ *"Nice switch up from regular lectures."*

+ *"I liked the real world application."*

If we compare this qualitative feedback from students with our former quantitative *t*-test, which showed a significant improvement in the students understanding of the cost accounting concepts, we dare to conclude that using this simulation game in class has been a positive success for both student engagement and student learning.

Teacher perspective

We enjoyed the experience, seeing students easily understand the concepts. It helped us to relate the different concepts to the game. Students became more engaged and were actively learning. It is clear from the above students' comments that the game helped them to grasp the concepts quite easily and that they enjoyed the experience. We are thinking of continuing to use this game (as it is) at this point, due to it being very convenient and inexpensive to conduct. Ninety-five percent (95%) of the student's comments were in favour of the game being introduced in class. The educator noticed the students' energy and enthusiasm rise significantly during the game exercise. There was a sense of 'fun competition' as to which group could finish the project first with the least amount of supplies.

Section 4: Moving forward

The initiative of bringing game to cost accounting concepts has gained significant support from students, instructors and even the Chartered Professional Accountant Education Foundation of Alberta, Canada. The Foundation sponsored development of the simulation game and the activities related to conducting and disseminating the research related to measuring the students' performance after using this educational tool. The funds from the sponsor were used for paying a student studying design to draw the layout of the house, printing the layout and worksheet, buying game supplies. In addition, they sponsored the presentation of the study of the effectiveness of this tool in a conference. This was one time funding opportunity.

We are thinking to continue working on developing the simulation game and making other products such as a boat or a plane. We believe that other disciplines such as engineering, law, HR, and others could benefit from this idea to develop similar engaged simulation games. It is important to engage students in designing the games as it would be designed from a student's perspective. We also agree with Oxarart *et al.* (2014) that more research is needed in the field of measuring the effect of using game in the classroom. This will help the concept of simulation games to spread among other disciplines.

Conclusion

We believe that the use of simulation games in higher education helps students to capture the main concepts taught in a way that it is difficult for them to forget. They have done it with their hands and related the concepts to the experience. It is important to involve students in designing the tool and consider the time spent in playing the simulation in a way that it does make significant inroads into class time. The instructions should be simple and easy to follow for both the faculty member and students. The timing of using the tool is also important, as the students should at least get the basic understanding of the terminology and main concepts upon which they can build their understanding by playing the simulation game. The result, in our case at least, was that students had a deeper understanding of the concepts that they learned through the simulation game, as well as their obvious enjoyment in playing it. We are advocates of experiential and active learning which is low cost, has simple instructions and requires only a small amount of class commitment. We will be working further to explore and develop more such simulation tools.

About the Authors

Sherif Elbarrad, Ph.D., CPA, CMA, is a Professor and Associate Dean – Students, at MacEwan University in Alberta, Canada. He can be contacted at this e-mail: elbarrads@macewan.ca

Franco (Frank) Saccucci, MBA is an Associate Professor at MacEwan University in Edmonton, Alberta, Canada. He can be contacted at this e-mail: saccuccif@macewan.ca.

Bibliography

Boyd, D. T., Boyd, S. C., & Boyd, W. L. (2000). Changes in Accounting Education: Improving Principles Content for Better Understanding. *Journal of Education for Business*, 76(1), 36–42.

Cruickshank, D. R., & Telfer, R. (2010). Classroom games and simulations. *Theory Into Practice*, XIX(1), 75–80.

Elbarrad, S., & Saccucci, F. (2016). The Effectiveness of Using Educational Tools To Enhance Undergraduate Students' Learning Experience To Cost Accounting Principles – an Applied Study. *The Turkish Online Journal of Educational Technology, Special issue* (December), 9.

Fouché, J., & Visser, S. (2009). An evaluation of the integration of a board game in introductory accounting. *South African Journal of Higher Education,* 22(3), 588–601.

Hicks, M. A. (2007). *Cognitive retention of Generation Y students through the use of games and simulations.* Argosy University – Sarasota.

King, G. H., & McConnell, C. (2010). Using a common experience to teach introductory managerial accounting. *Journal of Instructional Pedagogies,* 4, 1–8.

Leigh, E. (2003). A touchy subject—people factors in simulations. *SimTECT 2003,* Adelaide, Australia.

Oxarart, A., Weaver, J., Al-Bataineh, A., & Al Bataineh, M. T. (2014). Game Design Principles and Motivation. *International Journal of Arts & Sciences,* 7(02), 347–359.

Developing Undergraduate Students' Transferable Generic Skills through an Innovative Group Drama Project

Kayoko Enomoto & Richard Warner

Introduction

With our chapter, we contribute to this book *Innovative Teaching And Learning Practices In Higher Education* as we show how we have used an innovative group drama project as our pedagogical method for developing undergraduate students' transferable generic skills, with a particular focus on teamwork and communication skills, and intercultural competence. The innovative group drama project is part of a final (3rd) year Japanese course for undergraduates at The University of Adelaide, Australia. Nevertheless, our focus on teamwork and communication skills, and intercultural competence, does not come at the expense of language learning. Being a language course, the innovative group drama project is, in itself, designed to help students develop discipline-specific second language skills. Students enrol in this undergraduate course to learn the Japanese language, which is the primary learning outcome. However, the way we design the curriculum and scaffold the learning process of students, through the innovative group drama project, supports students' development of teamwork and communication skills, and intercultural competence – as additional key learning outcomes to learning the Japanese language in higher education. Such additional learning outcomes are crucial, because teamwork and communication skills, and intercultural competence – as we see it – are vital transferable generic skills, which as (stipulated) graduate attributes, help prepare students for their futures in the rapidly changing workplace.

Reading this chapter, you will gain the following three insights:

1. how we, as university educators, can effectively facilitate students'

teamwork and communication skills development through the group drama project;

2. how we can actively increase intercultural competence through the group drama project;

3. how effective this group drama project is in addressing transferable generic skills as university graduate attributes.

This chapter has four main sections. In Section 1, we discuss the issues of developing teamwork and communication skills. Following on from this, we examine the conceptual framework of intercultural competence which we used to underpin the process design of our group drama project in the context of a final (3rd) year Japanese course. In Section 2, we outline how the group drama project was scaffolded (Enomoto, 2011; Enomoto & Warner, 2014) and enacted to incorporate innovative practice at two levels: discipline-specific language skills and transferable generic skills, namely teamwork and communication skills, and intercultural competence. In Section 3, we discuss the outcomes of the project based on both quantitative and qualitative data analyses. This is followed by the teacher's reflective insights in order to add another layer of understanding and explanation. In Section 4, we look at how we will use the student feedback and teacher insights to inform the future application in other disciplines and development of this group drama project as an even tighter fit with university graduate attributes.

Section 1: The need for teamwork and communication skills, and intercultural competence

Today's universities need to prepare students for much more than having discipline knowledge and associated skills to take with them, into the workplace (see Enomoto et al. in this volume). The workplace scenarios of tomorrow appear to be largely unpredictable. However, what does seem predictable is an extension of further globalisation – increasingly enabled by technologies, which will continue to require our students to graduate with transferable skills to relate to others, whether it be in physical or virtual working environments. Thus, our focus, in this section, is on such transferable skills to relate to others, namely, teamwork and communication skills, and intercultural competence.

In Australian higher education, students of today face a very different academic environment from their yesteryear counterparts, including significantly larger class sizes, an abundance of learning enabling technologies and increasingly diverse student demographics. One of the constants emerging from this rapidly changing academic environment, is an increasing focus on working in groups – to the extent that the abilities to be a good 'team player and communicator' are distinct characteristics that strongly foreground Australian university graduate attributes. Graduate attributes are mandated for Australian Universities to make public, and are defined as *"the qualities, skills, and understandings a university community agrees its students should develop during their time with the institution"* (Bowden et al., 2002 in Channock, 2003:2). Furthermore, in many descriptions of graduate attributes, teamwork skills and communication skills are deemed to develop hand in hand, and are evidenced *"when they listen, understand and convey their ideas and issues..."* that are both *"...comprehensible and appropriate...teamwork hinges on effective communication skills that are equally about listening, as well as expression"* (Southern Cross University, 2018:NP).

Yet, invariably, we find ourselves having to 'sell' the value of doing group work to students, even in their final year. As Isaac (2012) observes, we regularly hear students say they 'hate group work', often stemming from negative group work experiences. This frequently overshadows their (initial) motivation to engage with a group work assignment for developing teamwork and communication skills. It is therefore crucial, when releasing a group assignment notice, to carefully unpack the value of working in groups as an activity that can bring about a positive, valuable learning experience. To realise this value, it is imperative that we carefully scaffold the process of working in groups, with both clear guiding steps and helpful tools, in a timely manner.

This current focus on the development of teamwork and communication skills in graduate attributes, does not exclude undergraduate language course curricula. In the case of a second language course curriculum, developing teamwork and communicative skills inevitably takes place within the reality of the language-culture nexus: *"linguistic competence needs to be enriched with deep intercultural competence"* (Byram & Wagner, 2018:140). That is to say, a second language cannot be learned to an advanced level in a vacuum away from the society and culture where the target language operates. Cultivating intercultural competence is particularly challenging when the socio-cultural context of the target language is markedly different from the student's own culture. The successful intercultural speaker is one who is 'at ease' with either target or mother tongue socio-cultural situation, and is according to Byram and Fleming (1998) (in Soler and Jordà, 2007), a person knowledgeable in terms of at least one or more cultures and aligned social identities and who appreciates both the discovery of and maintenance of relationships with those from different cultural settings.

However, the construct of intercultural competence has a chequered history, characterised by different cross-disciplinary interpretations. This is evidenced in an extensive study by Deardorff (2006) (in Borghetti, 2017). Despite the hope of encapsulating a cross-disciplinary lens to reach some sort of definitional unity for intercultural competence, Deardorff found a minimum of 49 studies with different definitions of intercultural competence, midst a variety of synonyms such as 'cross cultural competence' and 'cultural sensitivity'. Dervin (2010:158) also found similar definitional plethora, noting that intercultural competence is apparently "...*transparent, universally accepted and (ab)used*", a seemingly static phenomenon characterised by a multiplicity of definitions within academia and beyond. In contrast to such a static notion of intercultural competence, Borghetti (2017:2) provides a sufficiently succinct and focused definition of intercultural competence within higher education, viewing intercultural competence through a developmental filter: "...*as an integral whole of cognitive, affective and behavioural factors that influence...understanding of and interaction with diversity in a broad sense and...developed through education...*".

Building upon Borghetti's developmental interpretation of intercultural competence, Deardorff (2011:67) offers a developmental, process-focused model of what comprises intercultural competence. We utilise Deardorff's cyclic process model of intercultural competence, consisting of four Process Dimensions (PD), as the theoretical underpinning of this group drama project design. This is because the model provides a platform for students' intercultural competence to be fostered from the individual's internal level to the external interactional level as one cycle. Fundamental to this model is that intercultural competence development is incomplete until it is performed interactively in a simulated intercultural situation. The model also allows for the possibility that such an intercultural competence developmental cycle can be repeated and continued.

Figure 1, adapted from Deardorff (2011:67), shows the intercultural competence development from Process Dimension 1 (PD1) through to Process Dimension 4 (PD4), and then PD4 feeds back into PD1, so intercultural competence can be developed continuously. One cycle starts with PD1, that is the individual's attitudes to value other cultures and to accept differences and ambiguities without being judgemental. This then leads to PD2, the individual's cultural knowledge, awareness, comprehension and skills to observe, interpret and relate (Deardorff, 2011:67). According to Deardorff (2011:67), the degree of intercultural competence is determined by the acquired degree of both PD1 and PD2. PD3, then brings about the individual's desired internal outcome, by way of the informed terms of reference shift. The final process of the cycle, PD4, is the external interactional outcome demonstrated by the individual's effective and appropriate interactions in communicative behaviour in an intercultural scenario. This final performance stage, in a relevant situation, evidences a shift from the internal understanding to a demonstration of behavioural operative ability on the part of the individual. Thus, this interculturally competent individual values both diversity and similarity, and can communicate accordingly in different socio-cultural settings (Sercu, 2005) – 'living the language' through the performance stage.

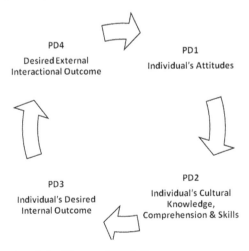

Figure 1: Process Model of Intercultural Competence (Adapted from Deardorff, 2011:67).

With the recognition of the need for embedding intercultural competence in second language curricula, we designed and embedded this group drama project in a final (3rd) year undergraduate Japanese course curriculum, following the cyclic process model of intercultural competence (Deardorff, 2011) that starts from PD1 (the individual's attitudes) in Week 1 through to PD4 (the drama presentations as desired external interactional outcome) in Week 12. We will outline this design in detail in Section 2.

Section 2: The Group Drama Project in more detail

Our group drama project is designed for students to work in groups of 4–5 persons. Each group creates an original, research-informed drama scenario on self-selected current social issues in Japan. This project gives scope, not only to ask individual students to play diverse roles in a Japanese socio-cultural drama scenario, but also to encourage them to identify, value and draw upon their own existing skill sets. In so doing, the project enables students to place themselves 'in the shoes of others' in different socio-cultural settings. We also demonstrate how this project clearly aligns with graduate attributes espoused by The University of Adelaide, Australia (2018).

Groups of 4–5 students wrote a drama scenario in Japanese that incorporated self-selected socio-cultural issues in Japan. This required each group to undertake online research in both Japanese and English, whilst exercising critical thinking to evaluate, discover and retrieve correct and relevant information amongst abundant online sources. The drama scenario that students write (as a group) has to incorporate and reflect an aspect of a socio-cultural issue current in contemporary Japan. This requires each group to research Japanese socio-cultural issues using online sources, both in English and Japanese. To begin with, they were provided with, as a scaffold, a list of several examples of Japanese socio-cultural issues for group discussions and online research (such as maternity harassment forcing women to resign before giving birth; the increasing number of middle-aged 'shut-ins' who live off elderly parents; and the aging population affecting working conditions of old age care workers). Their drama scenario needs not only to show their investigation into their chosen social issues, but also needs to conclude with (a) possible resolution/s within their scenario. Students were told, however, their scenario does not need to be serious in nature, and were encouraged to include humour, laughter and interactions with the audience.

Moreover, we structured this group drama project to utilise the skill sets that each student brings to the language classroom, in order to create an inclusive, active, student-centred learning environment in and beyond the classroom. Students in this course were enrolled in a wide range of undergraduate programs such as Engineering, Computer Science, Sciences, Commerce, Arts, Media, Teaching, Law and Music; and six students (out of 41) were international students from China, Singapore, and Malaysia. This diversity meant that the students brought into the 3rd year language course, a rich variety of skill sets from their major disciplines, as well as existing knowledge and understanding of other cultures. As we will discuss further in Section 3, the design of this group drama project gave scope to prompt this eclectic cohort to identify, value and draw upon each group member's diverse skill sets to foster inclusivity within a group. Thus, not only the small group parameter of the project (4–5 students), but also the diversity of the students' existing skill sets, enabled all group members to meaningfully and actively contribute to the process of developing teamwork and communication skills, and intercultural competence.

This group drama project is innovative, as it develops both discipline-specific language skills, and a wide range of transferable generic skills, with a particular focus on teamwork and communication skills, and intercultural competence, during one assessed task. Such discipline-specific language skills and transferable generic skills are outlined below.

Development of discipline-specific, language skills

Drama presentations are used to develop students' second language skills, allowing students to be more confident when speaking in a target language (Japanese), whilst improving fluency, intonation and pronunciation (Galante & Thomson, 2017). At the same time, students learn to match their emotional and physical expressions with what they are actually saying in Japanese, when within character. Doing so also helps reduce any inhibitions when speaking (in Japanese or English) in public. Students are also required to collaboratively write this drama scenario in Japanese. To do so, they put their previously learned knowledge of grammar and vocabulary into practice when writing their own scenario, whilst developing their skills to utilise various online language tools.

Development of transferable generic skills

Due to it being a group project, students are likely to encounter some (often challenging) situations, where there is a need for precise and effective communication within a group (Davies, 2009), as it is left to each group to arrange the time/dates for group scenario writing and practise outside the classroom. So, all group members are encouraged to work together collaboratively as a team, developing their transferable generic skills in the areas of interpersonal communication, teamwork, leadership, and emotional intelligence, through establishing trust and understanding amongst group members. Moreover, by way of their research into social issues in another culture and the sharing thereof, they could well be developing their intercultural competence. Such competence, coupled with the other transferable generic skills, such as critical thinking and research skills, that they gain through researching into social issues, can help them, beyond their university studies, to enhance their employability.

Amongst all the above-mentioned transferable skills, this group project's design focus is placed upon teamwork and communication skills; and intercultural competence which is facilitated through the utilisation of critical thinking and research skills. Yet, if successful, as Section 3 (the outcome) will show, this project as one assessed task, can extend to also address the full range of both discipline and transferable generic skills identified in the University of Adelaide Graduate Attributes (2018) below:

1. Deep discipline knowledge;

2. Critical thinking & problem solving;

3. Teamwork & communication skills;

4. Career & leadership readiness;

5. Intercultural & ethical competency; and

6. Self-awareness & emotional intelligence.

To effectively lead students to these graduate attributes, as one particular innovative feature of its design, this group project offers scope to ask students to work together to draw upon each other's skill sets that they bring with them. That is, it allows for a wide range of students' (language and non-language related) skill sets to be identified, valued and drawn upon by others – as one way to generate an inclusive learning environment. As a result, the design of this project process encourages students to recognise that each group member has a contributory role to play both in the project process and the final drama presentation performance itself.

A brief overview of the curriculum

One of the ways students can best learn, consolidate and retain their second language knowledge and skills is when they are involved in choosing what to say in a supportive, inclusive environment, and when they are using the language they would use in real situations. Yet, in reality, it is difficult to create such an ideal learning environment, when final (3rd) year language class sizes are still large (more than 40 students) and class contact hours are limited to 4 hours per week over 12 weeks. Furthermore, the 3rd year Japanese IIIB is a capstone course in the major sequence, and therefore, is required to serve as the culminating and integrative experience of Japanese Studies at the University. To fulfil this capstone requirement and to overcome the limitations of the current second language learning environment, activities towards completing the group drama project are carefully scaffolded and embedded in the curriculum throughout the semester, with two specific objectives:

1. to provide students with more student-centred, meaningful and authentic learning environments, rather than teacher-centred, controlled and textbook-based learning environments; and

2. to develop both discipline-specific language skills and transferable generic skills (teamwork and communication skills, intercultural competence).

This group project comprises 15% of the final grade, and consists of four assessed components: a) Group contract submission (2% assessed by teacher & peers), b) Storyboard submission (3% assessed by teacher &

peers), c) Drama presentation (8% assessed by teacher), and d) Individual contributions to drama presentation (2% assessed by peers).

Organisation of the innovative practice

A series of scaffolded activities are carefully mapped out and embedded from Week 1 to Week 12 within the curriculum, to effectively engage and facilitate students to continuously work on and complete this group project throughout the semester (Table 1). An advanced email notice on this project is given to students prior to Week 1 (during the Orientation Week), so students are prepared to organise by themselves to form small groups of 4–5 students in Week 1. This project culminates in a public presentation of a drama scenario in Japanese, presented to classmates and Japanese native speaker guests in Week 12. Throughout the whole process, the lecturer takes on the role of facilitator, providing guidance and appropriate support materials as scaffolds in a timely manner (Van de Pol *et al.*, 2015).

In Week 1, each group starts discussing in depth and writing down group-specific ground rules in concrete terms on the group contract, guided by the group contract template provided: individual responsibilities (such as researching social issues, scenario writing, storyboard drawings, preparing backdrops using Power Point slides for each scene, creating appropriate props for the presentation, booking venues for group meetings), timeline for the project progression with self-chosen deadlines for various agreed tasks, how to deal with a group member not fulfilling his/her responsibilities, and so on. The completed group contract, based on collective decisions, serves to hold group members accountable to allocated responsibilities which, the group feels, are important to a good working relationship. It is intended that this initial activity will help groups function in a more positive, productive way. After each group submits its own group-specific contract (in Week 3), they are then given a guiding handout outlining the process of completing the group drama presentation project consisting of Steps 1–5 as follows:

Step 1: Decide on your drama scenario content

+ Group members conduct online research on current social issues in Japan.

+ Group members each report and discuss what they have learned from their online researching activities.

+ Group members discuss their theme and ideas for scenarios by incorporating one or more current social issues into their storyline.

+ Then, discuss how you could act out a "resolution" to a chosen social issue/problem at the end of your play.

+ Note that the scenario does not have to be serious in nature and you are encouraged to include humour, laughter and interactions with the audience in your play!

Step 2: Create your storyboard as a group

+ Discuss what and how many characters appear in the scenario.

+ Allocate roles to each member.

+ Group members create a storyboard for their scenario. Use 'Storyboard Template Sheets' to create your group's storyboard.

+ Group members develop a sequence of scenes for their presentation, 1) by writing core messages to be conveyed in each significant scene and 2) by drawing a picture of such scenes, detailing which PPT slide backdrops are to be used, who is standing/sitting where, wearing/holding what props, saying basically "what", etc.

Step 3: Write your drama play script based on the decided scenario content and the storyboard

+ Based on the submitted storyboard, discuss and agree who is going to write the play script and who is in charge of which scenes, etc.

+ Discuss and agree how group members can work collaboratively to write scenario scripts for each scene and put them together and improve the entire play script.

Step 4: Rehearse, rehearse, and rehearse... also during the mid-semester break

+ Decide when and how many times, group members should meet to rehearse the entire script as a group during the mid-semester break.

+ Book an appropriate venue for this rehearsing purpose.

Step 5: Video record tricky scenes

+ Video record tricky parts/scenes and review the recordings as a group for further suggestions for improvement.

Week	PD	Scaffolds
1	1	In class (1 hour): Form a group. Watch example video recordings of drama presentations by past students. Begin discussing and creating the Group-Specific Contract. Start discussing and researching examples of Japanese socio-cultural issues provided, as a group.
2	1	In class (30 min): Japanese exchange students are invited to answer questions on socio-cultural issues in Japan, and to share their own personal experiences on such issues and problems. Outside class: Group Contract Discussion and Creation, Continue online research on socio-cultural issues.
3	2	In class (30 min): Group contract submission. Show video recordings of example drama presentations by previous cohort. Provide each group with the support hand-out outlining the process (Steps 1–5) of completing the group project. Outside class: Read the provided hand-out. Continue online research on socio-cultural issues, following Step 1.

Week	PD	Scaffolds
4	2	In class (20 min): Explain in detail the Steps 1–5 in the hand-out outlining the process of completing the group project and answer any questions. Outside class: Step 1.
5	2	Outside class: Step 1.
6	3	In class (20 min): Watch 'what is storyboard' YouTube links. Provide good storyboard examples done by previous year's cohort. Outside class: Step 2 and/or Step 3.
7	3	Outside class: Step 2 and/or Step 3.
8	3	In class: Storyboard submission. Outside class: Step 3 and/or Step 4.
Break	4	Two-Week Mid-semester Teaching Break: Outside class: Step 4.
9	4	Outside class: Step 4.
10	4	Outside class: Step 4 and/or Step 5.
11	4	Outside class: Step 4 and/or Step 5.
12	4	Drama Presentations.

Table 1: *Timeline for the Four Process Dimensions of Intercultural Competence Development and the Embedded Scaffolds.*

Preparation of the innovative practice

To assist each group to self-select a Japanese socio-cultural issue/s to be incorporated into their drama scenario, a list of example socio-cultural issues is prepared and provided in Week 1. We also showed students in Week 1, four recordings of past students' drama scenario presentations as a deliverable that they too can realistically produce. Some language students are not as interested in learning socio-cultural issues as they are in learning the language (grammar, kanji characters and vocabulary). Therefore, in Week 2, the provision of such a list is followed by Japanese exchange students' visit to the class (as guest speakers) to share their knowledge and personal experiences in relation to the listed socio-cultural issues. This helps motivate all students to start researching on Japanese socio-cultural issue/s for the project. In addition, helpful tools to prepare as hard scaffolds are:

+ A group contract template to facilitate each group to discuss and ascertain group-specific ground rules and individual responsibilities;

+ A storyboard template – when handing it out to each group in class, we shared with the students several examples of storyboard drawings from previous years, after showing a YouTube video on 'what is storyboard';

+ A handout that outlines the step-by-step process of completing the project consisting of the aforementioned Steps 1–5;

+ A video camera with a tripod (or equivalent) for recording and marking the group drama presentations; and

+ Marking rubrics designed for both teacher assessments and peer assessments.

Section 3: The outcome

In order to further develop the implementation of this group drama project, it was necessary to ascertain what outcomes Japanese IIIB students (n=41) in Semester 2, 2017, felt they achieved in the process of completing this group drama project. Therefore, a feedback questionnaire in hard copy form was administered by teaching assistants (who were not involved in the course), and completed in class following the drama presentations.

Student perspective

The questionnaire consisted of two parts. As Table 2 shows, Part I contained five categories of statements relating to: 1) Language Skills (3 statements: 1a–1c); 2) Teamwork & Communication Skills (4 statements: 2a–2d); 3) Intercultural Competence (1 statement: 3a); 4) Critical Thinking & Research Skills (1 statement: 4a); and 5) Project Scaffolds & Process (4 statements: 5a–5d). Students were asked to rate their agreement with each statement on a scale of 1 (strongly disagree) to 7 (strongly agree) with a choice of rating 4 (undecided). Part II contained two open-ended questions: Q1 – "What are the best aspects of the Group Drama Presentation Assignment, and why?" and Q2 – "Is the Group Drama Presentation Assignment effective as an assessment for your learning outcomes in terms of developing both language and employability skills at the University?" Then, the Broad Agreement (BA) percentages were calculated based on the percentage of students who were in agreement (marked a 5, 6 or 7) with any given statement.

Categories of Statements		Statements	BA%
1. Language Skills	a	This group assignment provided me with opportunities to develop and apply my Japanese language knowledge and skills into practice.	95%
	b	The drama presentation experience helped me feel more confident in speaking in front of audience in Japanese.	90%
	c	Writing a drama scenario helped me develop my digital literacy skills to use online language tools (e.g. dictionary, translation tools) independently.	88%
2. Teamwork & Communication Skills	a	This group assignment provided me with opportunities to develop my teamwork skills to discuss and allocate an appropriate share and type of work to each group member.	93%
	b	This group assignment provided me with opportunities to develop my teamwork skills to work responsibly on my share of the work.	93%
	c	This group assignment provided me with opportunities to develop my teamwork skills to work responsibly on my share of the work.	90%

Categories of Statements		Statements	BA%
	d	This group assignment provided me with opportunities to develop my communication skills to negotiate tricky or difficult social situations through discussions.	80%
3. Intercultural competence	a	This group assignment provided me with opportunities to deepen my intercultural understanding of Japanese society.	98%
4. Critical Thinking & Research Skills	a	This group assignment provided me with opportunities to practise and develop my online research skills and critical thinking skills, through researching Japanese social issues online.	93%
5.Project Scaffolds & Process	a	Discussing and signing the' Group Contract' as a group at the beginning, helped confirm each other's expectations and engage positively in the group assignment as a group.	68%
	b	The making of storyboard was useful for creating a drama scenario and deciding on how to present it.	88%
	c	Peer-assessment on each group member's contribution was effective and should be continued.	83%
	d	Overall, I feel that the process of developing a drama scenario and researching on Japanese social issues allowed me to engage in deeper, active learning beyond the textbooks.	93%

Table 2: BA % Results from Part I of the Questionnaire (n=41).

Results from Part I (Table 2) show that the BA in the Language Skills Category statements ranged between 88% and 95% with a high mean BA of 91%, whilst the BA in the Teamwork & Communication Skills

Category statements ranged between 80% and 93%, also with a high mean BA of 89%. In addition, the Intercultural Competence and the Critical Thinking & Research Skills statements both gained very high BA percentages of 98% and 93% respectively. The Project Scaffolds & Process category statements scored a slightly less mean BA of 83%, yet still ranging between 68% and 93%. One main reason for the relatively low 68% BA for Question 5a, points to the fact that the group-specific ground rules that each group had discussed and created, did not completely prevent a very small minority of students from unfulfilling their agreed responsibilities. To exemplify this, one student noted:

+ *"Some people just suck at getting stuff done on time :-(this makes it difficult and annoying for other group members."* (S4).

Indeed, some groups had to actually negotiate and overcome such problematic situations by using their teamwork and communication skills. This is strongly evidenced by their consistently high BA percentages across all the four Teamwork & Communication Skills Category statements (Table 2). Furthermore, the following comment is testament to the effectiveness and the value of discussing and writing down the concrete ground rules on the contract (such as small deadlines for agreed tasks or what they could do if someone was not being responsible), so each member engages and contributes to the project actively and responsibly to the best of their ability:

+ *"The small deadlines leading up to the presentation kept us on task (handing up the group contract in week 3, the storyboard in week 9, picking a topic in first term [=first half of the semester], etc.)... Group contract was a good idea. My group all put in their best but if they hadn't it was good to know I could anonymously report that [as all members had agreed]."* (S24).

Overall, these results in Part I are very positive in terms of student perceptions of how effective the group project was for their learning outcomes. This clearly indicates positive outcomes from the students' perspective.

For the analyses of the open-ended comments obtained from Part II, we adopted a phenomenographic approach for conducting the qualitative data analyses and sorted the collected commentaries into specific, emerging categories of description (Åkerlind, 2012). Such categories emerge from a collective analysis of the range of experiences, perceptions and understandings that this student group holds. In so doing, we explored the major compelling themes voiced by the students. As a result, several qualitatively discrete categories of description emerged.

An overwhelming majority of students considered 'the best aspects of this group assignment' (Open-ended Q1) to be the project's capacity to give students 'opportunities' to develop skills in two major categories of description: language-specific skills and transferable generic skills. These positive comments are consistent with the high mean BA percentages obtained in the Language Skills Category (91%) in Part I.

Language-specific Skills

+ "It is an opportunity for Japanese learner [sic] to combine what they have learned and to see how far they have come, their abilities." (S3).

+ "The best aspects would be the learning of social issues in Japan and the opportunity to use and apply the Japanese we've learned in class." (S28).

+ "It was useful having the opportunity to...use the grammar and vocab we have learned in class in a more practical situation." (S16).

+ "Opportunities to practise speaking Japanese in front of a group and [this project] allows us to practise speaking Japanese and receive feedback [from other members]." (S14).

Furthermore, a majority of students made specific reference to the following three sub-categories of emergent themes: 'teamwork & communication skills', 'intercultural competence' and 'critical thinking & research skills', within the transferable generic skills category of description.

Teamwork and Communication Skills

+ "[The best aspect is] to collaborate with other people and communicate to make sure that everyone does the part they were given." (S9).

+ "[The best aspect is] forming good friendships and building communication skills." (S7).

+ *"I found working in a team very rewarding and found that I enjoyed that part the most." (S8).*

+ *"I learnt to trust my team members...I had to know when their lines finished and when it was my turn to speak which really built team-work." (S24).*

Intercultural Competence

+ *"This [=the project] encourages the students to work together and widens the students' perspective of the language and culture." (S11).*

+ *"[The best aspect is] to explore one new topic with the people from different perspectives." (S27).*

+ *"Extremely useful and helpful way of learning more about the Japanese culture." (S9).*

· *"It gives us an opportunity to understand Japanese society better." (S21).*

These positive comments are particularly encouraging, as they are also corroborated by the high mean BA percentages obtained in the Teamwork & Communication Skills Category (89%) and the Cultural Competence Category (98%) in Part I. Finally, the third discrete sub-category emerged – Critical Thinking and Research Skills, as supported by the high BA responses of 93% in Part I. The students seem to have become more aware of the importance of building up their research skills and using their critical thinking to evaluate and analyse Japanese socio-cultural issues, whilst learning the language, as the following comments show:

Critical Thinking and Research Skills

+ *"[This project is] effective for serious learners so they know they need to concentrate on building their research skills and expanding on their language abilities." (S7).*

+ *"Researching current social issues is good, because a lot of Japanese students don't engage with negative aspects of the culture." (S5).*

133

- *"It allowed us to research more into things outside of what's taught in the textbooks, and gave us an opportunity to apply what we learned in class." (S9).*

- *"It allows us to research an issue of Japanese society independently outside the classroom and brings a cultural element to the course." (S13).*

Interestingly, other somewhat unexpected themes also emerged from the comments. These are 'new friendships' (10 students), 'fun' (9 students) and 'creativity' (8 students). The following comments encapsulate such experiences that the students have had through this group drama project:

- *"Having made friends through this exercise…makes the lessons themselves even more enjoyable and provides great motivation to push yourself harder so as either to not let them down or so you can keep up with their progress." (S1).*

- *"It's fun and people make friends – laugh together!" (S5).*

- *"It was rewarding and help to develop important friendships. It was really fun to meet up as well – we were also able to practice Japanese together." (S8).*

- *"Our group worked well together and we had fun doing it together." (S38).*

- *"The fact that acting out the assignment is so fun – I feel the best part of a drama instead of a [traditional oral] presentation." (S18).*

- *"Best aspects are being creative to write the script and come up with ideas to bring to the stage." (S29).*

- *"[The best aspect is] using our creativity to write the script and try to act to make it look real." (S3).*

There were also some negative comments (3 students) in Part II, yet they were in relation to the weighting of the project (15%) not matching its workload, rather than the project learning outcomes:

- *"It was a lot of effort for a tiny portion of the overall grade." (S4).*

- *"It sometimes felt like the amount of work and time spent on this assignment was disproportionate to the grade." (S1).*

✦   *"It involved a lot of work outside of class time considering it was only a small portion of our grade." (S6).*

This more negative feedback is something that we will take on board when considering any changes to the project weighting, as a part of moving forward with this group drama project in the future. Yet, this feedback is indicative of their primary focus on marks, rather than the processes of learning, including transferable generic skills. In addition, we should also highlight the fact that, despite the relatively small weighting, a large majority did actively engage with the group drama project, valuing the learning of both discipline-specific and transferable skills.

Teacher perspective – our reflections

The outcomes of this group drama project in the 3rd year capstone course, in terms of both student engagement and what they perceived they gained from it, in terms of discipline specific/transferable generic skills development and intercultural competencies, more or less met our expectations. What was a welcome surprise for us though, was the unanticipated positive outcomes, such as 'new friends', 'fun' and 'creativity' as significant outcome categories for many students. Such positive outcomes for students seem to suggest that if students are provided with appropriate, sufficient and timely 'tools' and 'scaffolds' to do the job, a group work task which aligns with their interests, coupled with a degree of autonomy, then they will extend themselves, laying the foundations for other positive outcomes to occur. Unpacking the value of developing transferable generic skills in this language course was a particularly crucial scaffold to provide at the beginning of the course. This meant taking five minutes at the end of each class to talk about past students' experiences of applying for a job and how necessary they had found the value of developing the generic skills during their university studies, for enhancing their employability. This (we feel) set the scene for their stated awareness of such skills development in the questionnaire responses of many.

Another reflection, not directly ascertainable from the students' questionnaire responses, is that those students who had been very quiet in the previous courses, became more and more active and visible in class. They were engaging in 'active learning', that was meaningful, authentic and relevant to their immediate realities. These were the students who have not gained high grades and have not been very strong in the language skills, but enjoy learning the language and have an affinity with the culture. They enjoyed the freedom to choose a socio-cultural issue/s, to share cultural knowledge and information and to create a scenario allowing them to be creative in a supportive group environment. The group drama project gave students the opportunity to contribute their other (non-language related) knowledge and skills from their other majors and degrees, such as Media, Computer Science, Music and Law, whilst also fostering their creativity. These students, who otherwise would likely have graduated from the University, with less confidence in Japanese Studies, had a chance to feel valued and shine as a group member, so boosting their confidence. This was particularly gratifying for us, as through this group project we have seen personal growth, particularly in this group of students, developing their teamwork and communication skills, and intercultural competence, as well as their critical thinking and research skills in this capstone course. Alluding to this issue of personal growth that one student felt through the project, s/he wrote:

+ *"At different skills-levels it [=the project] gives you the ability to learn new things in a way you may not know yourself"*. (S10).

We see such students' personal growth as positive outcomes not just for them, but for us as educators in higher education. Engaging such reticent students is always a challenge in any teaching and learning situation. Therefore, as teachers, such clear evidence of the engagement of these students in the group drama project, despite the project weighting being only 15% of the final grade, adds real value to the task for us.

Section 4: Moving forward

We will take on board students' feedback (both positive and negative) and continue to utilise the theory-informed design of this group drama project to help to better realise the goals of the University graduate attributes. Significant support for the continuation of this group drama project emerged from the students' comments, as they were able to recognise through doing this project, both discipline-specific and generic skills development as valuable learning outcomes that enhance their graduate attributes and thus, their employability:

+ *"It [the drama project] should be continued next year, it is a very good experience – students are able to improve all kinds of skills through [the] group assignment."* (S2).

+ *"I think the biggest skills learnt...are communication and presentation skills. I do think that this is important for future skills and do think that this type of [drama] presentation should continue in Japanese courses."* (S10).

+ *"The [drama] presentation was useful for learning and researching current issues in Japan which will help employability...It should be continued it's great for intercultural learning."* (S22).

Our next step is to work with colleagues in the School of Social Sciences at the University, to determine how the theory-informed organisational design principles and scaffolds of this group drama project can be applied and implemented in curricula in other disciplines. For example, in the case of a Sociology course, for the development of intercultural competence, we can utilise the fact that different cultures (and prejudice often against different cultures) exist within a society, based on: socio-economical class, race, ethnicity, age, disability, gender, sexual orientation, beliefs, and so on. Each student group could decide on one such socio-cultural issue as a theme of their drama scenario through their research. Such research-informed knowledge could then be incorporated into a drama scenario for each group member to play one of a number of diverse roles – stepping into the shoes of others, following the four-dimension cycle of the intercultural competence process model. Thus, there is realisable potential for the incorporation of intercultural competence development, informed by the intercultural competence process model, beyond the parameters of a second language learning context.

Conclusion

This group drama presentation project has demonstrated in one assessed task, an effective (and enjoyable) pathway to fulfilling the University graduate attributes, with a particular focus on the development of teamwork and communication skills and intercultural competence. Yet the success of the project has not been at the expense of discipline-specific skills development. Moreover, in addition to the expected project learning outcomes, the findings of the unexpected themes of 'new friendships', 'fun' and 'creativity' demonstrate that this innovative practice clearly engaged the students, including those who may not have been able to engage in the project due to their less developed discipline (language) knowledge, skills and confidence:

+ *"It encourages creativity and confidence."* (S40).

This is because the project allowed each group member's existing (non-language) skill sets to be also valued and drawn upon by others, generating 'a sense of belonging' in an inclusive learning environment where they can form friendships, be creative and have fun together in and outside the classroom:

+ *"working in a group was enjoyable, get[ting] to know others better... meant that I always had a group to sit with during class."* (S6).

Indeed, those students who had seemed less engaged previously came to attend every class because they had a group to sit with. A high level of course engagement by this student cohort throughout the semester was evidently reflected by consistently high attendance rates in all lectures and tutorials. In this sense, this group drama project is innovative in that the project makes it possible to engage both the engaged and the less engaged by double-tasking both discipline and generic skills development:

+ *"The work put into creating a drama performance helps people connect with their peers, all while learning more about Japanese culture and society along with practising language skills."* (S25).

Therefore, this innovative teaching and learning practice fosters not only discipline and generic skills, but promotes the individual's course engagement as a result. With all these innovative features outlined in this chapter, the organisational design principles of this group drama project have the true potential to be utilised in other disciplinary contexts.

About the Authors

Kayoko Enomoto is a Senior Lecturer, Head of Asian Studies and Director, Student Experience in the Faculty of Arts at the University of Adelaide, Australia. She can be contacted at this e-mail: kayoko.enomoto@adelaide.edu.au

Richard Warner is a Lecturer in the School of Education in the Faculty of Arts at the University of Adelaide, Australia. He can be contacted at this e-mail: richard.warner@adelaide.edu.au

Bibliography

Åkerlind, G. S. (2012). Variation and commonality in phenomenographic research methods. *Higher Education Research & Development*, 31(1), 115–127.

Borghetti, C. (2017). Is there really a need for assessing intercultural competence?: some ethical issues. *Journal of Intercultural Communication*, (44), 1–22.

Byram, M., & Wagner, M. (2018). Making a difference: Language teaching for intercultural and international dialogue. *Foreign Language Annals*, 51, 140–151.

Channock, K. (2003). *Challenges of the graduate attributes movement.* Paper presented at the Language & Academic Skills in Higher Education November 2003 Conference, http://www.aall.org.au/sites/default/files/kate%20Chanock.doc.

Davies, M. (2009). Group work as a Form of Assessment: Common Problems and Recommended Solutions. *Higher Education*, 58(4), 563–584.

Deardorff, D. K. (2011). Assessing intercultural competence. *New directions for institutional research*, 149, 65–79.

Dervin, F. (2010). Assessing intercultural competence in language learning and teaching: A critical review of current efforts. In Dervin, F., & Suomela-Salmi, E. (Eds.), *Intercultural Communication and Education. Finnish Perspectives.* Bern: Peter Lang, 105–127.

Enomoto, K. (2011). Fostering high quality learning through a scaffolded curriculum. In Nygaard, C., Courtney, N., & Holtham, C. (Eds.), *Beyond Transmission: Innovations in University Teaching*, 167–184. Oxfordshire: Libri Publishing Ltd.

Enomoto, K. & R. Warner. (2014). Promoting student reflection through considerate design of a virtual learning space. In Scott-Webber, L., Branch,

J., Bartholomew, P., & Nygaard, C. (Eds.), *Learning Space Design in Higher Education*, 127–150. Oxfordshire: Libri Publishing Ltd.

Galante, A., & Thomson, R. (2017). The Effectiveness of Drama as an Instructional Approach for the Development of Second Language Oral Fluency, Comprehensibility, and Accentedness. *TESOL Quarterly*, 51(1), 115–142. Retrieved from http://onlinelibrary.wiley.com/doi/10.1002/tesq.290/full

Isaac, M. L. (2012). "I Hate Group Work!" Social Loafers, Indignant Peers, and the Drama of the Classroom. *The English Journal*, 101(4), 83–89.

Sercu, L. (2005). *Foreign Language Teachers and Intercultural Competence. An Investigation in 7 Countries of Foreign Language Teachers' Views and Teaching Practices.* Clevedon–Buffalo–Toronto: Multilingual Matters Ltd.

Soler, E. A., & Jordà, P. S. (Eds.) (2007). *Intercultural language use and language learning.* Amsterdam: Springer.

Southern Cross University. (2018). GA6: Communication and Social Skills Retrieved from https://www.scu.edu.au/staff/teaching-and-learning/graduate-attributes/ga6-communication-and-social-skills/

The University of Adelaide. (2018). University of Adelaide Graduate Attributes. Retrieved from https://www.adelaide.edu.au/learning/strategy/gradattributes/

Van de Pol, J., Volman, M., Oort, F., & Beishuizen. J. (2015). The Effects of Scaffolding in the Classroom: Support Contingency and Student Independent Working Time in Relation to Student Achievement, Task Effort and Appreciation of Support. *Instructional Science.* 43(5), 615–641.

Section 3: Practice-Based Innovations

Chapter 11

An Introduction to Practice-Based Innovations in Higher Education

Christine Spratt, Christine Armatas,

Brenda Kalyn & Orcun Kepez

Introduction

The chapters in Section 3 present practice-based innovations, addressing important issues about the design and implementation of innovative practices. The chapters are embedded in the authors' interest and commitment to developing creative innovative pedagogies that can effectively engage students in active learning environments. In Chapter 12, Kalyn et al. explore an innovative approach to graduate teaching that arose from their long-standing commitment to critical pedagogy. In Chapter 13, Kepez sees his personal teaching philosophy lead an innovative practice in an undergraduate design program as well as influencing his institution's approach to learning and teaching quality. In Chapter 14, Kepez and Arsan continue by drawing the themes of Chapter 13 into a more detailed discussion of the integration of their research with collaborative teaching approaches and project-based learning in an innovative teaching space. In Chapter 15, in its exploration of a major learning analytics project, Armatas and Spratt demonstrate that organisational level innovation has the capacity to influence degree-level curriculum design and pedagogy.

Despite their diversity in topic, when seen collectively, the chapters in this section of the book all reflect innovative teaching and learning practices as it is described consistently both in this volume and the wider literature. One of the major areas of innovation in higher education globally in the recent past, has been the integration of new learning and social media technologies with pedagogical approaches that transparently support student engagement and active learning pedagogies. According to

Trowler (2010:3), student engagement can be seen as: *"…concerned with the interaction between the time, effort and other relevant resources invested by both students and their institutions intended to optimise the student experience and enhance the learning outcomes and development of students and the performance, and reputation of the institution"*. It is widely accepted that student engagement is closely linked to high quality learning outcomes (Krause & Coates 2008; Kahu 2013; Coates & McCormick, 2014). Alluding to this point, Trowler (2010:4) explains: *"…a sound body of literature has established robust correlations between student involvement in a subset of 'educationally purposive activities, and positive outcomes of student success and development, including satisfaction, persistence, academic achievement and social engagement"*. Indeed, the principles of pedagogical practice that have driven an improvement in student engagement strategies are seen across both undergraduate and graduate education; the chapters in this Section provide contemporary evidence of this in their particular contexts.

Description and synergy of chapters

The practices described in Section 3 are innovative, not just for the way in which they address local pedagogical problems, but the way in which they draw on the relevant literature to inform their innovative practices. Moreover, each chapter reflects the authors' explicit commitment to teaching and learning strategies that are based on humanistic pedagogies and principles of student-centredness. As practicing academics, the authors have been engaged in developing their own scholarship of teaching and learning. This serves to position the work in broader communities of practice (Lave & Wenger, 1991) that lead innovation in teaching and learning in higher education.

In Chapter 12, Kalyn *et al.*, teaching in graduate studies in Education, were particularly interested in developing an innovative teaching and learning approach where graduate students were part of a strong learning community. A fundamental theoretical and conceptual framework that leads their work is the *'situative perspective'* (Putnam & Borko, 2000, Greeno, 1997; Greeno *et al.*, 1996; Lave & Wenger, 1991). According to Putnam and Borko (2000), three main ideas underpin this framework. These are that cognition and learning are: i) situated in particular contexts, ii) social in nature and iii) distributed across people, resources and tools.

Situative theorists such as Brown *et al.* (1989) and Lave and Wenger, (1991) take the position that knowing and learning are not individualistic functions of the human mind nor based purely on individual experience. They argue, rather, that cognition takes place within particular physical and social contexts which deeply influence how and what an individual learns. In other words, that what we know, how we know it, and how we express ideas are products of interactions with other individuals and within groups of people, or *discourse communities* as Fish (1980), and Putnam and Borko (2000) have described it. According to Putnam and Borko (2000:5), "*...discourse communities provide the cognitive tools—ideas, theories, and concepts—that individuals appropriate as their own through their personal efforts to make sense of experiences*". In discourse communities, cognition is distributed, because it is "*stretched over*" (Lave, 1988), or shared, among participants who engage in collaborative meaning-making conversations about experiences, text and other artefacts. This approach is clearly directed at developing learners' engagement as partners with their teachers in collaborative, supportive learning experiences. In their chapter Kalyn *et al.* see their roles as academic teachers, to inspire learning and encourage creative passions in their graduate students. The Chapter illustrates how the authors encouraged an approach where graduate students were largely in control of their personal and cooperative learning experience.

Chapter 12 also describes how curricula and assessment practices included a variety of opportunities to demonstrate how learning strengthens personal practice. The innovative curricula included the application of creative and critical thinking practices inviting students to create new knowledge and explore deeper questions. Consequently, representations of learning were showcased through presentations, readings, writing, discussions, researching, and creative design in assignments. Students were challenged to interrogate theories and theorists through their work, critically analyse documents and engage in independent work and studies in their own areas of expertise and interests. Related assessment strategies included individual and theoretical explorations that linked students' ideas with theory, practice, and innovative thinking. This design aligns well with research such as that of Entwistle (2010) who argues that courses promoting deep learning pose broad questions, approach topics in an open-ended manner, and focus on authentic problems. Furthermore, students should be given choice in assignments, thereby promoting engagement and facilitating deeper learning.

While Kalyn *et al.* are writing in the context of graduate education in teacher education, one can see the synergies between their work and that of Kepez in Chapter 13 and Kepez and Arsan in Chapter 14. In Chapter 15, similar student-centred philosophies led the argument for developing the learning analytics project described by Armatas and Spratt—that project has its foundation in improving student learning outcomes by providing students and teachers with better evidence to improve both curricula and for students to take control over their learning experience and outcomes.

In Chapter 13, Kepez describes an innovative project-based learning curriculum in the design discipline that has been led by the authors' interest in creating a 'democratic classroom'; this is a particularly innovative and creative approach in his particular context, as his University has generally followed more traditional, didactic curriculum models. In the broader discussion of that project-based curriculum, in Chapter 14, Kepez and Arsan have developed their project-based curriculum drawing on their own research practices in the design of innovative learning spaces; their teaching and learning approach aims to bring a research-based design process to their pedagogy through the application of participatory design methods in the classroom. Participatory design is concerned with involving people who are affected by design decisions in the design decision-making process.

We can see, in Kepez's Chapter 13 and Kepez and Arsan's Chapter 14, a philosophy similar to that described by Kalyn *et al.* in Chapter 12 as they aim to develop a collaborative critical engagement with their students. In addition, Kepez and Arsan's collaborative practice sees students actively engaged in research problems drawn from the authors' own working and research lives. Chapter 14 describes how over the course of the semester, the student teams explore engineering design problems. These problems are associated with real-life problems the authors have faced, while developing new technologies to design a state-of-the-art active learning environment in collaboration with Steelcase Education. The pedagogy is described in Kepez's Chapter 13 and is a research-based approach to humanistic design, as it involves understanding the expectations of the people who will be the future users of the environments, observing their use of the space, collecting narratives about past experiences and finally including them into the design process. In this case, Steelcase Active Learning Centre acts as the Community Design Centre to initiate all collaborative efforts. The project-based learning design, which is presented in Arsan and Kepez's Chapter 14, sees students learn new techniques for analysis and revisit research questions as a learning community in the true spirit of engagement pedagogies. In both chapters, students and professors became a true learning community to pursue common goals with shared enthusiasm.

In the final chapter in this Section, Chapter 15, Armatas and Spratt present an innovative, creative approach to improving teaching and learning though the use of a new field of practice in higher education, the application of learning analytics to educational questions. Historically, curriculum review processes in higher education have followed standard evaluation methods employing both quantitative and qualitative research processes. However, the outcomes of such reviews have been generally limited to providing academic teams and other stakeholders with post-hoc strategies for curriculum improvement. Chapter 15 addresses innovation in teaching and learning by offering a model for evaluation that uses strategies drawn from the emerging field of learning analytics for curriculum review purposes. Harnessing discrete data sets, by using learning analytics in an integrated manner for curriculum review processes is innovative, creative and the authors argue, a new form of pedagogical practice. The chapter describes the preliminary stages of a major government-funded learning analytics curriculum review project at a university in Hong Kong, and includes the development of a practical, prototype tool to assist teachers in the process of review and development.

Chapter 15 overviews the project and concludes by considering the implications of this work for what Siemens (2013:1380) called the *"emerging discipline"* of learning analytics. The chapter describes a selection of data analysis techniques that were identified to analyse a range of available institutional data (including students' entry scores, grades, subject choices and relevant survey data). The chapter presents several examples of the outputs of the analysis and visualisation strategies; the results of which then provided curriculum review teams with additional evidence to inform decision making about curriculum improvement plans. Inherent in the approach described in the chapter is the authors' commitment to finding creative solutions to engage practicing teachers and students more directly in curriculum review processes. Historically, students' involvement as stakeholders in curricula review processes has been limited and has varied widely across institutions from involvement in governance structures to participation in routine surveys. (Trowler, 2010; Brooman *et al.*, Darwent & Pimar, 2015). In general, the student voice in curriculum review has been restricted to their voluntary participation in surveys and interviews usually at the completion of subjects and programs. However, in Chapter 15, Armatas and Spratt's work reflects Greller and Drachsler's view (2012:48) that learning analytics can lead to *"more learner oriented services and therefore improved personalisation"*. Indeed, learning analytics for curriculum review purposes has the potential to engage students more directly, both in the design of the curriculum and in providing students with immediate feedback in their current courses about how they might improve their current learning outcomes.

Conclusion

Each chapter in Section 3 demonstrates that creative, innovative teaching and learning has at its foundation a commitment to the development of students as equal partners in the pedagogical process. The chapters, while diverse in their disciplinary settings, each take a humanistic approach to pedagogy. The authors (in Chapters 12, 13 and 14) who are working with students directly, articulate an interest in developing "communities of practice" (Lave & Wenger, 1991), where students and teachers can create egalitarian, engaged learning environments as Kepez articulates in Chapter 13. The authors in Chapter 15, while less directly involved with students, have structured their project, so that the use of evidence to improve the student experience is central to their innovative use of learning analytics. We anticipate that from Chapter 12, readers will see the potential of critically reflective practice and innovative collaborative pedagogies as described by Kalyn *et al.* for their own practice. In Chapter 13 and 14, Kepez and Arsan raise for readers the notion of the "democratic classroom" as the starting point to integrate project-based learning, real-life research and new technologies into active learning pedagogies. In

Chapter 15, from Armatas and Spratt's discussion, the reader will gain an appreciation of the potential of learning analytics for curriculum review and the types of review questions learning analytics can address. Readers will also see how innovative data analysis has the potential to improve systematic curriculum review, the processes for academic advising and student learning outcomes and engagement. The experiential nature of the teaching and learning strategies described in this Section value shared processes to encourage critical reflection and risk-taking on the part of teachers and learners; as such in their specific contexts, the chapters describe work that is creative and innovative.

About the Authors

Christine Armatas, PhD, is Associate Director Educational Development at The Hong Kong Polytechnic University, Hong Kong, SAR China. She can be contacted at this e-mail: christine.armatas@polyu.edu.hk

Christine Spratt, PhD, is a Professorial Project Fellow at The Hong The Hong Kong Polytechnic University, Hong Kong, SAR China. She can be contacted at this e-mail: christine.f.spratt@polyu.edu.hk

Brenda Kalyn, PhD is an Assistant Professor in Curriculum Studies in the College of Education at the University of Saskatchewan, Canada. She can be contacted at this e-mail: brenda.kalyn@usask.ca

Orcun Kepez, PhD is an Assistant Professor in Interior Architecture and Environmental Design in the Faculty of Art and Design at the Kadir Has University, Turkey. He can be contacted at this e-mail: orcun.kepez@khas.edu.tr

Bibliography

Brooman, S., Darwent, S., & Pimor, A. (2015). The student voice in higher education curriculum design: is there value in listening? *Innovations in Education and Teaching International*, 52(6), 663–674. https://doi.org/10.10 80/14703297.2014.910128.

Brown, J. S., Collins, A., & Duguid, P. (1989). Situated cognition and the culture of learning. *Educational Researcher*, 18(1), 32–42.

Coates, H., & McCormick, E. 2014, (Eds). *Engaging University Students: International Insights from System-Wide Studies*, New York: Springer.

Entwistle, N. (2010). Taking stock: An overview of key research findings. In Hughes, J. C., & Mighty, J. (Eds.), *Taking Stock: Research on Teaching and Learning in Higher Education* (pp. 15–57). Kingston, ON: McGill-Queen's University Press.

Fish, S. (1980). *Is there a text in this class? The authority of interpretive communities*. Cambridge, MA: Harvard University Press.

Greeno, J. G. (1997). On claims that answer the wrong questions. *Educational Researcher*, 26(1), 5–17.

Greeno, J. G., Collins, A. M., & Resnick, L. B. (1996). Cognition and learning. In Berliner, D., & Calfee, R., (Eds.), *Handbook of Educational Psychology* (pp. 15–46). New York: Macmillan.

Kahu, E. (2013). Framing student engagement in higher education, *Studies in Higher Education*, 38(5), pp. 758–773.

Greller, W., & Drachsler, H. (2012). Translating learning into numbers: A generic framework for learning analytics. *Educational Technology & Society*, 15, 42–57.

Krause, K. & Coates, H. (2008) Students' engagement in first-year university. *Assessment and Evaluation in Higher Education*. 33(5), pp. 493–505.

Lave, J. (1988). *Cognition in Practice: Mind, Mathematics and Culture in Everyday Life*. Cambridge: Cambridge University Press.

Lave, J., & Wenger, E. (1991). *Situated Learning: Legitimate Peripheral Participation*. Cambridge: Cambridge University Press.

Putnam, R. T., & Borko, H. (2000). What do new views of knowledge and thinking have to say about research on teacher learning? *Educational Researcher*, 29(4), 4–15. https://doi:10.3102/0013189X029001004.

Siemens, G. (2013). Learning analytics: The emergence of a discipline, *American Behavioral Scientist*, 57(10), 1380–1400. https://doi.org/10.1177/0002764213498851.

Trowler, V. (2010). *Student Engagement Executive Summary*. York, UK: Higher Education Academy. Retrieved from https://www.heacademy.ac.uk/knowledge-hub/research-and-evidence-base-student-engagement

Chapter 12

Discourse Communities of Learning in Graduate School: An Authentic Transformative Experience

Brenda Kalyn, Lynn Lemisko.
Vicki Squires & Geraldine Balzer

Introduction

Our chapter contributes to this book on *Innovative Teaching And Learning Practices In Higher Education* by illuminating the educational experiences of 25 graduate students, who were teachers or administrators in the K to 12-school system, as they undertook their Master of Education (MEd) degree. They were graduate students moving in two directions – returning to university classrooms to pursue graduate studies while simultaneously moving back to their own classrooms with new experiences and approaches to education. As educational researchers, committed to innovative and relevant teaching practices, we wondered what impact our student-centered course design had on graduate students' experiences. We invited former graduate students who had completed their MEd to participate in focus groups or individual interviews, reflecting upon ways in which their graduate school experiences influenced their learning and transformed their practice. Within this chapter, the term 'graduate student' encompasses teachers and administrators who were in a graduate studies program and still actively teaching and/or acting in administrative positions within their own classrooms and schools during their studies. The term 'students' refers to classroom students of the graduate students (unless otherwise quoted or referenced), and 'teacher/teacher practices' reflects the graduate students' ongoing role and classroom practice.

In this chapter, we define innovative teaching and learning as strategies that enable graduate students to engage as co-learners with professors, challenge their assumptions about classroom practice, and question and explore new pedagogies of learning. We designed our courses around discourse communities of learning and authentic experience, with the student at the center of their learning. Understanding graduate students' experiences in graduate school fostered a greater understanding of the outcomes of graduate teaching and learning through our innovative approach to learning. Their experiences provided insight into the experienced pedagogical practices we designed as professors that subsequently influenced their professional practice and personal identity. We believed that planning for graduate students' learning should be visionary and innovative in the hope that valuable outcomes could be achieved. Therefore, we asked our graduate students about their experiences to learn if the approach was indeed, of value to them. The value emerged from their experiences, for they were the experts who made the journey.

The insights we gained through this research resulted in three learning outcomes that continue to shape our innovative practices:

1. graduate students' engagement with scholarly work and innovative approaches to learning re-shapes personal identity and impacts subsequent classroom or administrative practice;

2. recognizing the impact of graduate students' experience fosters greater understandings for us, as faculty members, regarding the outcomes of graduate teaching and learning;

3. the considerations that arise from examination of the data guides us to actively shape or re-shape our courses and our teaching to meet the needs of graduate student teachers in higher education.

This chapter has four sections. In Section 1, we outline in more detail, the background context and motivation for our innovative teaching and learning practice. This is followed by Section 2, that describes research-informed elements of practice and its curriculum and organisation. Section 3 discusses the outcome of our practice, in terms of emergent themes stemming from focus group data, and our reflections. Finally, this leads into our future direction moving forward with this innovative practice in Section 4.

Section 1: The background

Our graduate students' consistent enthusiasm within their courses and sharing of experiential change as a result, caused us to wonder exactly what they were experiencing within our courses and if indeed, their experiences aligned with our pedagogical goals as we designed courses within our program. To understand the experiences of graduate students within our MEd programs, our team investigated graduate students' engagement with scholarly work and innovative practices in higher education. We invited post-graduate students from our class lists to participate in the research process and we received 25 responses. Focus group discussions and phone conversations provided over 100 pages of data from which we drew our thematic outcomes, obtaining a reflective understanding of graduate students' experiences, so through this understanding we can continue to plan for innovative teaching and learning that will be valued by our graduate students.

We share more of an approach to innovation, rather than one specific innovation. Our program, in and of it-self is not innovative; however, our approaches to teaching and learning within that program are innovative. As teacher educators, we are committed to using best practices in our classrooms beginning with the acknowledgement that each of our graduate students is a legitimate source of knowledge. This approach honors graduate students as learners and recognises our role, as professors, to inspire learning and encourage creative passions. Ultimately, we encouraged an approach where graduate students were largely in control of their learning experiences. We embraced Anatole France's (n.d.) philosophy that stated: *"Do not try to satisfy your vanity by teaching a great many things. Awaken people's curiosity. It is enough to open minds; do not overload them. Put there just a spark. If there is some good inflammable stuff, it will catch fire."*

Another primary focus for our approach to innovative teaching and learning was to create a practice where graduate students were part of a strong learning community. Foundational to our approach to Graduate Studies in Education is the 'situative perspective' theory about cognition and learning labeled the 'situative perspective' (Putnam & Borko, 2000; Greeno, 1997; Greeno et al., 1996; Lave & Wenger, 1991). Three main ideas underpin this theory: that cognition and learning are (a) situated in particular contexts; (b) social in nature; and (c) distributed across people, resources and tools (Putnam & Borko, 2000). Situative theorists (Brown et al., 1989; Lave & Wenger, 1991) hold that knowing and learning are not individualistic functions of the human mind nor based purely on individual experience. They argue, rather, that cognition takes place within particular physical and social contexts which deeply influence how and what an individual learns – that what we know, how we know it, and how we express ideas, are products of interactions with other individuals and within groups of people, or *discourse communities* (Fish, 1980; Resnick, 1991; Putnam & Borko, 2000). According to Putnam and Borko (2000:5), "...*discourse communities provide the cognitive tools—ideas, theories, and concepts—that individuals appropriate as their own through their personal efforts to make sense of experiences.*" In discourse communities, cognition is distributed, because it is "*stretched over*" (Lave, 1988), or shared, among participants who engage in collaborative meaning-making conversations about experiences, text and other artifacts.

Given this theoretical perspective, we contend that innovative practice in our graduate program must include consistent opportunities for graduate students to build and engage within a community of practice, where they can explore and refine personal beliefs and values (Grimmett & Dockendorf, 1999), construct theories and philosophies based on their experiences and revisit and refine theories, philosophies and practice based on shared collegial experiences (Russell & Bullock, 1999). To be considered innovative, practice needs to move beyond reliance on the transmission of knowledge by an 'expert' and toward cultivation of "a community of inquirers" (Dana & Silva, 2009) where students and instructors engage in shared processes that encourage "*sensitive and supportive questioning*" (Grimmett & Dockendorf, 1999:100), critical reflection and risk-taking in an environment of trust. Biggs and Tang (2011) concurred, noting that learners need to engage in transformative reflection in order to apply their new understandings, to critically analyse their findings, or resolve problems.

Our collective goal was to provide insightful, stimulating, creative, and innovative opportunities for graduate students to emerge through their studies into more confident and critical thinkers. Expanding learning *through* the learner is gratifying for both teacher and student. One can see the learner change, think, explore, interrogate, and transform through quality learning experiences.

Section 2: The practice

To begin, we interrogated philosophical approaches to innovation and learning. In preparation for these experiences, we created syllabi and prepared course outlines complete with assignments and assessments to frame these experiences. Choreographing learning experiences that move from transmissional lecture style to student-centered and transformational methodologies required innovative pedagogical considerations where ideas merge with practice. We wanted to create experiences that were meaningful, relevant, and applicable to the learner's real practice. This act of innovation requires deliberate thinking by the instructor (Razeghi, 2008). Through innovative approaches to planning, syllabi and outlines, assignments become open frameworks, which invite graduate students to invent new and innovative ways to engage in thinking and demonstrate learning within their courses.

To create an innovative practice, one must begin with the imagination, recognize the power to imagine, and ask, *"Why imagine?"* Activating the imagination is born from a need to have or see something in a re-imagined and different way. Imagining is a desire for something better, more useful, and more meaningful. Creativity is at the heart of imagination and fuels our innovative ideas and practices (Branch *et al.*, 2017; Robinson & Aronica, 2015). Creativity is also about fresh thinking, not necessarily 'new' thinking, involves critical judgments, and is a dynamic process that often involves making new connections.

Creative innovations in teaching must be applied and experienced in order to learn of their value to the client (Branch *et al.*, 2017; Rust, 2017) in our case- the student. Graduate students are higher education clients; however, we regard instructors as clients as well. When instructors implement what they feel is an innovative practice, they also want to learn of and experience the value within the fresh practice. Teaching and learning is a reciprocal event and as we created what we hoped were innovative learning experiences for our graduate students, we observed their interactions with these opportunities and inquired to learn if in-fact our approach was valued because it made a difference, enhanced experience, and was worth keeping. Our approach was not a response to something that 'wasn't working'; rather, it was a deliberate response to our belief that if learning is to be meaningful, it must be self-directed, relevant, and social in context.

To effectively plan for and teach graduate classes, professors should be aware of the many reasons that graduate students return to university to further their education. The primary reasons teachers shared for entering graduate school centered round a desire to learn more and improve their practice. Many felt a void in their teaching and expressed that they *were missing something.*" Pursuing advanced studies also emerged from a love of learning, wanting to earn an MEd degree, creating career advancement opportunities, an interest in research, and the desire to become a better teacher, as demonstrated by the following two comments:

+ *"If I'm going to be a teacher I want to be the best I can be; I had so much more to learn and I felt I had more potential."*

+ *"I went into it [graduate school] with the hope that I would be able to learn how to inquire into my own practice."*

A brief overview of the curriculum

Courses and assignments for graduate students consisted of a variety of opportunities to demonstrate learning and strengthen personal practice. Ultimately, the application of creative/critical thinking practices invited graduate students to create new knowledge and explore deeper questions. Representations of learning were showcased through presentations, readings, writing, discussions, researching, and creative design in assignments. Graduate students were challenged to interrogate theories and theorists through their work, critically analyse documents, take on independent work and studies, all the while centering on their own areas of expertise and interests. Assignments made room for individual and theoretical explorations that linked ideas with theory, practice, and innovative thinking. This design aligns well with Entwistle (2010) who believes that courses promoting deep learning, pose broad questions, approach topics in an open-ended manner, and focus on authentic problems. Furthermore, graduate students should be given choice in assignments to promote engagement and facilitate deeper learning.

We invited personalised, original, and self-crafted assignment submissions where graduate students felt free to explore ideas and make course content applicable to their practices. This approach authenticated learning and created value in learning because it was important to their practice, resonated with their personal values, and was applied learning. The graduate students created innovative ways to demonstrate their learning and make sense of practice through theoretical constructs. Furthermore, the design of these courses and assignments facilitated self-directed learning for graduate students. Ambrose *et al.* (2010:191) noted, "*To become self-directed learners, students must learn to assess the demands of the task, evaluate their own knowledge and skills, plan their approach, monitor their progress, and adjust their strategies as needed.*" Carefully designed graduate studies can promote the development of these key competencies.

Organisation of the innovative practice

As researchers, we speak to our innovative approaches toward teaching and learning as a collective who approached the development and assessment within courses from a student-centered perspective, even though we prepared our own courses and taught independently. It was a defined belief that our graduate students come to our classes with knowledge of practice and the desire to explore deeper meaning in their work. Our belief is that the greatest transformation occurs through self-discovery.

As colleagues, we consciously used action verbs in our descriptions of assignments and learning outcomes with the intention of actively engaging graduate students in their learning. Some action terms used were: engage in, re-define, develop, apply, create, explore, analyse, synthesise, evaluate, demonstrate, reflect, construct, dream, and design. While these were not unique terms to ascribe to descriptive assignments or course outlines, the key was in the consistent *activation* of those words in real ways, through innovative practices, so graduate students actually *engaged in the action* of demonstrating learning through a variety of contexts.

Further, graduate students were invited and encouraged to represent their learning through creative design. They explored a variety of genres through assignments including: artistic expression through painting, music, dance, drama; DVDs displaying visual and audio representations of their work; creative curricula, written papers, and/or a combination of these. Book club approaches to readings and 'I-search papers' that moved beyond literature reviews and included the student's personal journey to increase understanding of issues were implemented . We engaged in pedagogical cinema to bring the realities of teaching to the forefront and explored ideas, theories, concepts, and the realities of practice. Graduate students were invited to engage in place-based practice through the inquiry approach. Within their educational contexts of classrooms and schools, graduate students developed an inquiry question of choice designed to improve pedagogical practice within learning environments. The ultimate goal of the inquiry was to investigate and improve practice and make specific links between theory and practice. Approximately 80% of the work was done within the graduate student's school or classroom/ place of work and culminated with an academic poster presentation at our Celebration of Research.

Figure 1: Representations of learning through creative design.

As a collective, we offered Selected Reading or Special Topics Courses for one or more graduate students. These specially developed, individualised courses focused on areas of student interest for which no regularly scheduled graduate course existed. These courses served to fill gaps in the student's research program or particular areas of study. Graduate students and professors in these courses meet regularly for approximately 13 hours per credit unit, which is typically 3 credit units. These courses were beyond the professor's normal assignment to duties and did not count within the credit hours of teaching required per academic year; however, credit for graduate work is noted within our CV and although we experience this as extra work, we believe in the value that graduate students experience as a result.

Each course had a syllabus approved by the College of Graduate

Studies, which included course objectives, course outline, reading list, and description of activities for evaluation with percentage allotments. Graduate students created this outline in collaboration with their professor and these students decided how they wished to demonstrate their learning and share the outcomes of their work.

The final capstone course within the course-based route in our MEd program challenged graduate students to research their experiences within a transformative and reflective learning culture. Each participant was asked to demonstrate his or her scholarship in teaching by developing a collection of academic and professional works and or artifacts, representative of their journey, knowledge, and academic growth. The work was crafted and represented through traditional formats, portfolios (including electronic portfolios), essays, multi-media presentations, performances or plays (games, simulations, models) or a combination of these. Ultimately, we respected individuals' learning styles and strengths and encouraged them to showcase their learning where most comfortable but to also explore areas of representation that were new.

As professors, we enjoyed showcasing graduate student learning experiences through a variety of venues that extended beyond the classroom to research symposia and presentations at conferences. Professors wrote papers with graduate students for publication arising from coursework to assist them in understanding the processes of presenting and publishing. Getting to this point required course work that challenged thinking and practice, with the classes containing both theoretical and lecture elements. Graduate students read, wrote, and discussed theoretical issues, learned about theorists, models of education, models of leadership, knowledge ideas and dissemination, all in relation to practice. As lecture time decreased, there was increased time for mulling over more extensive assignments and presentations.

This approach to graduate courses was deliberate and required constant vigilance and observation. It required aligning the context of the classes with the personal desires and interests of the students. We did not tell our graduate students what mattered or what was of value. That was a judgement call they made. Our goal was to create channels and pathways for students to explore and we hoped that this exploration would bring them to an important place within their professional practice and personal life. Through their studies, graduate students were invited to consider how they impacted the field of education and how they were subsequently impacted by it. They were challenged to face their assumptions, biases, perceptions, and personal identities. As professors who designed their courses, we were aware of the responsibility to honor our graduate students as learners with experience and create opportunities for each of them to uniquely encounter knowledge and ideas.

Section 3: Students' and teachers' perspectives on outcomes

We asked former graduate students how their scholarly studies impacted their practice and themselves as professionals. The ways in which graduate students explored their studies informed their experiences and grounded theory provided the foundation to investigate the phenomena of their experience (Mansourian, 2006). To honor their experiences, narrative quotes weave in and out of the discussion to elaborate on the five themes which emerged from the data: 1) experiencing innovative learning in graduate school; 2) observing students differently; 3) curricula and instructional outcomes in practice; 4) professional and personal growth; 5) relational growth and challenges.

The primary overarching outcome of graduate school for these teacher scholars was an increase in personal and professional confidence, resulting from the acquisition of new knowledge and a broadened understanding of education and educational practice. Confidence grew from collegial recognition of each person's knowledge within our learning communities. Every graduate student found their voice and our acknowledgement of that voice provided confidence. Graduate school provided space to question the purposes of education, realign and shift their beliefs and examine outcomes and consequences of actions within education as confirmed by one student, "*Graduate school influenced the way I think about education causing me to question why I was educating in the way that I was. I became very reflective about my work as a teacher.*" They appeared to appreciate the opportunity to think, reflect, act, and re-act to knowledge. It was a reflective time to recognize "*that's what I have been doing*" and realise the scholarship in their work and the fact that in essence they were re-searching their practice every day as scholarly professionals. Engagement in graduate studies assists graduate students with developing a disposition towards deeper learning. Entwistle (2010:43) agreed, *"that disposition brings with it deep approaches in studying – thinking critically about evidence and looking for links between new ideas and previous knowledge – processes which, in alternation, can lead to tight, integrated forms of understanding."* Their expanded understanding and growth impacted the students they taught, the families they encountered, and the communities within which they worked.

Initially, some graduate students were surprised by our approach to teaching and expected the traditional learning paradigms of undergraduate experiences, remarking, *"You're the professor. I was expecting that you, as the expert, would lecture and we would just take notes and write the paper."* Experiencing an invitation to explore and demonstrate their learning through flexible student-centered and open-ended approaches was new. Some were skeptical as they carefully merged into more open paradigms, while others just could not believe they were being invited to really explore, share in, and create new educational ideas and knowledge and they jumped in whole-heartedly. They also had to learn to trust themselves as learners. They were valued by their professors as learners but they had to recognize their own value. Their graduate level experiences were more aligned with the understanding that learning is a process, not a product, but the learning is only evidenced through the students' performances or products (Ambrose *et al.*, 2010). Furthermore, learning should result in changes in *"knowledge, beliefs, behaviours or attitudes"* (Ambrose *et al.*, 2010:3); these changes occur over time, but they have a lasting impact on the learner.

Graduate students showed demonstrable appreciation of the flexibility of their program and the variety of ways they were invited to demonstrate their learning. Writing a paper, making a video, creating a piece of artistic work, or any combination of ways to demonstrate conceptual ideas proved exciting for them. This approach honored the various ways that individuals learn and provided capacity for everyone to find ways to explore their learning, as one student commented: *"Although we shared common learning experiences, having the ability to demonstrate learning individually, not only valued our personal contexts, it also set an example for us as teachers to follow through with our own students in these ways."*

At the same time, creativity in assignments was also valued as one learning outcome: *"We were challenged to design our dream school based on the foundational aspects of schools, curricula, concepts, and theorists. I created an amazing school and designing this school taught me more about who I was as a person, a teacher."*

As they became immersed in academic reading graduate students discovered deeper meaning in their work, *"You start to see the reasons behind things and it changes your thinking about everything and I believe it changed me as well."* Graduate students appreciated the option of taking an independent reading course, as this involved working alongside one professor to focus on professional interests that affected their daily classroom practices. These courses often culminated in professor/student conference presentations, research, and published papers.

Engaging in the reading of theories and theorists, graduate students found allies and dissonance in the experience. They developed a greater understanding of theories and approaches to education that influenced their thinking. One student summarised a common experience, *"I began to re-evaluate everything including my assumptions about education. Everything just began to make more sense as a result of thinking through theory."* Recognizing theoretical frameworks within one's practice became exciting. It was easy to see how many graduate students recognized the traditional, factory, and management styles of approaches to education and how many of them aligned themselves with the humanistic approach to education (Ornstein & Hunkins, 2004). One student commented, *"Through the challenges and creative learning opportunities in graduate studies, I was awakened to the structure of schools historically and how they model a theoretical framework or design."*

While many graduate students could not recall particular theorists, theoretical information resonated with them, reflecting their personal philosophies. They could see the value in philosophical applications and approaches to curriculum for all grades but this took some time. One graduate student, who teaches high school, commented that he learned the most from one of his graduate peers who is a kindergarten teacher: *"I was drawn into the conversations about theorists and pedagogy and realized how many different points of view resonated with me within my practice. As a principal I began to ask questions about my identity, who I am, what I believe about education."*

Credit was given to professors who instigated an idea, a question, or a thought at the beginning of class that always led to a discussion or unraveling of a particular theorist and ideas as shared by one student,

"My professors were stunning models of teaching. I was so impressed and I carried this back to my classroom." One experience left another graduate student "stunned" when she was allowed to rewrite a paper because we [the graduate students] weren't happy with our marks: *"We had a conversation, went over the paper, and after a re-write I felt like I had earned a big gold star having improved my paper and my mark. No teacher had given that kind of time to my work in the past. I took that attitude back to my students in my classroom and it affected how I approached the work they did."*

Another graduate student shared a positive outcome emerging from her creative inquiry assignment through place-based learning, *"Working through a classroom-based project with my professor in relation to my work with autistic students was so rewarding. Publishing a paper with my professor was a bonus!"*

Graduate students applauded the innovative, practical, and student-centered experiences they encountered in graduate school that had direct application to their classroom practice sharing, *"I was able to interrogate my practice and apply research to my work. Instead of going through the motions and being on the 'treadmill' my practice became more thoughtful and meaningful."* And another commented, *"After I experienced, the theories of student-centered learning... I realized that it was sort of an innate response to my students' needs and gave me the vocabulary, understanding, and capacity to express my rationale for teaching the way I did."*

Graduate students' interactions with creative and critical approaches to learning in graduate school resulted in profound, shared comments, *"I feel like I have a voice and it counts and what I do in education is important for me as well as the students."* The learning experiences were empowering, *"We all have potential with the right people alongside us and the right mindset and I think that's exciting and a great thing. I honestly didn't want this learning experience to end. Everything about these experiences was transformative."*

Emergent themes: observing students differently

As a result of these graduate studies, teachers observed their students in new ways, which affected their practice. Many recognized that they had been seeing their students in short-sighted ways rather than as *"owners of their education."* One teacher said, *"They come with their own gifts and knowledge. We need to be aware of interactive strategies in our instruction so students become the voices of learning more often than teachers."*

Seeing their students as unique individuals in deeper contexts grew, and teachers described this transformation as moving beyond labels, curricular outcomes, data collection, and assessment of students as a primary focus to satisfy superiors. At times, it was a reflective wake up call to help them realise the reactive approach that teachers fall into due to hierarchical expectations and a focus on product-based outcomes. The shift in responding to students, curricula, and instruction came from their increased confidence. They began to take a stance and challenge the status quo. One teacher said, *"I look beyond my students and assess their needs and that becomes an act of really observing; rather, than just seeing a group of students in a classroom."*

Teachers found themselves interrogating their practice in new ways citing: being more selective regarding curricula; paying attention to the environmental factors such as lighting and seating and visual messages on the walls; and the language used in classrooms. They became mindful about the decisions they were making pedagogically and the impact of those decisions. They paid closer attention to new outcomes beyond measurements. Teachers felt better placed to foster school change for the advancement of all students and they expressed why change should occur. One teacher stated, *"I felt stronger with myself – a sense of self-efficacy that wasn't there before my graduate studies and that gave me new purpose in my teaching."*

As a result of studying narrative inquiry in graduate school, teachers became more aware of the importance of the narrative with their students: *"Through graduate school, I began to understand how important it is to move beyond labels or pre-conceptions and really observe students. I had to examine my own assumptions about all sorts of biases and beliefs and recognize my ignorance. Humility was a big part of this transition as well as self-reflection. It was about developing more patience and being a better teacher."*

Another teacher talked about thinking more deeply about the nuances of her students regarding gang paraphernalia such as the colors and headbands they wore, how they shuffle their power in the room, whom they sit with and where they sit. The teacher knew these behaviors influenced her classroom environment and practice; however, she probed the situation differently as a result of her experiences in graduate school. She developed a practice of trying to get to know her students instead of just *"dealing with them."* Her compassion grew and some of the theoretical work regarding relationships, curricula, and students resonated back into her practice. She changed tactics and shared herself with her students, as a person and not just the teacher, in order to invite them into a more personal conversation. She approached them and shook their hands and told her story to them. She said, *"I watch the students trying to figure out how to learn and what to learn. Their life tasks are huge."* One administrator shared: *"Rich conversations from graduate school fed my soul. We had a student who mis-behaved and many of the teachers wanted some sort of punishment placed on this child. Instead, I played cards with him. This strategy was a direct result of my graduate school experience. What I read, what I was challenged to think about went beyond basic management strategies. I knew I had to build a relationship with this student in order to move ahead and change his behavior."*

Teachers and administrators became enriched through graduate studies and the elements of humanistic teaching were prominent. They were naturally caring individuals; however, the elements of care within their practice intensified and with their growth in confidence they took command of their classrooms in new, deeper, and more meaningful ways.

Approaches to curricula and instruction

Educators who become more efficient observers in classrooms ask bigger questions about learning, and this leads to thinking about curricula in new ways. One graduate student described, *"The first day of class the professor asked, 'What is curriculum'? I didn't know and I was a teacher. I wrote, 'It's a book you follow, issued to us.' Three months later, I wrote pages of what I believed curriculum was. I questioned many pieces of curriculum structure."*

Many teachers gave themselves permission to move beyond curriculum as mandate and treat it as a guide. One teacher talked about switching from following curriculum in a linear approach to taking a backward approach, *"I don't look at the curriculum until after I find out what the kids are interested in and want to learn and then I look for outcomes and indicators to complement their interests and my teaching."* There was common agreement that, *"Curriculum should not dictate learning, childrens' passions, processes, or materials. Great learning and great teaching will always find a home back in the curriculum itself.*" Teachers valued their new insight into the curricula, "*The teacher is the guide of the curriculum.*" One teacher challenged the shift in curricula from the early years to grade 1 where the ideology of 'play' was no longer included. When she moved from a kindergarten to grade 1 class, she took a stand and brought the play philosophy forward into her grade 1 class, all the while meeting the outcome expectations. She just came at it in a unique and fulfilling way. This innovation was part of an inquiry project she did in graduate studies and ultimately produced a co-published article with her professor; a testament to the scholarly work of graduate students.

Teachers found these new approaches to curricula empowering and stated they were, "*resetting curriculum.*" They valued different types of learning and felt empowered to take action in their teaching and paid attention to areas of curriculum that lacked inclusion, sensitivity, or the wider views of others. One teacher stated, "*I don't think we teach curriculum; we teach kids*" and she developed a more personalised approach to curricula in her classroom. Teachers began to think about their students as lifelong learners and not just individuals needing to meet outcomes. One teacher shared, "*Curriculum became more about people and relationships and I feel much more at ease with the written curriculum because I realize it's just one piece of a lived or unfolding curriculum.*" Another expressed, "*Inquiring into curriculum the way we did in class helped me take matters into my own hands...I make choices about how I teach now. It's realizing that I have the freedom to explore ways of teaching the curriculum.*"

Words like freedom, flexibility, creativity, broad, adaptable all became a larger part of their vocabulary as they explored teaching curricula. They felt a sense of freedom to explore concepts and apply knowledge through innovative assignments to empower their own students. They became critical consumers of curricula and saw it with theoretical links and purpose, and they credited their graduate studies for this shift. These teachers agreed, "*I provide more student-centered choice for my students now. They learn best when they are choosing their learning and experiences. That's how it was for us in graduate school. We were all experiencing independent learning in our common classes.*" A further comment: "*Curriculum isn't just a book...I realize that a major part of my curriculum walks into my classroom every September. The students are my curriculum and how I meet all of their needs becomes a major part of my work.*"

Teachers believed that much of their new insight validated their instructional beliefs and choices made around instruction. Teachers gave themselves permission to teach in ways that suited them best. Others began to collect meaningful data about their practice and their students' needs in relation to instruction. Teachers agreed, *"Graduate studies has provided me with research-based knowledge to back up my decisions about curriculum and instruction and has caused me to change my practice of instruction."*

A primary impetus for changes to instruction was student engagement and meaningful learning, as one teacher noted, *"My students enjoy their learning now. I look at the whole child. I'm more relaxed in my approach to instruction. My kids talk more and I talk less. I take 'risks' to see what will unfold in the class."*

Studying different theoretical approaches to learning in graduate school was powerful. Exploring and adapting new ideas and innovations in their classrooms became an exciting shift that shaped their confidence, *"Our professors modeled several instructional models and I respect how much they crafted ways for our learning to emerge. We were encouraged to think about learning in new ways...Our professors demonstrated that and it caused our own changes in teaching."*

The concepts of 'accidental' versus 'deliberate' approaches to teaching and learning arose. Graduate students described the accidental as the teachers who not only followed the curriculum unquestioningly, but often taught as they were taught; on the other hand, in the deliberate approach teachers saw themselves as leading learning (Ritchie & Wilson, 2000). They deconstructed their personal identities in relation to instruction and many moved from the accidental to deliberate teaching. This shift did not come without struggle. One teacher shared how she ironically was an English teacher yet had lost her confidence as a writer. Graduate school assisted her in moving through her own mistakes, worries, and fears. These experiences transferred back into her own classroom where she began to *'slow things down'* and watch for her students to indicate when they were ready to move on in their learning. The focus of her instruction moved from attendance, attitude, and behavior to authentic learning, feedback, and the interactions within learning. Another teacher agreed, *"Graduate school was me having to figure it out. It was not always comfortable and I learned that you have to go through a lot of discomfort to get the greatest amount of learning. I had to be uncomfortable and grapple with ideas to grow."* Inviting graduate students to lead their learning was invaluable and observing the outcomes of this more relaxed, yet attentive approach to instruction was important for many. It took work and a sense of 'giving up control' by relinquishing so much direct instruction. When teachers trusted themselves and observed much richer learning outcomes, the transition was complete and met with a positive commitment to play with learning, grapple with new ideas and innovations, and enjoy teaching more.

Personal and professional growth

As stated earlier, graduate students felt like they had found their *"voice"* as educators and their feelings of self-efficacy grew as one graduate student shared, *"I just felt stronger within myself."* A sense of personal empowerment grew from their experience and was represented within their personal practice. Another took a stance and asked, *"what do I believe in education, what do I envision, and what do I see, what do I want from nobody's perspective but mine?"* Another remarked, *"My beliefs changed and my practice began to shift as a result of my growing confidence. I now believe I am who I am and I am valued for who I am and because of that I can give myself the permission to stop teaching the way I was taught."*

Graduate students reflected on going from their classrooms to graduate studies and back to their classrooms. They began to honor the *"complexities of teaching and learning"* and felt it was valuable to take the time to sit in graduate classes and reflect on the *"intense intellectual work of teaching."* Relationships to peers, colleagues, and the curriculum became key to deepening this understanding. Curriculum took on new meaning and expanded to an all-encompassing ideology of being *"alive and so much more than a document; it is what students and staff bring to schools, the knowledge we have inside of us and making space to realize we can create some of our own answers in education."*

As a result of increased confidence, personal and professional contributions to their practice increased. Comments affirmed, *"I felt like I could contribute more because of my new knowledge"* and *"I understood educational paradigms in new ways and as a result my contributions were greater. Instead of just 'participating' in education I began to shape outcomes and have an impact in my practice."* Shaping outcomes resulted in feeling more passionate about being professional. Teachers reflected on how they were using their students' time: *"I am more thoughtful in my teaching considering everything from the space, my language, my assumptions, the perspectives I bring to the class"* and *"I am more purposeful in my teaching and my planning... I became a more critical thinker as a result and this was an important step within my professional career."* Tensions arose through educational interrogation, *"Sometimes I think graduate school made me think too much about education. Now, I think too much and have become a more critical thinker about the curriculum"* and a colleague agreed, *"Getting a Masters degree has complicated my teaching. Now, I hold everything to a higher standard in my teaching and I am not as spontaneous. I am a better teacher now."*

Changing relationships

Graduate school resulted in changes to professional and personal relationships. Fostering a discourse community with each other produced a camaraderie amongst graduate students that they valued. There were also some difficult relational outcomes that emerged as a result of their new experiences and advanced education. At times, graduate students felt shunned by colleagues back in their schools who did not see the value in graduate school. They were chastised, and in some cases, told to keep their scholarly ideas to themselves and not interfere with the *"way things have always been done."*

Graduate students recognized the importance of connecting with other learners and sharing their perspectives, *"Meeting and talking with others in graduate school was significant. Graduate school increased my circle of belonging. We all shared and became leaders in a way. Our opinions mattered."* They recognized the value in extended relationships and larger partnerships in education including their own students, teachers, and families, *"We learned how to welcome parents in new ways and value the fact that they are their children's first teachers. Some of us feared parents in our classrooms but we learned to broaden these relationships in deeper ways."* One administrator was influenced by the readings and discussions about parents and their relationship within the school, *"How we talk to parents about their children became a significant question for me... Learning about the children from the parents is crucial. I began to see my role as an administrator as one who should facilitate these ideas."*

Cultural contexts are a major part of the changing landscapes within many classrooms. Teachers struggle to understand and implement best practices when faced with as many as 14 different languages within their classes, the unique needs of immigrant students, and honoring Indigenous students. In our province, Indigenous content is expected to be taught within every subject area. Some school populations have few or no Indigenous students, while other schools may be all Indigenous students. Teachers openly admit the challenge of understanding cultural knowledge/s and teaching it.

Experiencing readings and other forms of literacy, such as movies and documentaries, opened their eyes to matters not previously considered relevant to their teaching. Their relationships with the knowledge grew. One administrator shared that in her school there were no First Nations students and teachers struggled with presenting the cultural aspects of residential schools and said generally students were not interested. After learning more about First Nations' culture and curricula through the academic lens, the administrator was able to offer media and literary supports for her teachers, that resulted in major impacts for teaching and learning. The principal said, *"We all grew together in a better understanding about truth and reconciliation teachings which is an important piece of learning and moving forward as a society."* Another agreed, *"Through graduate studies I had to face my assumptions, my stereo-typical views. Professors wouldn't let me settle with the 'well that's the way it's always been done'. They challenged me to answer the bigger 'why' questions. I became more humble."*

Acquiring knowledge and humility through graduate studies transformed teachers and administrators within their practice; changing their understanding of self and their relationships with their students, colleagues, and education itself. We can expect great changes along the journey. How we experience those changes is the challenge.

Our reflections

As a result of investigating the experiences of graduate students within graduate studies, we learned about the outcomes of our approach to teaching and learning and affirmed that much of what we are doing through our programs and innovative practices has been a rewarding experience for them. We are humbled to know that they feel transformed by their experiences and that we have been instrumental in this process. The observations of our graduate students at work, hearing them think, and watching them emerge as teacher scholars is the ultimate reward. We will continue with our approaches to innovative teaching, and honor what graduate students believe we are doing well, by continuing with these practices. We, as professors in higher education, are challenged to continue to develop new and exciting approaches to learning.

Every-day challenges in teaching provide little time for teachers and administrators to reflect on their practice. Engaging in graduate studies provided much appreciated time for graduate students to think, discuss, plan, dream, construct new ideas, and discover new philosophies and foundational frameworks of education. They grappled (Sizer & Faust Sizer, 2011) with ideas and realized that curriculum itself with over 120 different definitions was much more than a document (Marsh & Willis 2003). They discovered new theories and theorists to challenge their thinking and push the boundaries of their biases, comfort zones, and ultimately, their practices.

Positioning our courses within the beliefs that knowing and learning are not individualistic functions, but are strengthened through discourse communities of learning, we learned that graduate students did find strength and breadth of learning through these interactions. Interrogating ideas and theories alongside the realities of the classroom, created authentic and meaningful learning outcomes. Graduate students appreciated the social support from colleagues and professors, as well as the open-ended creative approach to demonstrating learning through a wide variety of creative assignments. Graduate school became largely self-directed and personal which transformed their practice, identity, and passion for education.

Hørsted (2017:10) stressed that positive learning experiences are fostered by educators who make a difference because they *"inspire, motivate, and involve students in their own learning; act as guides, treat students as explorers, and encourage students to find their own way while assisting students to make connections between the subject and students' interests."* When this occurs, heightened value is experienced through the learning process. Further value is seen in the ways that personal and professional life are intertwined for instructors and their students (Hayes, 2017). Value improves the practice of teaching and enhances student learning in higher education (Branch *et al.*, 2017). Understanding graduate students' reasons for entering graduate school, we remain better equipped to prepare and plan approaches to innovations in our teaching to assist them in achieving their personal goals. Creating courses and planning syllabi for learning engagement must be creative, challenging, thought provoking, learner centered, and cover a wide range of interests and intellectual areas.

Graduate students appreciated professors who shared their expertise and stretched their thinking. *"Pushing them"* was invaluable because they felt that push challenged them in so many ways. There was large agreement that many of them felt like imposters when entering into graduate school, *"Entering graduate school I felt like an imposter; wondering "what am I doing here?"* Another commented, *"I felt very stupid in the beginning because I hadn't written an essay in a long time."* Another lamented, *"I didn't even know how to find a journal article!"* And another, *"When I began I felt out of touch and reluctant to share in the conversation. People began to share their stories and experiences. Everyone listened and slowly, everybody in their right time, shared themselves."* Professionally, they gained friends and colleagues. Conversation communities became a valued by-product of their experiences. Ultimately, our graduate students felt a sense of validation in their work as professionals and as individuals, as a result of their experiences. One graduate student summarised, *"The expanded notion of who I am as a teacher and who I want to be in the classroom emerged through my studies. I questioned how students learn and how we teach. We are constantly re-searching as we are teaching."* The guidance, prompting, feedback, and professional interactions with faculty were highly regarded. Graduate students agreed, *"A spark was ignited within us and we carry on these educational conversations when we meet or have time within our schools. It speaks to that need and desire to keep the academic conversations going."*

Section 4: Moving forward

Within the focus group conversations, our graduate students left us with some advice and reflective thoughts. Many believe that all educators should have to attend graduate school after five to ten years in the classroom.

The growth in their practices has convinced them that everyone would benefit from this experience and the result would be better teaching, more efficient and caring schools, better student outcomes, and better working relationships. Many expressed the belief that research should be a part of the graduate experience.

As professors, we applaud our graduate students and the tremendous effort it takes to be a graduate student. They are juggling time, finances, family routines and work to make their dream a reality. We acknowledged the participants as experts within their graduate experiences. Their passions spoke from the heart and we honor this passion through their voices and concluding wonders, *"Where do we go from here? Publish! Take another Masters degree! Do a PhD! I need the conversations, I don't want to become stagnant and fall back into the place where I was before I began,"* while many echoed, *"I did not want graduate school to be done."* They encourage others who are thinking about doing an MEd degree, *"Absolutely you should do it because it gives you space and knowledge to think about school, ask what education is, think deeper about the purpose and your role in education."*

One graduate student reflected, *"Teaching is the best job on earth."* When I began my Masters, I had a mentor with 34 years of teaching experience. She said, 'Never stop asking questions because the day you stop asking is the day you stop learning.' For her final graduate project, this graduate student created a book of questions that was a summary of key questions she took from each of her graduate courses. The project became a reflective piece about asking the right questions. This in turn affected the questions she asked her students to think about.

As a result of their experiences in our program within discourse learning communities and student-centered courses, graduate students transformed in so many ways. We are paying attention to and honoring our graduate students as teacher scholars and believe that the best way for them to emerge as professionals within their practice is to make learning personal and authentic within an environment of community and trust. They told us how much they valued their experiences and they did not want it all to end. We conclude that we are on the right track and the focus on student-centered, action-based learning is a vital approach moving forward in our practice as professors in higher education.

Conclusion

Graduate students' engagement with scholarly work clearly impacted their subsequent practice. These graduate students-teacher-scholars became more purposeful in their work and began to explore a richer philosophical practice. Their thinking became more critical and analytical and they were willing to take risks as a result of their deeper theoretical understanding and new foundations. A major increase in confidence occurred and a sense of validation empowered them to act, think, and respond professionally in new ways. Their imaginations were ignited and their thinking *slowed* (Jack, 2017) and became more deliberate. They considered leadership roles that never occurred to them previously and developed greater compassion in their work.

Relationships changed as a result of graduate school. Many were positive and some produced a sense of isolation. Ultimately, their experiences increased their resilience and as professors we need to be mindful of both the positive and negative impacts that graduate school may have on our graduate students' work and subsequent relationships. Pro-active discussions in class, regarding these experiences, will assist graduate students in dealing with a change that may or may not have been expected.

They all agreed that their experiences have impacted them beyond anything they might have imagined. Graduate school was not merely an intellectual exercise; it expanded their feeling, actions, re-actions, and practice in many new ways. There was an overwhelming desire by graduate students to continue learning and engage in educational conversations. They felt a strong sense of sadness when they were done and they asked, *"now what and where do we go from here?"* Another commented, *"Graduate school is addictive."*

Added value was experienced when graduate students had the opportunity to reflect on their practice and themselves. Hutchings and Wutzdorff (1988:12:15) believed that learning is deeper and more meaningful when learning *"touches on things we care about."* These authors further stated, *"Reflection is the ability to step back and ponder one's own experience, to abstract from it something meaningful. The capacity for reflection is what transforms experience into learning."* Dewey (1916) agreed that knowledge and experience must be linked and education must involve the learner in active ways. Meaningful education must be grounded in daily reality and the opportunity to engage in personal work-related outcomes was immeasurably beneficial to the graduate students.

One day, I asked my graduate students *"what does thinking mean"* or *"what is thinking?"* We use the word so easily but do we interrogate it? We ask students to "think about this or that" but do we teach thinking? Silence abounded, eyes shifted, thinking about thinking happened. I did not record their answers but I challenged them to ask their students what thinking is and here are some responses from children aged 4–10: *"it's like parts of your brain are having a party; to be smart and make the right choices; caring for people in your heart; visualizing and inferring; thinking about something you don't know and your brain turns on and starts working; getting your brain going deep."*

As we think, we interrogate ideas in new ways. We wonder, imagine, create, apply new strategies and look for outcomes that inform if we think we are on the right track, or in some cases, have a winning innovation! Regardless, of the definition or approach to innovation, we believe that our graduate students are innovators of practice as they deliberately approach their work. We applaud their professionalism and passions and we are very proud to be a part of their educational quest.

Their passionate observations and sharing of experience through our research highlighted the impact of graduate studies on teacher practice. We know just a little more about how we, as professors, impact and influence their experiences by paying attention to our learners and their courses. Honoring who they are and what they bring to our graduate programs inspires us to continue to be innovative planners and educators in order to ignite that spark within each graduate student. In doing so, we participate in our graduate students' lived experiences. We all strive to impact the lives of the students we teach whether it is in graduate school or pre-school. We are all learners and the joy of learning from each other is a gift. Teaching really is the best job in the world!

About the Authors

Brenda Kalyn, PhD is an Assistant Professor in Curriculum Studies in the College of Education at the University of Saskatchewan, Canada. She can be contacted at this e-mail: brenda.kalyn@usask.ca

Lynn Lemisko, PhD is a Professor in Educational Foundations, College of Education, University of Saskatchewan, Canada. She can be contacted at this e-mail: lynn.lemisko@usask.ca

Vicki Squires, PhD is an Assistant Professor in the Department of Educational Administration in the College of Education at the University of Saskatchewan. She can be contacted at this e-mail: vicki.squires@usask.ca

Geraldine Balzer, PhD is an Associate Professor in Curriculum Studies in the College of Education at the University of Saskatchewan. She can be contacted at this e-mail: geraldine.balzer@usask.ca

Bibliography

Ambrose, S. A., Bridges, M. W., DiPietro, M., & Lovett, M. C. (2010). *How learning works: Seven research-based principles for smart teaching.* San Francisco, CA: Wiley and Sons.

Biggs, J., & Tang, C. (2011). *Teaching for quality learning at university* (4th ed.). New York, NY: McGraw-Hill.

Branch, J., Hayes, S., Hørsted, A., & Nygaard, C. (2017). An innovative teaching and learning in higher education. In Branch, J., Hayes, S., Hørsted, A., & Nygaard, C. (Eds.), *Innovative Teaching and Learning in Higher Education* (pp. 1–20). Oxfordshire: Libri Publishing Ltd.

Brown, J. S., Collins, A., & Duguid, P. (1989). Situated cognition and the culture of learning. *Educational Researcher,* 18(1), 32–42.

Dana, N. F., & Silva, D. Y. (2009). *Learning to teach and teaching to learn through practitioner inquiry* (2nd ed.). Thousand Oaks, CA: Corwin Press.

Dewey, J. (1916). *Democracy and education.* Toronto, ON: McMillan.

Entwistle, N. (2010). Taking stock: An overview of key research findings. In Hughes, J. C., & Mighty, J. (Eds.), *Taking stock: Research on teaching and learning in higher education* (pp. 15–57). Kingston, ON: McGill-Queen's University Press.

Fish, S. (1980). *Is there a text in this class? The authority of interpretive communities.* Cambridge, MA: Harvard University Press.

France, A. (n.d.). *AZQuotes.com.* Retrieved March 22, 2018 from AZQuotes. com http://www.azquotes.com/quote/602085

Greeno, J. G. (1997). On claims that answer the wrong questions. *Educational Researcher,* 26(1), 5–17.

Greeno, J. G., Collins, A. M., & Resnick, L. B. (1996). Cognition and learning. In Berliner, D., & Calfee, R. (Eds.), *Handbook of educational psychology* (pp. 15–46). New York: Macmillan.

Grimmett, P., & Dockendorf, M. (1999). Exploring the labyrinth of research teaching. In Loughran, J. (Ed.), *Researching teaching: Methodologies and practices for understanding pedagogy* (pp. 83–110). London: Palmer Press.

Hayes, S. (2017). Introduction. In Branch, J., Hayes, S., Hørsted, A., & Nygaard, C. (Eds.), *Innovative Teaching and Learning in Higher Education* (pp. 1–20). Oxfordshire: Libri Publishing Ltd.

Hørsted, A. (2017). Introduction. In Branch, J., Hayes, S., Hørsted, A., & Nygaard, C. (Eds.), *Innovative Teaching and Learning in Higher Education* (pp. 1–20). Oxfordshire: Libri Publishing Ltd.

Hutchings, P., & Wutzdorff. A. (1998). Experiential learning across the curriculum: Assumptions and Principles. In Hutchings, P. , & Wutzdorff, A. (Eds.), *Knowing and Doing: Learning through experience* (pp. 5–19). San Francisco: Jossey-Bass, Inc.

Jack, K. (2017). Exploring feelings through reflective poetry writing. In Branch, J., Hayes, S., Hørsted, A., Nygaard, C. (Eds.), *Innovative Teaching and Learning in Higher Education* (pp. 83–91). Faringdon, Oxfordshire: Libri Publishing Ltd.

Lave, J. (1988). *Cognition in practice: Mind, mathematics and culture in everyday life.* Cambridge: Cambridge University Press.

Lave, J. and Wenger, E. (1991). *Situated Learning. Legitimate peripheral participation,* Cambridge: University of Cambridge Press.

Mansourian, Y. (2006). Adoption of grounded theory in LIS research. *New Library World,* 107(9/10), 386–402.

Marsh, C. J. & Willis, G. (2003). *Curriculum: Alternative approaches, ongoing issues.* (3rd ed.). Upper Saddle River, NJ: Pearson Education, Inc.

Ornstein, A. C. & Hunkins, F. P. (2004). Curriculum: Foundations, principles, and issues (4th ed.) Boston, MA: Pearson Education, Inc.

Putnam, R. T. & Borko, H. A. (2000). What do new views of knowledge and thinking have to say about research on teacher learning? *Educational Researcher*, 29/1, 4–15.

Razeghi, A. (2008). *Where ideas come from and how to have better ones.* San Francisco, CA; Jossey-Bass.

Resnick, L. B. (1991). Shared cognition: Thinking as social practice. In Resnick, L. B., Levine, J. M., & Teasley, S. D. (Eds.), *Perspectives on socially shared cognition* (pp. 1–20). Washington, DC: American Psychological Association

Ritchie, J. S., & Wilson, D. E. (2000). *Teacher narrative as critical inquiry: Rewriting the script.* New York: Teachers' College Press.

Robinson, K., & Aronica, L. (2015). *Creative schools: The grassroots revolution that's transforming education,* New York: Viking Press.

Russell, T., & Bullock, S. (1999). Discovering our professional knowledge as teachers: Critical ideologies about learning from experience. In J. Loughran (Ed.). *Researching teaching: Methodologies and practices for understanding pedagogy.* (pp. 132–151). London: Palmer Press.

Rust, C. (2017). Foreword. In Branch, J., Hayes, S., Hørsted, A., & Nygaard, C., (Eds.), *Innovative Teaching and Learning in Higher Education* (pp. ix–xii). Oxfordshire: Libri Publishing Ltd.

Sizer, T. R., & Faust Sizer, N. (2011). Grappling. In Ornstein, A., Pajak, E. F., & Ornstein, S. B. (Eds.) *Contemporary issues in curriculum* (5th ed.) Upper Saddle River New Jersey: Pearson Education, Inc.

Chapter 13

The Steelcase Active Learning Centre as a Community Design Centre

Orcun Kepez

Introduction

This chapter contributes to this book on *Innovative Teaching And Learning Practices In Higher Education* by showcasing the research-based design of a state-of-the-art learning environment, its adoption by students and how it has facilitated institutional change in education. The main practice-based innovation in this chapter is the teaching practice that has been brought to design education through the adoption of participatory design methods that lead naturally to active learning. The Community Design Centre is a physical place, where members of the community gather to make design decisions via participatory workshops. In this case, the learning environment serves as the Community Design Centre, where students come together to participate in workshops that aim to facilitate collaborative learning based on reflecting on their experiences in campus environments.

The design discipline is often misinterpreted as if it were solely based on artistic pursuits. However, as opposed to art, the act of design is more complex, since the artefacts of design, whether they be products, interiors or buildings, play a great role in the quality of the daily lives of their users. The focus of innovative educational practice here is on Interior Architecture, but the lessons here are easily applicable to other design disciplines as well as other fields. As most of Earth's population now lives in cities, approximately 87% percent of our daily lives are spent inside buildings (Klepeis *et al.*, 2001). Thus, even small changes in interior environments can make big differences to our experiences and lead to better outcomes. Understanding the expectations of those who will be the future users of the environments, observing their use of the space, collecting narratives about past experiences and finally including them into the design process is a research-based approach to humanistic design. Building on Boyer's (1990) seminal work on defining scholarship, Boyer and Mitgang (1996) helped the architectural community to set a vision for design education. This has now lead to over two decades of planned efforts, protecting curriculum design from the risk of being dominated solely by knowledge transfer from ongoing design practices that may be significant today but will be irrelevant tomorrow.

International accreditation boards and professional organisations often emphasise the importance of bringing research-based decision making into the discipline of Interior Architecture (Kepez, 2015). Yet, there are still disparities in how research is integrated into education and into practice. In an earlier study, 80% of interior architecture faculty were found to believe that research findings provided useful information for their profession, but still unsure about how to integrate research into education (Dickinson, et al., 2009). The design studio, which is the heart of design education, requires careful planning and strategising to include research as an integral part of the curriculum (Salama, 1997, 2015; Kepez & Ust, 2017). Aligned with the innovative practice of this Chapter, the U.S. based Council of Interior Accreditation (CIDA) places a constant emphasis on understanding human behaviour, by setting an entire standard, entitled "Human-Centred Design" as a requirement among its accreditation standards (CIDA, 2018). This professional standard (7) reads as follows (p. II–20): "Interior designers apply knowledge of human experience and behavior to designing the built environment." and its intention ensures that "graduates understand theories of human-centered design, and identify, analyse, and apply information from a variety of stakeholders and sources to develop a successful response to user needs and to promote health and wellbeing."

From my experience, it is hard to apply behavioural research in the design studio for three main reasons. First of all, the studio schedule is tight and most of the research time is spent on analysis of existing projects, often referred to as predecessors. Through this research, students come to understand the history and logic behind more recent examples. Second, the type of knowledge acquired in the studio mostly comes from the experiences of different professors including adjuncts, most of whom are not experts in the topics listed above. Third, selected sites and buildings for study can usually only be used for a short time and cannot be used as research sites with their community. Thus, the innovation in teaching and learning that occurred in the 'Human Behaviour and Environmental Design' course specifically developed to cater to the aforementioned professional standard on *"Human-Centred Design"*.

Reading this chapter, you will gain insights into the following three topics:

1. Pedagogical strategies to bring about research (mapping, postoccupancy evaluations, systematic observations, visual auditing, content analysis, environmental assessment, and participatory design) in the discipline of Interior Architecture;

2. Redefining the Campus Environment (and Steelcase Active Learning Centre) as the case study and including students as everyday users making research-based design decisions;

3. How to use the Steelcase Active Learning Centre (SALC) to design each class as a collaborative design thinking (participatory design) workshop.

Section I: The background

A recent survey reports that 26% of architecture students said that they were being treated or had been treated for mental health issues related to their course (Waite & Braidwood, 2016). Such issues notwithstanding, it can be stated that design/architecture students are universally some of the most solitary students on campus due to the long hours they have to spend on individual projects. Although they will work in teams when they graduate, teamwork is seldom practised at university level. Students' creativity is mostly defined as an individual 'talent' rather than something that can be nourished collectively. In design juries, students learn how to present and defend their ideas as individuals. Given this focus on the individual, together with the aforementioned mental health issues, perhaps partially the result of such isolation, the creation of collaborative learning environments where students learn to design together becomes even more crucial. They help isolated students to become a community by providing social interaction without the usual competition.

When I joined my faculty back in 2008, there were no classes linking humanistic values and research to interior architecture. Theory classes were given in the traditional way, and practical classes, other than those in the studio, were solely focused on the practice of technical skills with nearly no theoretical background. Coming from a background in architecture, but having grown into the community design of learning environments, and specialising in working with special populations and well-being, I wanted to make a difference. At the time when I was hired, there was a transition in the university from a teaching-oriented to a research-oriented basis, but without sacrificing the learning experiences of students. So, this gave me an edge when redesigning the course (at the time named Environmental Design) to serve both to defined mission of the University and to make a healthier difference in the lives of my students.

When I began serving as the Chair of the Department two years after my appointment, I also established a curriculum that incorporated research-based design at the studio level and documented outcomes that resulted in international exposure at the 1st and 2nd *Istanbul Design Biennial* (2012, 2014) and at the *1st Biennial of Architecture in Thessaloniki* Architecture and the City in Southeast Europe (2012). Our analysis of the campus environment, in these courses that focused on human behaviour and design, was also used by the university to make future decisions about the campus (Kepez, 2010). My own research in observing students' in-class behaviours resulted in my establishing a research-based design for the very first Active Learning Centre in our country, through grants received from Steelcase Education and PolyVision. As a team of researchers, we continue our research on understanding the use (e.g. interactions between students, occupancy of furniture) of the Active Learning Centre to inform the future design of learning environments.

Section 2: The practice

My new motivation in teaching and learning in higher education can be summarised as bringing about a research-based design approach by applying participatory design methods in the classroom. Participatory design is all about involving people in the design decision-making process who will be affected by design decisions (Sanoff, 2000, 2010). When lay people are given an introduction to the multiple factors that play a role in experts' design decision-making processes, they can make meaningful choices for themselves. Thus, empowering the community through teaching this kind of information helps community members to become aware of trade-offs and decide what is good for themselves. Known also as community design and democratic design, this approach is widely employed in the design of learning environments, workplace and housing.

When we select our campus as the case, then it is a learning environment for students and a workplace for faculty and staff. Thus, we work in a real environment that each student is able to experience on a daily basis. I design participatory design workshops to enable students to uncover the problems they face and explore their link to environmental factors. They collect data around the campus through multiple field techniques including systematic observation, photo taking and surveying people. But first we start by collaboratively designing a syllabus in which we 'plant the seeds of democracy' in the classroom. In order to achieve results with this kind of approach, one needs to give students control while they are participating in the workshops and making decisions. So being a facilitator in the learning community is more important than being a professor. In a class like this, it is impossible to have a syllabus with a linear progression; instead, students experience all content during a carefully designed series of workshops, where they feel that they can also conduct workshops like these.

Community design has been found to be an effective way to involve students in the challenges of the real world and counted as one of the teaching methods that can be applied in the design studio (Salama, 2015). Yet, it is a rare case where the same approach is taken by classes outside the studio. This practice can be best explained by *Situated Learning Theory* developed by Lave and Wenger (1991). Situated Learning Theory proposes that learning is unintentional and situated within activity, context and culture. Wenger (2008) extended their work on this theory to the concept of 'Communities of Practice', which is used for groups of people with shared concerns or passion to something they do. When these group members come together regularly and collaborate over an extended period of time, their interactions nurture their practice through sharing ideas, determining solutions and building innovation. This process of social learning also puts emphasis on presentation of knowledge in authentic contexts, settings and situations that would normally involve knowledge.

This case, with the Steelcase Active Learning Centre (SALC) as the context, includes embedded knowledge about community design, since the design of the centre was built on the collected needs of generations of students over the years. We used to arrange heavy furniture to create a collaboration surface, carefully tape maps so as not to peel off the wall paints and carry around extension cords for laptops. Most of the time small group work would not be effective, since we would have used all tables and chairs to create one big table to serve for mapping. When we used projection, we would be limited to a particular place in the classroom. Since projection curtains were folded and covered whiteboard surface when opened, it was not possible to use the board during a projection. There were no individualised controls in any of the rooms where we gathered. The exhibition space inside the classroom was very limited. Based on all these experienced needs I designed the SALC in collaboration with Steelcase Education to be the very first custom designed centre supported by an Active Learning Grant.

The centre has all moveable furniture that can be easily grouped based on the activity and can serve for multiple activities with different group sizes. It has a ceramic steel wall all around that can be written or projected on and is magnetic to allow for the hanging of posters. In addition to two projectors on the ceiling, there is a moveable projector table. There are writing boards that can be hung on the walls or displayed in a moveable caddy. All ambient control is given to users by providing adjustable lighting and HVAC system, and openable windows. The Human Behaviour and Environmental Design class is designed as workshops that foster social interaction and collaboration. Finally, students who are daily users of the campus are the community of practice who bring their daily experiences into the environment when they arrive for classes. When combined, all of these factors enable situated learning in the SALC and make it more work and act like a Community Design Centre that welcomes communities of practice for situated learning (Figure 1).

Figure 1: Steelcase Active Learning Centre @ KHas.

An introduction to the innovative practice

Starting each workshop with a big question, to which students need to tailor field research to gather data and perform collaborative analysis to find the answer, has always served students' best interests, rather than didactic learning methods that provide the answers. When we study our campus, students simply start by walking around and noting problems they experience on a daily basis on plan layouts. They also take photos. Later these textual and visual datasets are used to carry out multiple analyses including content analysis to determine codes, multiple task sorting, and mapping where students also provide ratings of importance (Figure 2). This leads to a giant mapping exercise that includes hundreds of stickers representing specific themes with individuals' ratings. This data also enables me to run analysis in software such as ArcGIS and report back to students via thematic maps created for each problematic theme. The visual database is also used to show that similar problems can be photographed differently and different students experience different problems, provoking discussion in terms of environmental perception and cognition. Students also locate their favourite spots and write about their memories there, exploring the types of environmental qualities we associate with positive feelings. In the end, based on all the workshops, students work in teams to come up with research-based design guidelines for the campus environment where they generate reports about the changes they expect to happen and which behaviours these changes should support. They are also given alternatives, allowing them to respond to these guidelines by designing or finding successful cases that can represent the changes they have written about.

Figure 2: Collaborative Mapping of the Problems in the Campus at Steelcase ALC.

A brief overview of the curriculum

The course, entitled "Human Behaviour and Environmental Design", that serves as a case study for this chapter, was run during the 2017 Spring semester, as a component of a four-year Interior Architecture and Environmental Design Program. The course has been designed to be inclusive to all students regardless of their skills. Nurtured by the participatory design approach, none of the tools used in the classroom require any special artistic or technical skill, since members of the community design workshops can come without these talents. With this approach, the course has gained popularity and attracted students from diverse departments outside the faculty. The pedagogical approach is open-source and can be repeated with professors who do not have a design background. The field techniques used in the classroom can be replicated with other purposes and help professors to carry out research in undergraduate education. Overall, the design thinking concept is followed in the course, which is similar to participatory design in terms of its emphasis in involving the community in the creative decision-making process.

The organisation of innovative practice

As the teacher, I am a facilitator during workshops. I also present theoretical and real-life applications from completed or on-going research and research-based design projects. Having completed research projects which employ techniques used throughout the course and using learning environments designed by the community enables me to fully engage students in the class, by sharing real-life experiences. We always have collaborative practice. Students are expected to go out, tour the campus and collect data without knowing how it will be analysed. Each week they learn a new technique for analysis, most of which they carry out in teams. As a learning community, we revisit research questions, and our aim is to connect the results of our workshops to them. Students also provide their viewpoints by writing short reflection papers.

For announcements and sharing content we use the Blackboard course site during the lecture. We use both analogue and digital technologies side by side. The content of workshops is uploaded and made accessible to students for analyses they wish to carry out outside the classroom.

The preparation of innovative practice

The Steelcase Active Learning Centre, specially designed to support various group formations during the workshops that I have observed over the course of seven years, has served as a great environment. Surrounded with a PolyVision Duo-Wall system, the classroom enables a seamless transition between collaborative mapping (analogue) and data entry, analysis and the exchange of information (digital) (Figure 3). The physical setting is important in many different ways. First and foremost, it supports what we want to accomplish by transforming into any seating arrangement with ease. Second, as it is so different from the rest of the classrooms on campus, the active learning classroom communicates (silently) that students will have a once in a lifetime experience during the class. Finally, it is a lively environment in which, combined with the democratic approach in the class, students can be themselves and engage in leadership by taking on responsibilities.

Figure 3: Collaborative Data Entry and Analysis Workshop. Note that one wall is used to reflect data tables whereas the other used for mapping.

Students use MS Office programs (Word, Excel, Power Point) and AutoCad vectoral drawing software for point data entry (which is not necessary if teachers do not perform further data analysis). I use ESRI's ArcMap and extensions to demonstrate further spatial analysis. These may not be necessary since thematic maps showing problem groups (observed and categorised by students) can also be produced using workshop materials. Occasionally I use additional research software to engage with data such as Space Syntax and Atlas.ti but they are not vital to the success of the projects. For textual analysis, we use open source online software such as Cloud Tags. We have used an off-site scanner to digitise the big maps, since we do not possess one on campus. Beyond these technical requirements, which seem neither too many nor too complex, I think our weekly research on our research questions and the supporting efforts for them are transferrable to those who would have similar motivations.

Section 3: The outcome

The outcome of the reported innovative practice, in terms of student behaviours, is retrieved for this particular class from an end of year survey that is designed by Steelcase Education to measure the effectiveness of the classroom. The survey was originally designed as a web-survey but was applied as a self-administered survey to maximise participation. The survey was conducted at the end of the semester in the Active Learning Centre. The survey was handed out and collected by other professors, assuring students that we only gain access to them after assigning the final grades. Only the part of the survey relevant to the scope of this chapter will be reported here to give insights about the main outcomes. Also, my personal observations and students open-ended responses will be reported in the upcoming sections.

A total of 40 (90% [36 female and 4 male]) out of 44 students in two sections of the Human Behaviour and Environment Spring 2017 class, took part in the survey.

When students were asked about their *"overall view of the type of instruction that they experience in the class during the course's term"*, only one student (2.5%) selected that the course was *"mostly lecture"*. Two students (5%) reported that it was *"only student to student work"* and 60% of the class (24 students) believed that the course was *"mostly student work"*, whereas 32.5% (13 students) stated that the course was *"equally balanced between lectures and student work"*. The majority of students reported that the course provided an experience for 'student work' during class hours, an indicator of the raised self-awareness on their community of practice.

Students loved to be in the SALC for their course. When they were given the phrase *"I want my other classes to be held in the Steelcase Active Learning Centre"*; 37.5% (15 students) reported that they *"Strongly Agree"* and 52.5 percent (21) said they *"Agree"*. One student (2.5%) was *"Undecided"*, and another one (2.5%) was negative. No one said that they *"Strongly Disagree"* with the statement. One student (2.5%) skipped the question.

Another reason why students seemed to love to be in the SALC was the pedagogy I followed in the class that redefined my role as a facilitator rather than a professor. When students were asked about their opinion on *"the effectiveness of instructor's helpfulness on their learning experience"*,

40% (16) of them said "very effective" and 50% (20) of them reported "effective". Three students (7.5%) stated that the instructor's helpfulness was *partly effective* in their learning experience. One student (2.5%) was neutral and two students, or 5% of the respondents, said *"partly ineffective"*. Two students skipped this question.

Students were also asked to provide an overall view of their level of engagement and contribution during the lecture part of this course through responding to questions, asking questions or making comments. 10% of the students (4) reported that they were *"extremely"* engaged and 21.5% (19) of the students stated that they were *"very"* engaged. 37.5% (15) of the students said they were *"moderately"* engaged in the course. Two students (5%) reported that they were *"slightly"* engaged. It should be noted that this question was directed at revealing how students felt like when I made a formal presentation about the theoretical part of the class. Overall, nearly one in three students were very or extremely engaged, participating orally in the class, in which lectures were given solely in English to Turkish students. From my experience of teaching this class in traditional learning environments, this represents a significant increase.

Based on their experiences of the new classroom, students were also asked to rate its contribution to increase of four outcomes: their *ability to achieve higher grades, ability to be creative, motivation to attend class* and *increase in their engagement in this class*. As Table 1 summarises, nearly half of the students (47.5%) reported that their experience contributed to an *"Exceptional"* increase in their ability to achieve a higher grade. 35% of students reported a *"High"* increase and 15% reported *"Moderate"* rating for the increase in their ability to achieve higher grade. It can be concluded that apart from one student, who represented 2.5% of the respondents, all reported that the new classroom had led to experiences that enabled them to achieve higher grades.

Students reported in equal numbers an *"Exceptional"* and *"High"* increase in their ability to be creative, adding up to 85% of the responses. The same equal trend was observed when students reported their motivation to attend the class, where 40% of the students each reported that experiences lead to an *"Exceptional"* and *"High"* increase, adding up to 80%. 37.5% of the students stated that their engagement in this class was exceptionally increased by their experiences in the new classroom and 42.5% rated this increase as *"High"*. There was only one student (2.5%)

reporting that his/her experiences in this classroom had no effect on his/her engagement in this class.

	Not at all	%	Low	%	Mod-erate	%	High	%	Excep-tional	%
Your ability to achieve a higher grade	0	0.0	1	2.5	6	15.0	14	35.0	19	47.5
Your ability to be creative	0	0.0	1	2.5	5	12.5	17	42.5	17	42.5
Your motivation to attend class	0	0.0	1	2.5	7	17.5	16	40.0	16	40.0
Your engagement in this class	1	2.5	1	2.5	6	15.0	17	42.5	15	37.5

Table 1: The rate of contribution to an increase in experiential outcomes taking place in the new classroom (number and percentage of students).

Finally, it can be concluded that the research-based design of the SALC supported new experiences for this learning community that led to positive outcomes. In following this pedagogical method, student learning went beyond the scope of this particular course, with students questioning the approach they followed in the design studio. They adopted the participatory design approach for learning environments. The course was held in the SALC, which was designed to respond to students' observed in-class behaviours when this pedagogy was followed in traditional learning environments (theory classes and design studio) by moving around furniture. Hence, the students experienced how design with community input makes all the difference.

The presence of a learning environment like this and a course with this innovative pedagogy empowered students to take control in their learning and perceive classes as planned interactions with learning opportunities. Thus, at the end of the day, they realised that it is their presence and participation that matters. Even the best classroom with an award-winning teacher would have no meaning without students who are eager to be part of a learning community. With the onset of the SALC, I enjoyed my classes more, seeing how the environment complemented my goals and how it helped us to become one big learning community.

Student perspective

Students tended to come to class early and leave some time after the end of class, which is to me an indicator that they loved to spend time in this classroom. They often asked to use the space outside class time when it was available. When they first encountered my innovative practices, they were surprised. As we progressed, they appreciated my effort in workshop design and other activities. They loved to go out and collect data, and to make sense of it collaboratively. They showed interest in the formal presentations when I presented theory in terms of its practical implications. They really loved the fact that I do not know what we will find out when we first start a workshop. They have become critical of other learning experiences they have had and have considered how these former experiences could be modified to be more like this class.

What do students learn? Students learn core concepts in Environmental Psychology such as Personal Space, Territoriality, Behavioural Settings, Theory of Affordance, Environmental Assessment, Perception and Cognition. They also learn Participatory Design Methods, post-occupancy evaluation and data collection techniques such as observation (direct/indirect, structured/unstructured observation and conducting interviews). They use analysis techniques such as mapping and content analysis (from text and images). They learn the needs of special populations (such as children of different ages and the elderly) and universal design guidelines.

How do you know what they learn? Their weekly participation in workshops and our interactions during class hours provide cues about their learning experiences. Each workshop ends with a presentation of findings by each team where each team member talks about their reflection. From time to time, these reflections are handed in in the form of short papers. They carry out a group and an individual project for the finals based on data from the entire semester.

How is it different from other types of teaching and learning? Students were generally used to classes where they were expected to perform alone. Design schools in particular generate students as 'islands' surrounded by weekly tasks in the studio and other courses but left alone to achieve. This kind of curriculum is often associated with the misconception that creativity happens alone – when you work on your own. Students are expected to defend their projects in design juries against groups of critics, and over time they may become over defensive about their ideas. This is the type of student which we are dealing. So they were surprised when they first faced a class where their attendance was a must for the class to happen, their group work was as important as their individual work, where it was possible to maintain a good mood in the class throughout the semester, and where they could have fun while they were learning. My personal belief is 'If it's not fun, why do it?'. I have seen that they initially associated fun with 'easy', but they later realised that fun could also be overcoming challenges.

What do students say? I handed in a sheet of paper for the overall evaluation of the class that was to be collected by a student who volunteered. Without my presence in the class, the students collected the papers. The envelope was sealed and remained with the student until all the grades were in. This is how professors receive feedback in my university, where they collect evaluations themselves before assigning the final grades. Apart from the heartfelt thank-you notes, here are some narratives that represent the nature of comments representing the overall evaluation of the course:

✦ *"It's a course that doesn't feel like a course."*

✦ *"Every week I look forward to coming here to do the things we never did before. I wish all my educational experiences has been like this so far."*

✦ *"The classroom is amazing! We are now cool people in a cool classroom."*

✦ *"I like the fact that we have various roles in this class... We are students, we are interior architects, we are community designers, we are map makers, we are data people, we are the design people..."*

✦ *"I really liked working with my classmates and finally get to know some people in my class I had never talked to before..."*

+ *"I wish I could do studio projects like this."*

+ *"I like the fact that I can have access to everything before and after the class...We can't see some professors' presentations after class in other courses but we can see your presentations before you present them."*

I can state that open-ended comments in my personal evaluation fall into one of the four categories: 'fun', 'pedagogy', 'active learning classroom features', or 'other personal reflections'.

The survey that was conducted to measure the outcomes of the SALC also contained one open-ended question for reflection. Most of the comments focus on how the mobility of the furniture, the presence of multi-purpose boards in all walls and the presence of outlets on the ground and on the walls enabled group study. One student stated that: *"The furniture on wheels helped us to form groups with ease. The classroom with boards everywhere also supported us to write everywhere. This freedom in the classroom was by design."* Another one mentioned that *"The classroom provides freedom to move and be active. It also provided options to select a table at which to sit with a friend or alone. Both options support group study and also support interaction between groups."* These open-ended responses revealed the fact that students were fully aware of how design features of this classroom helped them to achieve the goals of the course.

As a professor teaching the core concepts of Environment Psychology in this course, the most interesting finding, from combing through the open-ended responses, was noting how nearly all of them stated how design aided positive behavioural changes such as an increased motivation to attend classes, an increase in participation and increased social interaction. One student wrote: *"This class gave me a positive mood. I usually use all my permitted leave in the classes, but I loved this class and attended every week. I love coming to this classroom and being part of it. This course demolished my prejudice that all courses are boring."* Another student wrote about how the design the classroom and the course helped her to feel better, naturally leading to an increase in her participation. She wrote: *"I'm shy and generally avoid talking in front of the crowd. In a regular class, I don't like to participate. However, the freedom to move in this classroom, the group work and the teaching method enabled me to actively participate to this class."* Peer-to-peer social interaction was mentioned several times in relation to group studies. However, the interaction between professor and students was also mentioned several times. One student stated that the classroom had changed the way how she perceived professors: *"The classroom design and the way this course is thought through revolutionise traditional student-professor interactions. Here, students are not under any threat and they are not afraid to speak their minds regardless of whatever they want to say. It's a friendly social environment with open minded people."*

The teacher's perspective – my reflections

The greatest gift in teaching is seeing students excited about your class and witnessing their success in it. As a teacher I learnt that all my sincere efforts had succeeded. Being critical about design education and its unchanged attitude towards the student population, since the time when I was a student, encouraged me to design my own approach after years of experience working with other communities. It is likely that the success of our students lies in the promotion of the feeling that none of them is better than any other, or making them compete to be stars in their studio classes. Instead, we worked through a participatory design pedagogy, in a supportive active learning environment, where students shined through their own strengths. All went well, as expected. What did not go well was breaking the old habits that came from traditional teaching when we first began. Grading becomes a challenge when you have so many people doing better. Sometimes it feels like doing small good (e.g. writing better reports) or bad things (e.g. missing more than one class) consistently separated students from each other in terms of grades. I wish I could have simply given a fail or pass grade to this class, which was not possible with this curriculum. It is hard to keep tabs on interactions, since they happen a lot and everywhere, and showing interest in them for the purpose of assigning grades conflicts with the nature of this course and the classroom. In a course that is focused on improving students' self worth, creating a sense of community through learning experiences, in a democratic environment, does not easily match grade-focused assignments that lead to an ease in the calculation of final grades.

Through this experience I have learned and confirmed that I feel I am a good teacher and I certainly love what I do. The SALC at Kadir Has University was designed to respond to the observed needs of students in participatory design workshops that make up the core of the pedagogy

I followed. Being the only custom-designed Active Learning Centre, funded with grants received from Steelcase and PolyVision, this whole experience made me realise that, if you do your job well, there may be someone from another part of the world who appreciates what you did.

Section 4: Moving forward

The university, in which I work, recently established a Centre of Excellence in Learning and Teaching (CELT) and invited me to serve as one of their Advisory Board Members. The press kit that publicised the opening of the new centre mentioned the establishment of SALC as one of the two events that had led to the opening of the CELT. Having no Faculty of Education among its faculties, this was a bold move. The SALC has been widely used by diverse courses from different faculties. I have received incredible feedback from design and non-design students, who have taken my classes, and say that they have used techniques that they learnt in my class for other classes and in their professional life. As I continue using the SALC on a daily basis to conduct classroom research with a multi-disciplinary team of scientists, I have recently developed an interest in developing wearable technology that helps to keep track of interactions happening during the class to provide feedback for students (not for grades). As an interdisciplinary team, we follow a collaborative approach together with students from College of Engineering and Natural Sciences to work on real-life problems where the active learning centre serves as the test-bed. This effort is also described in Chapter 14 of this book. I have recently started to transfer my knowledge of conducting design workshops to learning communities outside my institution and providing consultancy to help people design their own learning environments.

Conclusion

In this chapter, I discussed how learning space design can be thought of as a multi-subject facilitator, involving students as members of the campus community. Students not only collected data based on their own experiences but are also expected to analyse and make design guidelines out of this data. The course communicates multiple subjects both directly and indirectly (through experience and then reflection). The active learning environment that served as the basis for this course was also established by taking observed community needs into account. Students encounter these concepts and pedagogy of this kind for the first time and complete the semester with positive outcomes and outlooks towards the future of their education. The outcomes such as increase in engagement, interactions, participation and attendance have been reported in other studies measuring effectiveness of active learning pedagogy and active learning environments (Prince, 2004; Scott-Webber *et al.* 2013; Nissim *et al.* 2016). From this perspective, the findings reported are in parallel with the literature. However, defining an Active Learning Centre as a Community Centre through the pedagogy that relies on participatory design is a new approach. In terms of the design of learning environments, the designers often focus on number of students, courses and expected increase in the future. Similarly, for a professor, it is easy to be caught up in designing a course where x amount of topics will be taught in y amount of weeks to a class size of n. Yet, when making design decisions about environments for learning or the curriculum, one needs to think about how these decisions play an important role in learning experiences that lead to students gaining an attachment to their institution and building a sense of community. In addition to all the extra-curricular activities and administrative efforts in a university that supports students in building a community, the course content and learning environments can be geared towards the same ends.

From this perspective, the Steelcase Active Learning Centre did indeed serve as a Community Design Centre, supporting students' sense of belonging and attachment. The pedagogical approach we followed, combined with a supportive learning environment, bonded students to one other, to the humanistic values of design and ultimately to their university as well.

About the Authors

Orcun Kepez, PhD is an Assistant Professor in Department of Interior Architecture and Environmental Design in Faculty of Art and Design at Kadir Has University, Istanbul, Turkey. He can be contacted at this e-mail: orcun.kepez@khas.edu.tr

Acknowledgement

Steelcase Active Learning Center was established by grants received from Steelcase Education and PolyVision (Internal Grant Numbers 2015-DK-05 and 2015-AP-04 respectively).

Bibliography

Boyer, E. L. (1990). *Scholarship reconsidered: priorities of the professoriate.* Princeton, N. J.: Carnegie Foundation for the Advancement of Teaching.

Boyer, E. L., & Mitgang, L. D. (1996). *Building community: a new future for architecture education and practice: a special report.* Princeton, N.J: Carnegie Foundation for the Advancement of Teaching.

Council for Interior Design Accreditation (2018). *Council for Interior Design Accreditation Professional Standards 2018.* Council for Interior Design Accreditation.

Dickinson, J. I., Anthony, L., & Marsden, J. P. (2009). Faculty Perceptions Regarding Research: Are We on the Right Track? *Journal of Interior Design,* 35(1), 1–14.

Kepez, O. (2010). Use of Behavior Mapping and Space Syntax Methods Inform Design of a Museum Path Located in University Building: Case Study of Rezan Has Museum in Kadir Has University. In Meldrena Chapin (Ed.), *Proceedings of EDRA 41: Policy and Environment* (p. 252). Oklahoma: EDRA.

Kepez, O. (2015). Graduate Education as a Research Environment (Original Title: Bir Arastirma Ortami Olarak Lisansustu Egitim). In Cordan, Ö. (Ed.), *Book of Full Paper Proceedings ICLEK: National Congress (I) on Graduate Studies in Interior Architecture* (pp. 45–52). Istanbul: Istanbul Technical University.

Kepez, O., & Ust, S. (2017). Post Occupancy Evaluation of a Transformed Design Studio. *ITU AZ Journal,* 14(3), 41–52.

Klepeis, N. E., Nelson, W. C., Ott, W. R., Robinson, J. P., Tsang, A. M., Switzer, P., & Engelmann, W. H. (2001). The National Human Activity Pattern Survey (NHAPS): a resource for assessing exposure to environmental pollutants. *Journal of Exposure Analysis And Environmental Epidemiology,* 11, 231.

Lave, J., & Wenger, E. (1991). *Situated learning: legitimate peripheral participation.* Cambridge, UK: Cambridge University Press.

Nissim, Y., Weissblueth, E., Scott-Webber, L., & Amar, S. (2016). The Effect of a Stimulating Learning Environment on Pre-Service Teachers' Motivation and 21st Century Skills. *Journal of Education and Learning*, 5(3), 29.

Prince, M. (2004). Does Active Learning Work? A Review of the Research. *Journal of Engineering Education*, 93(3), 223–231.

Salama, A. M. A. (1997). *New trends in architectural education: designing the design studio*. Cairo, Egypt: Anglo Egyptian Bookshop.

Salama, A. M. A. (2015). *Spatial design education: new directions for pedagogy in architecture and beyond*. Farnham Surrey, England; Burlington: Ashgate.

Sanoff, H. (2000). *Community participation methods in design and planning*. New York: Wiley.

Sanoff, H. (2010). *Community participation in school planning: case studies of engagement in school facilities*. Saarbrucken: VDM Verlag Dr. Müller.

Scott-Webber, L., Aileen, S., & Kapitula, L. (2013). Built Environments Impact Behaviors: Results of an Active Learning Post-Occupancy Evaluation. *Planning for Higher Education*, (October–December), 28–39.

Waite, R., & Braidwood, E. (2016, July 28). Mental health problems exposed by AJ Student Survey 2016. *Architect's Journal*.

Wenger, E. (2008). *Communities of practice: learning, meaning, and identity*. Cambridge: Cambridge Univ. Press.

Chapter 14

Steelcase Active Learning Centre as a Testbed for Engineering Design Projects

Taner Arsan & Orcun Kepez

Introduction

This chapter contributes to this book on *Innovative Teaching And Learning Practices In Higher Education* by presenting how we can use the Steelcase Active Learning Centre as a research environment for students to engage in active learning. This chapter follows on from Kepez's Chapter 13 in this volume, in which he shared the background behind the Steelcase Active Learning Centre and how it serves as a community design centre for his class. This chapter describes the use of the Steelcase Active Learning Centre as a research environment where students work on engineering problems that require effective technical solutions. These engineering problems are real-life problems we face in the real world and given to students as multi-disciplinary engineering design projects. Although these engineering design problems could be seen as marginal to the research challenges we face in the real world, they do fill a gap and contribute to real projects. To engage students in active learning, this chapter also outlines the use of the sensor technology we developed to track people's positioning and movements, and how we can use this technology to assess the uses of the Steelcase Active Learning Centre.

Reading this chapter, you will gain the following three insights:

1. how we can utilise sensor technologies to understand the uses of active learning environments;

2. how effectively our engineering design projects facilitate students to recognise the transferability of their skills to real-world application;

3. how effectively engineering design projects can develop students' teamwork skills that they need as professionals.

Section 1: The background

We were interested in understanding how campus indoor environments could be used through methods established in engineering and design research. Previous engineering research conducted on the campus where the active learning centre was located tested the potential of Wi-Fi, Bluetooth low-energy beacons and ultra-wide band technologies to solve location-based well-defined engineering problems such as tracking people and objects as they moved around the campus (Arsan, 2016). At the same time, the behaviour mapping of the campus was conducted by the design researcher through systematic observations of individuals (Arsan & Kepez, 2017). The university administration used the findings of both studies to make spatial decisions for the future development of the technology. When both researchers teamed up to apply for a Steelcase Active Learning Grant, they joined together their research agendas to focus on indoor positioning in active learning environments and the development of automated behaviour mapping through sensor technology.

Upon the establishment of the centre through an Active Learning Grant received jointly from Steelcase and PolyVision, we developed the design of the physical environment in collaboration with Steelcase Education. The design put in place was a state-of-the-art active learning environment, which is a classroom furnished with moveable furniture, providing multiple choices for seating. The walls were clad with ceramic-steel surfaces that could be used for projection, writing or displaying posters through the attachment of magnets.

As we progressed with our research agenda, new engineering design problems that emerged have been assigned as graduation projects to prospective engineering students. Among the population of students who chose to participate in this research, three teams of four students were established to work on three distinct real-life engineering design problems under the supervision of a multi-disciplinary team of professors. These three projects, focused on understanding the uses and resource management of sensor technology and increasing the accuracy of the sensors, were developed right inside a test bed that was already developed as part of our continuing research project. As the classroom was used heavily within a regular schedule, we reserved time slots for engineering design projects as well. These groups may have been small but nevertheless required the use of the entire classroom for testing (software and hardware) and technology development.

Section 2: The practice

The innovation that we bring to teaching and learning in higher education is introducing a multi-disciplinary approach to solving engineering design problems related to user activity in active learning environments. This multi–disciplinary element can be seen from the fields of expertise of the students' advisors and professors. The following fields were represented: Computer engineering, electrical-electronics engineering, industrial engineering, energy systems engineering, data mining, interior architecture and environmental design. As a team of researchers, we openly share problems that we encounter with a community of students who are required to participate in engineering design projects in order to graduate. When students are aware of the real-life contributions of their project, then they are no longer students but real engineers who collaborate with us. Thus, the undergraduate students who take part in our multi-disciplinary research project have different experiences from those who self-selected various topics independent from their advisors' research agenda. The multi-disciplinary nature of our team also provides them with new challenges that may otherwise not be available in terms of their development as a team member. We devoted our efforts in this approach to increase the agile skills of engineering graduates to compete in professional career planning where they will face similar challenges.

The background to our innovative practice

Generally, professors in our context are expected to include Masters and PhD students in their research projects. Given the small number of graduate students and the eagerness of our institution to involve undergraduates in research projects, we announce projects that cluster around our needs in the laboratory on a daily basis.

The Association for Evaluation and Accreditation of Engineering Programs (MUDEK) is a non-governmental organisation aimed at evaluating undergraduate engineering programs and supporting the continuous development of such programs in order to meet their expectations.

The Computer Engineering, Electrical-Electronics Engineering and Industrial Engineering programs at Kadir Has University's Faculty of Engineering and Natural Sciences were accredited by MUDEK in 2016. Our innovative practice in the Engineering Design Project course led to contributions to outcomes 1–7, and 10 out of 11 which are required in the evaluation of bachelor engineering programs (MUDEK, 2016). Four of these outcomes (2, 3, 6 and 7) are indispensable in any graduation project, whereas the others may be met to different degrees depending on the content of the project. The four crucial outcomes (2, 3, 6 and 7 respectively) are:

+ *"the ability to identify, formulate, and solve complex engineering problems; the ability to select and apply proper analysis and modelling methods for this purpose (2)"*;

+ *"the ability to design a complex system, process, device or product under realistic constraints and conditions, in such a way as to meet the desired result; the ability to apply modern design methods for this purpose (3)"*;

+ *"the ability to work efficiently in intra-disciplinary and multi-disciplinary teams; the ability to work individually (6)"*;

+ *"the ability to communicate effectively in Turkish, both orally and in writing; the knowledge of a minimum of one foreign language; the ability to write effective reports and comprehend written reports, to prepare design and production reports, make effective presentations, and give and receive clear and intelligible instructions (7)"* (MUDEK, 2016).

The traditional flow of a course in an engineering curriculum is a linear progression, where each week is dedicated for communicating a topic (Figure 1). By assigning weekly homework or an in-class quiz, the instructor measures the success of the class. A midterm or a final exam generally measures if distinct weekly topics are well understood. A complicated question that requires a questioning of the topic matter as a whole is seldom asked in either type of evaluation.

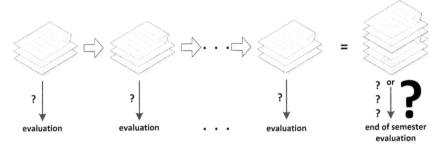

Figure 1: Traditional flow of an engineering course curriculum.

In our Engineering Design Course, we follow a project-based approach where we assign a real-life engineering problem and expose students to all key resources at the beginning of the semester. In the progress of working throughout the semester, students also look for other resources they believe serves the project. As a team, they divide up tasks, and actively assess themselves as individuals and as a team during the entire project timeline. So as instructors, we focus on feedback during the process rather than giving grades for individual evaluations. Since the goal of the project is clear, students already know whether they have reached the milestone events or not. In the end, they know that they need to find a solution (whether software or hardware, or both) in order to succeed and that this requires going beyond answering some questions in an examination. In order to keep up a steady progress, our teams have realized that they need to incorporate project management skills from day one (Figure 2).

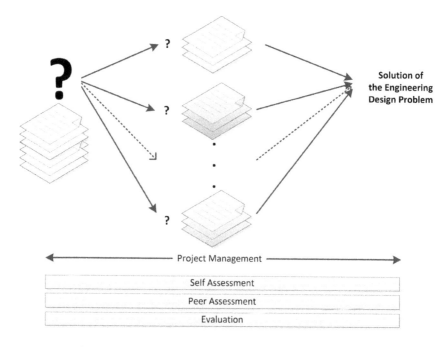

Figure 2: Flow of engineering design course.

Project based education is often described as assigning individual projects, usually to an individual student and sometimes to a small group, in a regular course where students are expected to follow a linear progress similar to a traditional class (Thompson & Beak, 2007; Wurdinger & Bezon, 2009). Within the broad sphere of project based education, Fan *et al.* (2018) define project-based learning (PBL) as a unique form of pedagogy designed to help improve students in their self-learning and active practice. PBL has developed over many decades in the realm of medicine and has been adopted worldwide in other discipline areas, including the field of engineering education. The study by Li and Wang (2018) is a creative example of how PBL can be used to apply a theoretical knowledge of engineering and develop problem-solving skills. PBL, whereby students explore real world problems, promotes active learning and higher-order thinking through the investigation of complex questions and challenges (Savery, 2006) and was critical to our course design. This form of classroom activity, also allows students autonomy over how they solve the problems entailed by the project they are working on, how it will finish, and what the end project will be. In addition, in our situation, by removing regular contact hours, leaving the traditional classroom environment for an active learning "lab" space, and employing real-life problems, our teams built leadership skills.

In our innovative engineering design project, due to the complexity of the real-life project we ensured that the expected product was well-defined and clear from the beginning in the PBL approach we used. However, this complex project could also include smaller problems that students could tackle separately. These smaller projects included the interface design (mobile and/or desktop) and the project branding (whether software or hardware). We gave students free reign to design these according to their personal tastes and were less critical about the end product on these measures, since their individualised solutions for these smaller problems also helped them to cultivate their attachment to the bigger project.

A brief overview of the curriculum

In the final year, all engineering students took the Engineering Design Project course for graduation after they successfully completed the Engineering Problem Solving and Project Management course in the fall semester. The three teams, that selected topics which we announced, came from the Computer Engineering Department. The projects that were given were as follows:

+ a smart-ceiling system project that helped researchers to move ultra-wide band (UWB) receivers that helped to locate sensors worn by students and professors;

+ behaviour mapping software that plotted retrieved sensor data to the classroom plan layout automatically;

+ a geo-fencing application that automatically detected entrances to and exits from the active learning classroom, good for automatic attendance logging for students and resource tracking.

Each project used sensor-based technology and we were challenged to develop an application for it.

Organisation of the innovative practice

Our approach required us to act as a learning community rather than as formal educators. Thus, we established teams as research groups where we participated as consultants. We adopted the motto of *"Good engineering design does not happen overnight"* which was a call for going beyond the regular contact hours. As a team, we meet once a week, but also provided time in our schedule for impromptu walk-ins by students. We also established a WhatsApp group for each team to resolve instant conflicts and to enhance communication. The progression of the projects contained steps starting from product design and manufacturing planning to prototyping, testing, documenting, and presentation. We added input from the design disciplines at all steps and empowered students to question their decisions in relation to design problems with more than one solution. We also provided the Active Learning Centre to act as their testbeds.

Active learning and blended learning are two concepts that are mostly associated with using the learning environment more efficiently for meaningful activities rather than spending time on traditional teaching (Baepler *et al.*, 2014; Garrison & Kanuka, 2004; Prince, 2004). Our innovative practice in Project Based Teaching is threefold: First, we used a real active learning environment as a test bed for projects that are usable in learning environments. Second, we employed real-life digital communication interfaces such as cloud services and instant messaging that mimic interactions in a professional environment. And third, we removed regular classes in favour of face-to-face planned meetings and impromptu walk-ins that replaced their expectations of professors in a regular class to a shared excitement about all their interactions.

Preparation of the innovative practice

Indoor positioning systems research requires knowledge in coding and sensor technology. Sensor hardware is also necessary. Based on the needed accuracy of measurement, one can select different sensor technologies. In our research, we found that ultra-wide band (UWB) sensor technology is best for capturing the location of people in an active learning classroom (Arsan & Kepez, 2017). We currently use a decaWave Trek 1000 kit

(DecaWave, 2016). The decaWave Real-Time Location System (RTLS) interface is limited to displaying the last 99 records of coordinates sensed by UWB sensors to monitor collected data visually (Figure 3).

Obviously, we used computers to retrieve sensed data and work on coding. But most importantly, we needed to understand human behaviour to make sense of the collected locations of people. We used ESRI ArcMap, and Spatialist extension to run analysis and make heat maps, as well as using social theories to understand the big data that was captured by the sensors.

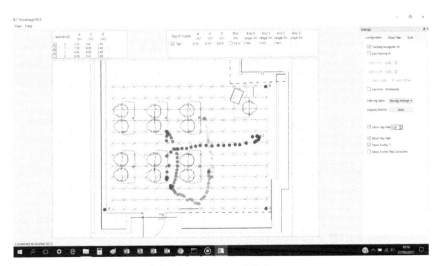

Figure 3: The interface of the decaWave RTLS system.

Section 3: The outcome

A recent effort in following a similar curriculum, focused on smart systems, was found to be effective (Arsan, 2016). However, when focused on a real-life environment and informed by an inter-disciplinary approach including the discipline of Design, the end products went beyond our working models. Given real-life problems in a real-life context – in this case an active learning centre – students became aware of concepts that may otherwise not concern them. Originality in innovative problem solving, design considerations, multi-disciplinary thinking, and the user-friendly design of interfaces and documentation are listed as developed skills that we observed. As graduating students, our team members had experienced what it felt like working in a research environment by means of their intellectual and professional contributions. If we had solved the same problems on our own, it would have taken less time than the time we spent on our students. Yet, as we support research in undergraduate education, the transfer of knowledge through more informal means, such as the research teams we established, is a must. Similarly, if students selected other topics, they might have studied less since they would not have been under pressure to deliver an answer for a burning research question. Therefore, we can state that the experience based on both parties was based on pure interest in the topic, and the mutual sacrifices that came with that. In the end, we were all content to do the hard work with working prototypes of apps and sensor-based devices (Figure 4 & 5). The three projects given to the three teams that took an interest in joining our research groups in the scope of the aforementioned course were:

+ a mobile app-controlled ceiling system that can lift sensors to the desired height automatically;

+ an indoor geo-fencing app that can be used for the management of people and resources; and

+ an app that plots the coordinates of the sensed people/objects to make automated behaviour maps.

Figure 4: Smart ceiling system; manual system, mobile application-based remotely controlled motorised system, and the project group.

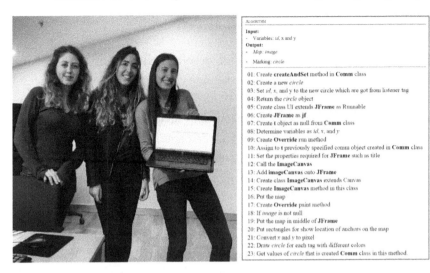

Figure 5: The Engineering Design Project group developing the code for the geo-fencing system for the Active Learning Centre.

Student perspective

To ascertain the effectiveness of our innovative practice, we conducted focus groups interviews with each team and also collected their written statements reflecting their thoughts about their own experiences. We analysed the statements obtained from the focus groups sessions and the written statements by way of grouping them into major Categories 1 to 4:

1. emphasis on the transferability of their skills to real-world application;

2. emphasis on the multi-disciplinary nature of the projects;

3. emphasis on their team-work skills development; and

4. comparison of their learning experiences with other students who were working with other professors

Category 1

Students stated that tackling real-life problems throughout their course gave them the opportunity to take this as a challenge to grow into professionals. One student stated that: *"I think that this project also influenced my professional career by teaching me viable skills sought in the field. Our project can be integrated into so many industries and that has served my competitiveness as a new graduate."* Another mentioned that: *"Through this project, we were able to conduct research, follow different methods and use various applications. I think these skills helped me to develop as a professional engineer rather than spending last year as a fourth-year student."* Students believed that this experience helped them to make easier real-life transitions, since their project required more complex structures including hardware development, mobile application development, cloud service, web services and software development. One student stated that: *"Our project has never been a single-application project. We have mobile applications, cloud services, measurements, and mapping. At the end of the day, these are skills that it takes to deliver a project when we graduate."*

Category 2

The students felt lucky to be part of a greater good in the bigger projects pursued by their professors in multiple disciplines and this made them take this challenge more seriously. One student shared her excitement, saying *"Working with a team of professors who represent engineering and design disciplines, has been an excellent experience for me."* Similarly, another student mentioned that *"bringing a multi-disciplinary point of view to this project by representing the engineering and design fields has been a significant benefit of this course"*. Students also pointed out that the multi-disciplinary nature of our research group enabled them *"to develop their skills in disciplines including mechanical, electrical, electronics, and computer engineering disciplines' points of view."* They also responded to the design experience, saying *"doing something that works is not enough: it should work beautifully by taking into account user experience too."*

Category 3

They enjoyed that they were responsible for each other's work. Students mentioned that they had to carry out teamwork effectively from the beginning by assigning realistic goals and roles from day one. One student wrote: *"Teamwork has never been as important as in this project where active contribution of everyone is a must in order to deliver. This has helped us to learn how to work together to achieve our common goals."* Another stated: *"I and my team mates put a lot of collaborative effort into the system selection, design, and implementations. Without any of us, this project would not be possible."*

Category 4

Compared to their peers, our teams felt more pressure in terms of time-management and expected outcomes in the beginning, but this feeling turned into a calmer professional experience as they received continuous support from us. They praised our approach by comparing their peers' experiences. One student wrote that: *"Because we are part of a real ongoing research project, our professors respond to our questions very openly and clearly. In many of our friends' projects, the real-life connection is made up and they lose the track of how their project will be used. That was never the case for us."*

Students' comparison of their learning experiences with those of other students have helped us to understand the merits of our approach. Students made comparisons based on the applicability of their project to daily life. One student wrote: *"Our project makes daily life easier and increases the quality of life. We built this project on interactive software and services. This is completely different than other students who work on just one of them."* Another supported this by writing *"When we complete our project, it's ready to be used. That's what we aim for, and why we work. This is not happening in other students' projects."*

Some students claimed that their group is different compared to others because working with us provided a medium to involve in the university community in a way that other groups don't have. A student wrote: *"I think the main difference between us and other students is that as a group, we are part of a real research group that pursues innovative practices in our university. We are contributing to the goals of the group and serving to university while we are working on this project."*

Thus, getting student feedback as a focus group as well as written statements helped us to evaluate ourselves as professors. It also informed us that we can act as a team, regardless of roles, in order to improve our communication. Students were able to express their feelings freely during the focus groups. Since we carried them out at the end of the semester, students' fear of dealing with the complexity of the projects regularly turned into pride and self-confidence according to many of our students' reflections.

Teacher perspective – our reflections

What did you learn? The Engineering Design Project course has followed the same structural format for the past decade and we have observed that time management, weekly meetings for mentoring, and suitability of the student team structure for selected projects are key points for overall success.

What do you get from this particular innovative teaching and learning practice? In our innovative teaching and learning practice, we experienced better outcomes (report quality, prototype or end-product quality and user experience quality). Most importantly, students in these teams are competitively ready for professional life. Alternatively, they can continue graduate degrees (at our university or at another institution) or can work in research environments.

What went well? We were happy to observe our students' passion, confidence and their dedication to the multi-disciplinary approach. They also carried out teamwork effectively, which has always been a problem for undergraduate students in our cultural context. We supported experimentation but also allowed room for failure. For example, the selection of the motor used in the Smart Ceiling System in order to allow movement is left to the students. They already know that stepper motors need to be used in such systems. It has been observed that students have always made the correct choice to make stepper motors for their systems. At one important point, it was observed that students used their own creativity to transfer stepper motor movement to the plate carrying the sensor: at first they thought of a screw system, but immediately realized that it was not the right choice, and immediately afterwards they transferred the motor movement to the plate with a belt-and-pulley system. The mobile application was developed by the students and they made the whole design themselves. In the geo-fence system, the students used their own programming skills and creativity in transferring the data from the sensors to the desktop applications they developed. The behaviour mapping group was able to design an interface to visualise the collected data. All these products were the result of free experimentation that fostered creativity.

What went not so well? In rare cases, some individuals were not effective in the teamwork environment and asked to change their teams or complained about their teammates. Yet as a rule, when students sign up for projects with their team members, leaving a team does not reduce the expected workload, and the leaving member automatically fails the course. Thus, it is not allowed, unless there is a medical reason.

We carried out some teambuilding activities aimed at conflict resolution. When individual students came to meet with us alone, we told them to come with their teams. We showed them our working schedule as a team and told them how we plan to work together and how we would resolve conflicts similar to theirs or explained why we would not have problems similar to theirs.

What did you learn yourself? We learned that being patient pays off and as a team of professors we have to manage our patience to a level where we see progress. Teams progress at different speeds, based on the different challenges they face during the timeline. We realised that when we expect real products, we have to have a project management approach that is different from regular mentoring. Yet, this management should be humanistic, including tolerance for error that gives students room to grow. We realised that communication is the key for success.

What would you do different next time? We realised that weekly meetings may have been necessary in the beginning but not all the way through the course. As students progress, sometimes they need a couple of weeks to resolve issues and weekly meetings can be over-stressful for them. So, next time we will list milestone events and let them schedule meetings whenever they reach them. We believe that this will give them more control over the timeline of the project.

Section 4: Moving forward

We are a multi-disciplinary team of authors representing Design (Interior Architecture and Environmental Design) and Computer Science who served as advisors for teams of students for the Engineering Design Course that we outlined as the innovative practice of this chapter. As a research team, we work in the field of indoor positioning systems through sensors. We focused on sensing the location of people and furniture in the Steelcase Active Learning Centre and understand in-class interactions through automated behaviour mapping. Our innovative practice extends the Steelcase Active Learning Centre beyond being our testbed outside class hours, by defining it as a learning laboratory for students who took our course. Our university supports our approach that overlaps with their policy of supporting research from undergraduate level onwards. We received a seed grant to continue our research from our institution and are preparing for bigger grants.

Conclusion

Innovative practices in higher education do require preparation and teamwork. As a multi-disciplinary team of researchers, our years of effort spent establishing a joint research agenda with regard to indoor positioning systems and applying our knowledge to understand learning environments really proved their merit. This was the demonstrated when we came to understand that the daily problems we faced in developing hardware, software and prototypes specialised for our purposes could be shared with community of students. Being swamped with even more complex problems, we also realised that in order to save more time in the long run, we also needed to have teams to develop solutions. We were aware that creativity can only be nurtured when students are allowed to make autonomous decisions. This creativity was showcased by the students in such examples as the selection of the motor for the Smart Ceiling System, the design of the mobile application, their programming and creativity in the geo-fence system in data transfer from sensors to desktop applications and an interface to visualise collected data. All of these products represented the result of open experimentation that nurtured their creativity and ingenuity.

The Steelcase Active Learning Centre continues to serve as the testbed for our now-extended research groups. Given the real-life challenges, and the high expectations of the multi-disciplinary group of professors, students tried to make the most of their team abilities, and our mentoring skills. We also made ourselves available in the project specific WhatsApp groups for quick questions that could hasten students' decision-making processes. Finally, all students succeeded and provided positive feedback. We learned that bringing top quality research to the undergraduate level takes more dedication in terms of time from both students and professors side but it pays off when both parties know that the end-result goes beyond a project to receive a passing grade.

About the Authors

Taner Arsan, PhD, is an Assistant Professor in the Computer Engineering Department in the Faculty of Engineering and Natural Sciences at Kadir Has University, Istanbul, Turkey. He can be contacted at this e-mail: arsan@khas.edu.tr

Orcun Kepez, PhD, is an Assistant Professor in the Department of Interior Architecture and Environmental Design in Faculty of Art and Design at Kadir Has University, Istanbul, Turkey. He can be contacted at this e-mail: orcun.kepez@khas.edu.tr

This research was funded by grants received from Kadir Has University, Grant Number 2017-BAP-09. Steelcase Active Learning Center was established by grants received from Steelcase Education and PolyVision (Internal Grant Numbers 2015-DK-05 and 2015-AP-04 respectively).

Bibliography

Arsan, T. (2016). Smart Systems: From design to implementation of embedded Smart Systems. In *2016 HONET-ICT*, pp. 59–64.

Arsan, T., & Kepez, O. (2017). Early Steps in Automated Behavior Mapping via Indoor Sensors. *Sensors*, 17(12), 2925.

Baepler, P., Walker, J. D., & Driessen, M. (2014). It's not about seat time: Blending, flipping, and efficiency in active learning classrooms. *Computers & Education, 78*, 227–236.

DecaWave, (2016). *TREK1000 User Manual, How to Install, Configure and Evaluate the Decawave Trek1000 Two-Way Ranging (TWR) RTLS IC Evaluation Kit, Version 1.06.*

Fan, C., Jiang, B., Shi, X., Wang, E., & Li, Q. (2018). Update on research and application of problem-based learning in medical science education: Problem-Based Learning in Medical Science Education. *Biochemistry and Molecular Biology Education, 46*(2), 186–194.

Garrison, D. R., & Kanuka, H. (2004). Blended learning: Uncovering its transformative potential in higher education. *The Internet and Higher Education, 7*(2), 95–105.

Li, Y., & Wang, L. (2018). Using iPad-based mobile learning to teach creative engineering within a problem-based learning pedagogy. *Education and Information Technologies, 23*(1), 555–568.

MUDEK – Association for Evaluation and Accreditation of Engineering Programs. (2016). Criteria for Evaluating Bachelor Engineering Programs. Retrieved April 12, 2018, from http://www.mudek.org.tr/doc/en/MUDEK-Evaluation_Criteria_(2.1.1–11.03.2016).pdf.

Prince, M. (2004). Does Active Learning Work? A Review of the Research. *Journal of Engineering Education, 93*(3), 223–231.

Savery, J. R. (2006). Overview of Problem-based Learning: Definitions and Distinctions. Interdisciplinary *Journal of Problem-Based Learning, 1*(1).

Thompson, K. J., & Beak, J. (2007). The Leadership Book: Enhancing the Theory-Practice Connection Through Project-Based Learning. Journal of Management *Education, 31*(2), 278–291.

Wurdinger, S. D., & Bezon, J. L. (2009). Teaching practices that promote student learning: Five experiential approaches. *Journal of Teaching and Learning, 6*(1).

Chapter 15

Evidence, Analysis, Action: Using Learning Analytics to Direct Curriculum Review and Improve Student Learning Outcomes

Christine Armatas & Christine Spratt

Introduction

With our chapter, we contribute to this book *Innovative Teaching And Leanring Practices In Higher Education* by demonstrating that learning analytics as an integral part of curriculum review can highlight factors impacting on student success. We present our innovative practice that can both lead the development of improvement strategies and prompt teachers to ask important questions about the curriculum they may not have previously considered – and this is achieved through the use of predictive capabilities of learning analytics in curriculum review.

We use Siemens' (2013:1382) definition to define learning analytics as *"...the measurement, collection, analysis and reporting of data about learners and their contexts, for purposes of understanding and optimizing learning and the environments in which it occurs"*. Learning analytics can be used to predict student performance, understand the causes of at-risk learning behaviors and student attrition and for assessing institutional performance (Greller & Drachsler 2012; Ravishanke, 2011; Gašević *et al.*, 2016). However, there is little research on its use for curriculum evaluation and review (Méndez *et al.*, 2014).

In defining innovation for this chapter, we draw on the influential work of Rogers (1995) that equated innovation with the communication of new ideas across a social system. The definition of innovation developed by Rogers (1995:11) still resonates twenty-five years after he described it as: *"...an idea, a practice or an object that is perceived as new by an individual or other unit of adoption. It matters little so far as human behavior is concerned whether or not an idea is objectively new as measured by the lapse of time since its use or discovery. The perceived newness of the idea for an individual determines his or her reaction to it. If the idea seems new to the individual it is an innovation".*

Therefore, the application of learning analytics approaches to curriculum review is innovative as there has been little work reported on its application for this purpose. Rogers (1995) went on to demonstrate empirically, that it is the identification of a problem that usually generates the innovation-development process. Consistent with this, as we will demonstrate, for the work reported here, we have used learning analytics as part of curriculum review to address challenges with traditional approaches. Consequently, we define innovative teaching and learning for this chapter, as any new or established pedagogical practice that aims to create change and improvement in curricula and student learning outcomes. In other words, such pedagogical practices have to generate additional values to be deemed innovative. Harnessing discrete data sets by using learning analytics in an integrated manner for curriculum review is therefore innovative, creative and a new form of pedagogical practice.

The chapter describes the preliminary stages of a major government-funded learning analytics curriculum review project at The Hong Kong Polytechnic University, including the development of a practical, prototype tool to assist teachers in the process of review and development. The chapter outlines the progress of our project and concludes by considering the implications of our work for what Siemens' (2013:1380) called the *"emerging discipline"* of learning analytics.

Reading this chapter, you will gain the following three insights:

1. An appreciation of the potential of learning analytics for curriculum review;

2. An understanding of the types of review questions learning analytics can address;

3. How innovative data analysis has the potential to improve systematic curriculum review, the processes for academic advising and student learning outcomes and engagement.

We have structured our chapter in four main sections. In Section 1, we outline a learning analytics curriculum review project at The Hong Kong Polytechnic University. Section 2, the practice, describes the project and the development of a prototype tool for the data analytics phase of the review process. It uses examples from specific curricula case studies to illustrate how the outcome of analyses has led to immediate curricular change and assisted academic teams to generate curriculum review questions they would not have otherwise. Section 3, the outcome, overviews the benefits of learning analytics to the review of curricula beyond post-hoc approaches. Section 4, moving forward, concludes with progress in relation to ethics and data governance, curriculum review models, student learning outcomes, and student academic advising.

Section 1: The background

In 2009, the Hong Kong Education Bureau mandated that all universities in Hong Kong implement a four-year undergraduate curriculum, increasing the duration of an undergraduate degree by one year. At our University, this curriculum model includes General University Requirements, where the first-year curriculum introduces students to broad learning experiences so they begin to develop skills and behaviors related to critical thinking, effective communication, innovative problem-solving, lifelong learning, professional competence and ethical leadership. Discipline specific areas of study with major specialisations commence subsequently with opportunities for elective study and a capstone project concludes year four. The project described in this chapter arose from the lead author's interest in using learning analytics for curriculum review and coincided with the first graduates of the new four-year curriculum model in Hong Kong. The funded project is across three Hong Kong Universities, but this chapter describes the way our university has begun to use learning analytics to review the four-year curriculum.

In general, research and development that has begun to apply learning analytics in higher education has focused on academic success and retention (Siemens *et al.*, 2014), rather than as an approach to program curriculum review ("program" in our case, refers to the duration of a degree). Learning analytics, specifically for curriculum review purposes, is under-explored but has considerable potential (Komenda *et al.*, 2015;

Méndez *et al.*, 2014; Toetenel & Rienties, 2016). This is because we know that curriculum evaluators have access to many data categories to help in the understanding of factors impacting on past students' successes and challenges which could be used to help current students. Data, relevant to students' learning behavior, are held in student administration records, the learning management system (LMS), the library, IT services and other sources. Unfortunately, data often exists in silos and are rarely aggregated, analysed and applied to specific curriculum questions. Institutional data governance frameworks are important strategies to avoid local debates about data storage, ownership and management so the potential of learning analytics for curriculum review can be met.

Section 2: The practice

An introduction to the innovative practice

This section presents examples of applications of learning analytics (using anonymized data) for curriculum review at the program level. We outline the simple model we developed to guide the learning analytics strategy in Section 2b; in Section 2c we present specific examples from actual program reviews. At the program level, some of the review questions we have addressed are in relation to defining and measuring how difficult a program was as a whole, how student grades were related to student satisfaction, and whether the assessment mix was appropriate. Section 2d briefly describes the prototype tool we are developing to undertake the analyses and our progress to date.

A brief overview of the approach

In conceptualizing our learning analytics-based curriculum review approach we drew on program-level and subject-level data available at the University from various sources including enrolment records, grades and institutional surveys. We developed a simple model to guide our practice (Figure 1) that was informed by the work of Siemens (2013) and Greller and Drachsler (2012).

P-MAI: Prepare, Map, Analyse, Implement
A model of learning analytics for curriculum review

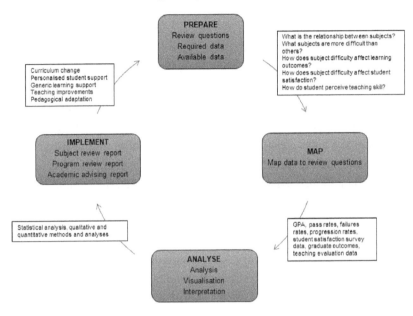

Figure 1: P-MAI Prepare, Map, Analyse, Implement: A model of learning analytics for curriculum review.

Siemens (2013:1386) describes learning analytics as having two intersecting components which are *"...techniques and applications"*. Techniques, according to Siemens (2013:1386), are the *"specific algorithms and models for conducting analysis"*. In our model, technique, is situated in the preparation and mapping cycle. He goes on to describe applications as *"... the way in which techniques are used to impact and improve teaching and learning"*. In our model this is integrated in the analysis and interpretation cycle that leads action. Siemens' (2013) work also assisted us to conceptualise our work as a cyclical review process linked to the principles of the University's existing quality improvement framework. The model was also informed by the work of Greller and Drachsler (2012:44–45) who proposed a detailed design framework for learning analytics in six dimensions, that is *"stakeholders, objectives, data, instruments, external constraints and internal limitations"*.

Data analysis techniques in our project were identified to analyse a range of available institutional data (including students' entry scores, grades, subject choices and relevant survey data). In the reviews, we have conducted to date, analysis using techniques such as cluster analysis were conducted to identify sub-groups of students with different learning pathways (such as different subject choices and major areas of study) and/or learning outcomes. Importantly, the work we have undertaken in the data analysis stage helped us to conceptualise a bespoke prototype tool for analysing and visualising data, which is discussed in Section 2d.

Organisation of the innovative practice

The curriculum review questions we have identified can be categorized as being about the curriculum, students or student behavior/characteristics, subjects and teaching. For example, an important curriculum question for all academic teams is whether the subjects across a program are appropriately developmental towards graduate exit behaviors or graduate attributes. As this is an important question, we explored the issues of assessing program difficulty, identifying subjects that need revision and the program learning outcome and assessment mix.

Assessing program difficulty

We interpreted the difficulty of one program as the level of challenge across subjects that all students have taken as part of their degree. While student grades could be used to address this question, our approach was to conduct Rasch analysis to compare subject difficulty against students' ability to determine the overall difficulty of the program. While a full description of Rasch measurement is beyond the scope of this chapter, one of its advantages is that Rasch analysis can calibrate the person estimates (ability) and the item estimates (difficulty) on the same unidimensional scale. In our case, an "item" represents a subject. For Rasch analysis, the difficulty of a subject was estimated from all of the grades that students who took the subject received in the program, while student ability was determined from their performance in all subjects.

Another benefit of conducting Rasch analysis to compare students' ability and subject difficulty is that both use the same scale units, logits (log odds units), which are linear and can be compared on the one scale. When a student's location (ability) on the unidimensional scale is equal to the difficulty of getting a certain grade in the subject, the student has a 50% probability of obtaining that grade. Figure 2 shows the item-person map for Rasch analysis for one program we reviewed. As this figure shows, for this program the mean student ability is above the mean subject difficulty, which indicates that, overall, the program could be made more challenging as the average difficulty level of subjects is below the ability of the average student.

The usefulness of this analysis is that it gives an overall indication of the level of challenge across the subjects in the program that all students complete, which for the program in Figure 2 is 27, while also assigning a difficulty score to each of the subjects in the program. The analysis does not shed any light on why a subject is relatively more difficult or easy. This needs to be examined at the subject level and could be due to many factors such as the learning and teaching approach used in a subject. However, using these scores to categorise subjects according to difficulty level – for example, high difficulty, moderate difficulty, low difficulty – can help the review team to determine if the difficulty level of each of the subjects is appropriate or not, and if it is not appropriate, to then formulate a strategy to increase (or decrease) the overall difficulty of the program by targeting specific subjects. Conducting this analysis provides information to assist with developing such a strategy.

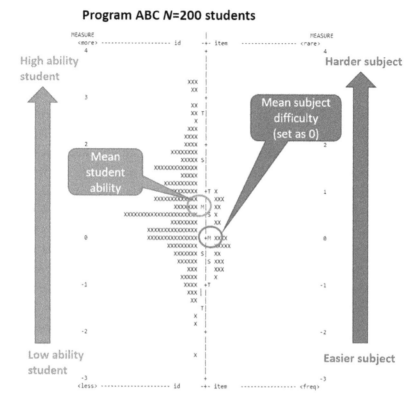

Figure 2. Item-person map showing student ability against subject difficulty. On the right hand side, one x equals one subject (N=27), while on the left hand side, one x equals two students (N=200).

Identifying subjects that need revision
Programs have a large number of subjects that students take, so decisions about what subjects need revision can be difficult. Figure 3 shows subject difficulty scores plotted against the subject's mean evaluation score on the end of a semester evaluation of teaching survey. In the figure, the lower the subject number, the earlier in the program the subject is taken by students. As shown in Figure 3, subjects 1, 2 and 4, which are taken by students in the first semester of their first year, receive quite low subject satisfaction scores and are relatively more difficult compared to other

subjects. In contrast, subjects 7, 14 and 16 are relatively easier than other subjects in the program, but also have lower satisfaction scores. Although it does not explain why this pattern of results occurred, this analysis and visualization suggest that review of these subjects (i.e., subjects 1, 2, 4, 7, 14 and 16) to determine how to improve satisfaction, student performance or both is needed. It also provides the curriculum review team with evidence to identify and prioritize subjects for revision as part of the review. However, it does not provide information on what revisions need to be made – this needs to be determined by further analysis at the subject level.

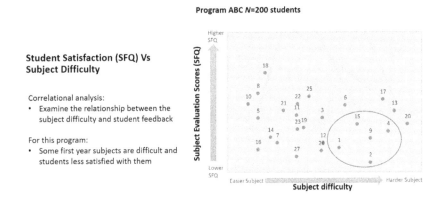

Figure 3. The relationship between subject difficulty and student satisfaction with the subject. Subjects are numbered according to the order in which students complete them in the program.

A second analysis and visualization that provides information about subjects in the program is shown in Figure 4. In this figure, the thickness of the line joining nodes in the diagram indicates the strength of the correlation between subjects – the thicker the line the stronger the correlation. From the figure, students' performance in ABC2006 and ABC3001 is strongly correlated with their performance in ABC4001. Similarly, performance in ABC3004 is strongly correlated with both ABC2004 and ABC4006, the latter being low on student satisfaction and low on subject difficulty. Based on this analysis, revision of the lower level subjects (i.e., ABC3004 and ABC2004) to increase their difficulty could be undertaken to better prepare students for the upper level subject ABC4006. Again, what revisions need to be made to achieve this would be determined by further analysis and review of the subjects themselves.

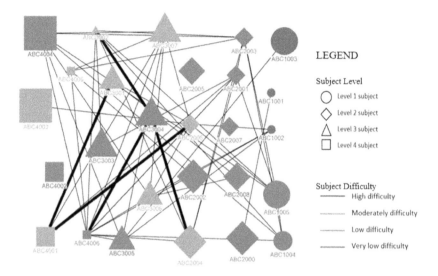

Figure 4. Visualisation of the relationship between subjects together with subject level (indicated by node shape), average student satisfaction with the subject (indicated by node size – the larger the node, the higher the average satisfaction rating for the subject) and subject difficulty (indicated by node colour – see legend for details).

Program-level assessment mix

Depending on the program or learning approach, some assessment types may need to feature more prominently than others – for example with problem-based learning, a higher proportion of assessment that is project-based might be appropriate. By calculating the proportion of assessment at each level that is obtained by different assessment methods, the assessment mix can be visualised to ensure it is appropriate for the program. Figure 5 exemplifies an assessment profile across a program, showing a mix of assessment types in Year 1, while assessment type is less varied in Year 2. There is also more assessment by examination in Years 1 and

2 and comparatively less in Year 3. Similar to Year 1, in Year 3 there is also a greater variety of assessment types compared to Year 2. A similar analysis of the proportion of group versus individual assessment tasks could be used, if feedback from students or staff has been received that suggests there is too much group assessment in the program. A similar analysis and visualization can be produced to check that the relative contribution each assessment type makes towards the student's overall performance on the course is appropriate and that one assessment type (e.g., examinations) does not contribute disproportionately to students' grades in the program.

Figure 5. Frequency of assessment types across the program.

2d: Preparation of the innovative practice

The project has involved team members with expertise in curriculum and learning design, statistics and software development from a University-wide educational development unit. In the first instance, we worked closely with a number of program leaders in one disciplinary area. However, now that we have formalised our approach and begun to develop tools to assist with conducting analyses, we are actively recruiting more programs to be reviewed using a learning analytics-based approach. The development of tools for the analysis and visualisation of the learning analytics data, Siemens' (2013) *"techniques"*, is an important aspect of our project and contributes to its innovativeness. The design and development of a prototype, Excel-based tool to enable us to better integrate data sources for analysis and synthesis purposes was crucial as a preparatory stage. While it is still under development, our aim is for the tool to be used by faculty themselves to conduct analysis for a review without the need for sophisticated technical or statistical knowledge or assistance which we do currently need while the tool is being designed and adapted.

Section 3: The outcome

Objectives

Building on the work discussed in Section 2, a major outcome of the project is to document a formal approach to curriculum review that incorporates learning analytics to address questions that are not easily answered using traditional approaches. These questions include what factors impact on students' academic success within a program, the effect that these factors have, that is, as Siemens (2013:1391) describes how we might create "... *predictive models of learner success*" and how to support students to mitigate them. Importantly from an innovation diffusion perspective, these questions have to be answered by both 'bottom-up' and 'top-down' support and strategies in our view.

We also would like to be able to use our prototypical tool and others we may develop to assist us to design and review curricula that are flexible and responsive to evidence that learning analytics generates. Such tools as we have already noted, need to be developed for user engagement and user acceptance.

Student Perspective

Historically, students' involvement as stakeholders in curricula review processes has been limited and has varied widely across institutions, from involvement in governance structures to participation in routine surveys. (Trowler & Trowler, 2010; Brooman *et al.*, 2015). In general, the student voice in curriculum review has been limited to their voluntary participation in surveys and interviews, usually at the completion of subjects and programs. Our University engages students, to varying degrees of success, in such standard quantitative and qualitative evaluation and quality assurance strategies. However, we agree with Greller and Drachsler (2012:48) who suggest that learning analytics can lead to "*more learner oriented services and therefore improved personalisation*". Indeed, learning analytics for curriculum review purposes has the potential to engage students more directly, both in the design of curricula and in providing students with immediate feedback, in their current courses, about how they might improve their current learning outcomes.

Moreover, learning analytics can play a major role in the development of academic advising programs and in the professional development of staff engaged in academic advising. Such strategies for academic advising might include using learning analytics outcomes to advise students prior to University enrolment and to assist students to more directly monitor their own progress, and thus take on more responsibility for their learning development, during the course of their studies.

Teacher perspective – our reflections

In our experience, program leaders have found the actionable insights generated from the learning analytics approach most useful; they have commented to us that our analyses provide concrete evidence for their 'hunches' so they can implement strategies for improvement. Furthermore, our analyses have told them things about the program that they would not have otherwise known. While the feedback from our colleagues has been positive and supportive, we want to formalise our approach and make it systematic. To do this we intend to map data types to analyses that address specific curriculum review questions and detail related strategies for analysis, visualization, interpretation and reporting when using learning analytics for program review.

In addition, for learning analytics to be useful to teachers, it needs to suit their teaching and learning needs, which can be very diverse. Therefore, further development of the described tool prototype will continue to include teachers in the design process, as we have done from the beginning, to help promote user acceptance and adoption.

Section 4: Moving forward

A reporting mechanism, based on progress so far, will be developed for academic teams, academic advising and students. The reports to be produced include a Program Review Report (PRR) which details the key factors and associated measures of student success identified from the program review. The PRR will be used in academic advising to provide general information to help students make informed and effective choices in relation to things such as subject choices, co- and extra-curricular activities, study behaviors and employment commitments. Customised subject reports will be devised that provide information on the progress of individual students and which can be used for monitoring their progress and projected learning pathway, and, if necessary, provide advice or an intervention to avert a likely negative outcome. A framework to embed such planned reporting will be developed for current curricula, academic advising practices and quality assurance processes. A website with online resources will also be developed in order to assist others to use the curriculum review methodology to establish student activity and performance data reporting processes for their own programs.

A key challenge to using learning analytics is having access to relevant institutional and program-level data. Sometimes this is because the data exist in silos and bringing it together for analysis is difficult due to institutional constraints, such as data "ownership". In our situation, data that would be useful for program (and subject) review has not been collected consistently or are not available to our department. One of the review recommendations then becomes creating a data collection plan that maps to a curriculum review framework and ensuring that the data are collected for future evaluation exercises.

Our recent experience has also emphasised the need for Universities to develop appropriate governance frameworks that link to relevant regulatory legislation for the ethical use of data, as well as strategies to better integrate institutional data sets. Siemens (2013) and others have also alluded to these issues as key considerations in furthering innovation with learning analytics (Gašević et al., 2016; Daniel 2015). Our University has recently implemented a new Data Governance Framework to facilitate the rigorous, ethical management and integration of institutional data-sets. There are of course complex ethical and confidentiality concerns in Universities and other educational settings that may constrain the expansion of learning analytics for curriculum review processes. However, a data governance framework is crucial to manage the use of data for learning analytics.

Conclusion

In summary, analysis of our work to date and our learning analytics approach has revealed interesting correlations between student performance and curriculum design at the program and subject level. In this chapter, we have described how we have used a learning analytics strategy to analyse data from students collected across their studies to identify factors that impact on students' learning and academic success. Even with the limited data we have used, which is mainly performance data based on student grades, the learning analytics approach to curriculum review provided useful insights that inform curriculum enhancement. Including a wider range of measures, such as students' previous study experiences and demographic information, in the data analysed, will further enhance the approach and will provide additional information on the factors that impact on student success. Measures of these factors can be incorporated into formal reports and used with existing student support systems to assist academic advisors, program leaders, teachers and students in monitoring and responding appropriately to students' learning progress in a timely and effective manner. In addition, learning analytics holds the promise to assist Universities to design curricula and curricula review strategies that situate the learner at the centre of their concerns. We believe learning analytics for curriculum review purposes can do this because it can be aggregated, analysed and applied to specific curriculum questions and that learning analytics outputs can generate predictive models to guide success.

About the Authors

Christine Armatas, PhD, is Associate Director Educational Development at The Hong Kong Polytechnic University, Hong Kong, SAR China. She can be contacted at this e-mail: christine.armatas@polyu.edu.hk

Christine Spratt, PhD, is a Professorial Project Fellow at The Hong Kong Polytechnic University, Hong Kong, SAR China. She can be contacted at this e-mail: christine.f.spratt@polyu.edu.hk

Bibliography

Brooman, S., Darwent, S., & Pimor, A. (2015). The student voice in higher education curriculum design: is there value in listening? *Innovations in Education and Teaching International*, 52(6), 663–674. https://doi.org/10.10 80/14703297.2014.910128

Daniel, B. (2015). Big data and analytics in higher education: Opportunities and challenges. *British Journal of Educational Technology*, 46(5), 904–920. https://doi.org/10.1111/bjet.12230.

Gašević, D., Dawson, S., Rogers, T., & Gašević, D. (2016). Learning analytics should not promote one size fits all: The effects of instructional conditions in predicting academic success. *Internet and Higher Education*, 28, 68–84. https://doi.org/10.1016/j.iheduc.2015.10.002

Greller, W., & Drachsler, H. (2012). Translating learning into numbers: A generic framework for learning analytics. *Educational Technology & Society*, 15, 42–57.

Komenda, M., Vita, M., Vaitsis, C., Schwarz, D., Pokorna, A., Zary, N., & Dusek, L. (2015). Curriculum Mapping with Academic Analytics in Medical and Healthcare Education. *Plos One*, 10(12), e0143748. https://doi. org/10.1371/journal.pone.0143748

Méndez, G., Ochoa, X., & Chiluiza, K. (2014, March). Techniques for data-driven curriculum analysis. In *Proceedings of the fourth international conference on learning analytics and knowledge*. (pp. 148–157). ACM.

Ravishanke, G. R. (2011). Doing academic analytics right: intelligent answers to simple questions, *Research Bulletin 2, 2011*, Boulder, CO: EDUCAUSE Center for Applied Research.

Rogers, E. (1995). *The diffusion of innovations*. New York, NY: The Free Press.

Siemens, G. (2013). Learning analytics: The emergence of a discipline, *American Behavioral Scientist*, 57(10), 1380–1400. https://doi. org/10.1177/0002764213498851

Siemens, G., Dawson, S., & Lynch, G. (2014). *Improving the quality and productivity of the higher education sector – Policy and strategy for system-level deployment of learning analytics*. Canberra, Australia: Office of Learning and Teaching, Australian Government. Retrieved from http://www.olt.gov.au/ system/files/resources/Solearning analyticsR_Report_2014.pdf

Toetenel, L., & Rienties, B. (2016). Analysing 157 learning designs using learning analytic approaches as a means to evaluate the impact of pedagogical decision making. *British Journal of Educational Technology*, 47(5), 981–992. https://doi.org/10.1111/bjet.12423

Trowler, V., & Trowler, P. (2010). *Student engagement evidence summary*. York, UK: Higher Education Academy. Retrieved from https://www.heacademy. ac.uk/knowledge-hub/research-and-evidence-base-student-engagement